MEMBERS OF BLACK HAND ARRESTED AT FAIRMONT, W.VA.

676-6

THE ATLAS OF TRUE CRIME

Si presento lo mano Nero

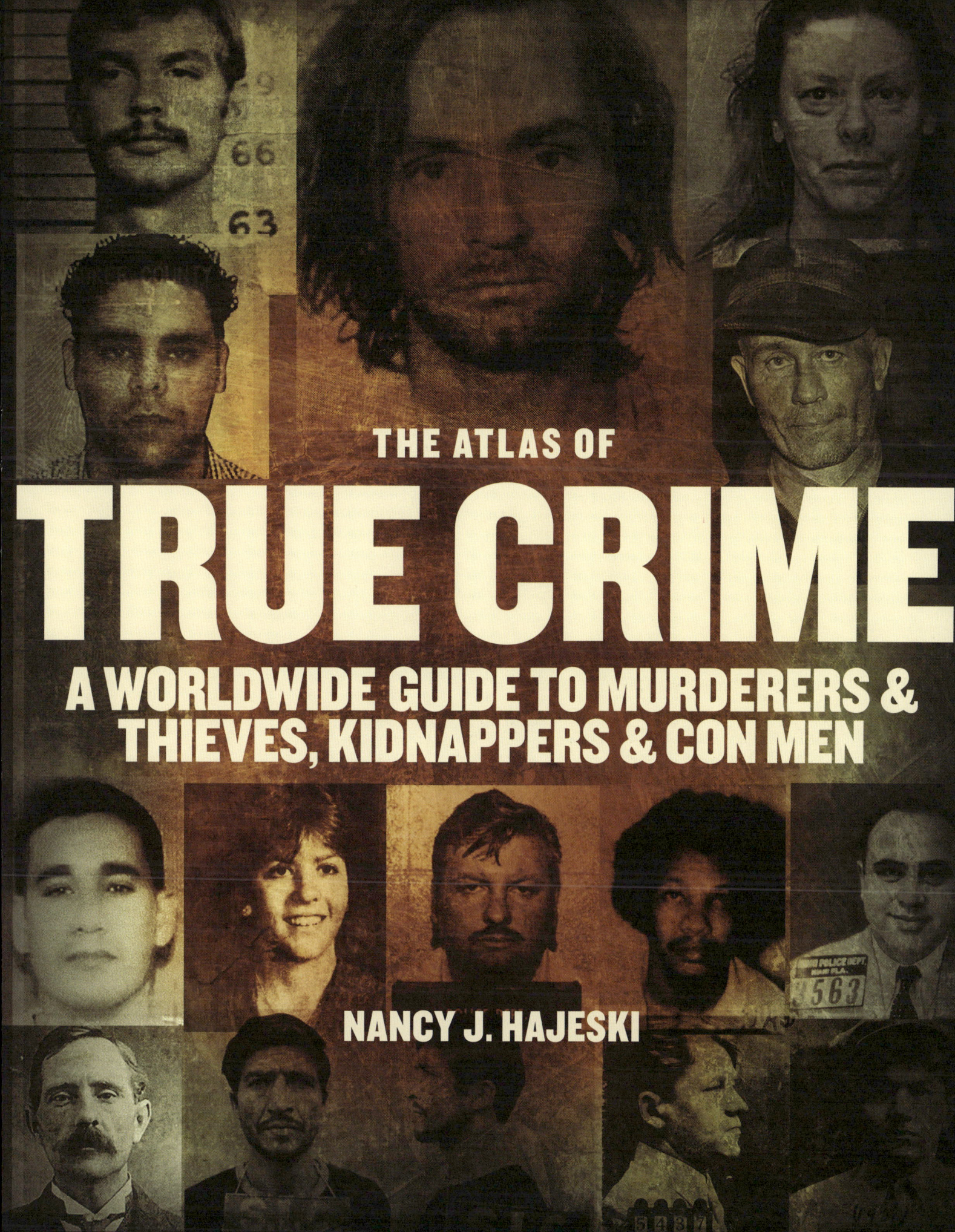

THE ATLAS OF
TRUE CRIME

A WORLDWIDE GUIDE TO MURDERERS & THIEVES, KIDNAPPERS & CON MEN

NANCY J. HAJESKI

MOSELEY ROAD INC.
International Rights and Packaging
22 Knollwood Avenue
Elmsford, NY 10523
www.moseleyroad.com.

President **Sean Moore**

International Rights
Karen Prince: kprince@moseleyroad.com

Written by **Nancy J. Hajeski**

Picture research, mapwork, art direction, and design
Duncan Youel at oiloften.co.uk, London

Printed in Hong Kong

ISBN 978-1-62669-221-3

10 9 8 7 6 5 4 3 2 1   21 22 23 24 25

CONTENTS

07   **Introduction**

10   **Chapter One: Crimebusters**

12   Branches of Law Enforcement

14   Bow Street Runners, Bobbies, and Scotland Yard

16   Taming the Wild West

18   Calling in the Feds

20   **Feature: The Advent of Forensic Science**

22   International Law Enforcement

24   **Chapter Two: Bootleggers and Bank Robbers**

26   Challenging Prohibition

28   Mayhem in the Midwest: Depression Desperados

32   **Chapter Three: The Rise of Organized Crime**

34   The Mafia's Origins: Italy and America

36   The Mafia in America

38   **Feature: Top Crime Bosses of the Past Century**

40   The Irish and Russian Mobs

42   Asian Crime Syndicates: Tongs, Triads, and Yakuza

44   Drug Cartels

46   **Chapter Four: Murder Most Foul**

48   Victorian Poisoners

52   Unsolved Murders

54   In Cold Blood

56   **Feature: Hollywood Homicides**

58   Shocking Murders of Music Legends

60   The Preppy Murderer and the Menendez Brothers

62   Parents Who Kill Their Children

64   ...And Children Who Kill

66   Homicidal Husbands

68   High-Profile Mystery: JonBenét Ramsey

70   **Chapter Five: Romance Gone Wrong**

72   Evelyn Nesbit: The Floradora Girl

74   The Crippen Case

76   Deadly Love Triangles

78   **Feature: Black Widows**

80   Grim and Grisly: Fred and Rosemary West

82   Death in Brentwood: O.J. Simpson

84   **Chapter Six: The Mind of a Serial Killer**

86   Jack the Ripper and his Victims

88   H.H. Holmes: The Master of "Murder Castle"

90   John Christie: 10 Rillington Place

92   Albert DeSalvo: The Boston Strangler

94   Ted Bundy: "Total Possession"

96   Ted Kaczynski: The Unabomber

98   **Feature: Profiling Psychopaths**

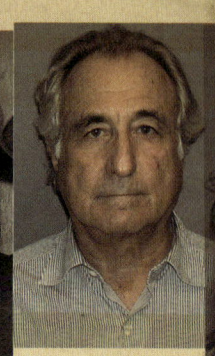

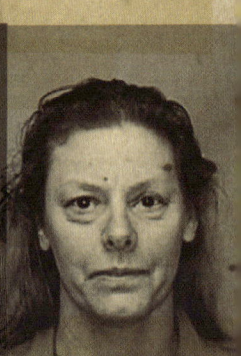

100	David Berkowitz: Son of Sam
102	John Wayne Gacy: "Killer Clown"
104	Dennis Nilsen: Bodies in Bin Bags
106	Aileen Wuornos: Deadlier Than the Male
108	High Body Counts
110	Angels of Death: Nurses Who Kill
112	West Coast Killers
116	**Feature: The Yorkshire Ripper**
118	Andrew Cunanan: Celebrity Assassin
120	South American Serial Killers
124	British Serial Killers
126	The Moors Murders
128	European Serial Killers
132	Asian Serial Killers
134	African Serial Killers
136	**Chapter Seven: Rampage Killers**
138	Richard Speck: Born to Raise Hell
140	Sniper Attacks: Death From Above
142	The Manson Murders
144	**Feature: Crime Goes To The Movies**
146	Rampage Killers of Latin America
148	Rampage Killers of Europe
150	Rampage Killers of Africa and Asia
152	**Chapter Eight: Cannibals in our Midst**
154	Ed Gein: The Plainfield Ghoul
156	Jeffrey Dahmer: The Milwaukee Monster
158	English and European Cannibals
162	Dishonorable Mentions
166	**Chapter Nine: Kidnappers**
168	Leopold and Loeb: Thrill Killers
170	The Lindbergh Abduction
172	Celebrity Abductees: John Paul Getty III and Patty Hearst
174	**Feature: Kidnappings That Created Change**
176	Captives in the Basement
178	Media Storms
180	**Chapter Ten: The Big Heist**
182	The Great Train Robbery
184	Terrorists and Militants
186	The Lufthansa Heist
188	**Feature: Stealing Masterpieces**
190	Bullion Galore: The Brink's-Mat Break-in
192	The Knightsbridge Security Deposit Robbery
194	Targeting Iraq—Twice
196	Hostage-based Heists: The Northern Bank Robbery and The Securitas Depot Robbery
200	Going Underground: Banco Central
202	**Chapter Eleven: Con Men and White-collar Criminals**
204	Ivar Kreuger: The Match King
206	**Feature: "Psst, Buddy, Wanna Buy a Bridge?"**
208	Ponzi Schemers
212	Big-Time Embezzlers
214	Successful Imposters
218	Legendary Charlatans
220	**Index**
224	**Credits**

A FASCINATION WITH CRIME... AND PUNISHMENT

Murder, robbery, kidnapping . . . when most people read about violent crimes they react with feelings of dismay. But their initial distaste is often quickly followed by an eager curiosity: "How did it happen?" "Why did it happen?" And perhaps most importantly, "Could it happen to me?"

Criminals, likewise, have long excited the human imagination. From Biblical times onward, crowds have flocked to view trials and executions. During the French Revolution, guillotines were set up in public squares, where viewing the handiwork of the gruesome machines was a popular entertainment. In some cultures, attending an execution was even mandated by the authorities, who believed that seeing criminals being put to death had a cautionary effect on potential wrongdoers. Yet did such things ever really act as a deterrent? In spite of all the grisly means of execution, all the fearsome threats warning humans not to err, crime has always found a way . . . and, furthermore, continued to enthrall the public.

The Psychologist's Viewpoint

A fascination with crime is part of our primal human make-up, and there is nothing weird about it. According to Dr. Michael Mantell, former chief psychologist of the San Diego Police Department, "It says that we're normal, and we're healthy." Other mental health professionals concur, pointing out that our interest begins when we're young . . . that even as children, we're drawn to the tension that exists between good and evil.

Listed below are some factors that account for this attraction to dark deeds and those who perform them.

■ Evolutionary psychologists believe we have a profound interest in crimes like murder, rape, and theft because they were critical parts of human society going back to our time as hunter-gatherers. As a species we are ultra aware of criminal behaviors and we seek to know what makes these lawbreakers rebel against society's strictures. In this way we can better ensure our

Top: The Death Chamber and electric chair at Sing Sing Prison, 1923; **Above:** The last public execution by guillotine in France was in 1939.

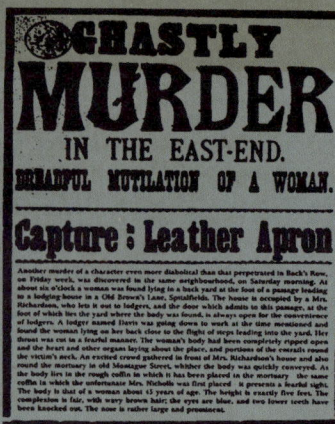

GHASTLY
MURDER
IN THE EAST-END.
DREADFUL MUTILATION OF A WOMAN.

Capture : Leather Apron

Another murder of a character even more diabolical than that perpetrated in Back's Row, on Friday week, was discovered in the same neighbourhood, on Saturday morning. At about six o'clock a woman was found lying in a back yard at the foot of a passage leading to a lodging-house in a Old Brown's Lane, Spitalfields. The horror is occupied by a Mrs. Richardson, who lets it out to lodgers, and the door which admits to this passage, at the foot of which lies the yard where the body was found, is always open for the convenience of lodgers. A lodger named Davis was going down to work at the time mentioned and found the woman lying on her back close to the flight of steps leading into the yard. Her throat was cut in a fearful manner. The woman's body had been completely ripped open and the heart and other organs laying about the place, and portions of the entrails round the victim's neck. An excited crowd gathered in front of Mrs. Richardson's house and also round the mortuary in old Montague Street, whither the body was quickly conveyed. As the body lies in the rough coffin in which it has been placed in the mortuary—the same coffin in which the unfortunate Mrs. Nichols was first placed—it presents a fearful sight. The body is that of a woman about 45 years of age. The height is exactly five feet. The complexion is fair, with wavy brown hair; the eyes are blue, and two lower teeth have been knocked out. The nose is rather large and prominent.

Tabloid Journalism

For more than a century the public's tendency to obsess over crime has been spurred, even encouraged, by sensationalized coverage in the press. It started in earnest in the late 1880s, during Jack the Ripper's London murder spree, when the penny press purposely ramped up levels of fear and pandered to reader fascination with bloody crimes—giving birth to tabloid journalism. At first, any entity posing a public threat became the new sensation: mummies, cannibals, ghosts, and other occult manifestations were reported on with little regard for research or facts. And soon real crimes were being treated with the same hyperbole as fabulous ones.

From that time to the present day, the press has created media circuses over certain high-profile police investigations. Recipients of this tabloid treatment include the Lindbergh baby kidnapping; the murder trials of Harry Thaw, Leopold and Loeb, Charles Manson, Robert Chambers, Ted Bundy, Jeffrey Dahmer, Casey Michaels, O.J. Simpson, and Amanda Knox; and the abduction of toddler Madeleine McCann in Portugal. A sardonic newspaper slogan of the 20th century, "If it bleeds, it leads," has never gone out of style—and today it is estimated that 25 to 30 percent of most media news deals with violent predatory crime and murder.

own safety: History shows that those attuned to potential danger, those who avoided it or thwarted it, left more descendants.

■ **A 2010 study at the University of Illinois, Urbana-Champaign, reported that women** are more drawn to true crime stories than men, especially crimes that feature female victims, shed light on a killer's motives, and show how victims escaped. It is not surprising that women want to be prepared with information on how to outwit a felon in case something similar happened to them.

■ **Some people are enticed by the puzzle-solving aspects of true crime investigations** and enjoy coming up with their own theories. If their deductions prove correct, they may feel a great sense of satisfaction and, indeed, closure.

■ **Many criminals—especially serial killers, spree killers, and cannibals—attract people** the same way that motor vehicle accidents or natural disasters draw onlookers. It is tantalizing to them, admits Scott Bonn, professor of criminology at Drew University. It is logical that

people would feel relief that they are not the victim, but there is also a real possibility that some feel relief that they are not the perpetrator, the monster who let his or her jealousy, rage, lust, or other base instincts take control.

■ **There is also the rush that some people experience when reading about true crimes.** It has been described as similar to the euphoric effect of riding a roller coaster.

Ultimately, humans enjoy being scared... providing the experience takes place in a safe and controlled setting. True crimes are the equivalent of kid's monster stories, only for adults. And, like fairytales, these crime stories are not only entertaining, they are also comforting if they contain a happy ending, one where justice is served.

The Atlas of True Crime . . .

No matter what types of crimes intrigue or gruesomely fascinate, you are likely to find them within the pages of this book. Here you will meet both the lawbreakers and the dedicated law enforcement officers who battle them.

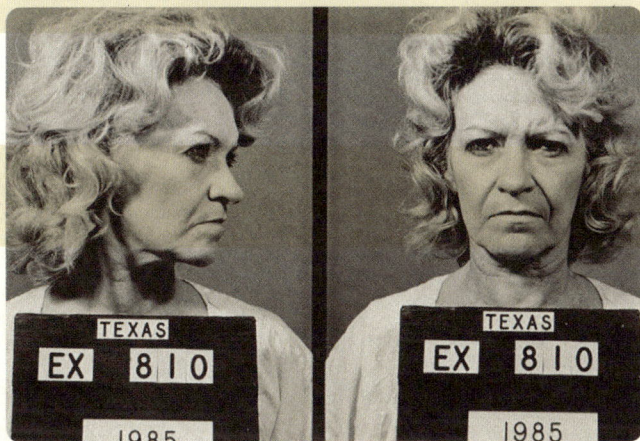

Follow the evolution of crime syndicates in other countries and study their growth in America. Learn about early versions of the police force and the modern organizations that currently combat national and global crime. Encounter a rogue's gallery of bootleggers, gangsters, drug cartel bosses, murderers, poisoners, serial killers, rampage killers, and cannibals, along with infamous kidnappers. History's most daring bank robbers and greatest heists will also be revealed, along with tales of brazen con men and scheming white-collar criminals.

Each chapter provides evocative archival photographs, mementos of crimes, and maps of the locations where certain key crimes took place. Special Features throughout the book offer detailed looks at the birth of forensic science, the profiling of psychopaths, show business homicides, cases that prompted laws to change, and the portrayal of crime in the movies. Ultimately, you can savor the drama, shudder at the horror, and relish the downfall of the perpetrators of the world's most notorious crimes.

Top: Analyzing DNA samples in a forensics lab; **Above left:** Multiple husband-murderer Betty Lou Beets; **Above, from left:** Johnnie Cochran , Robert Shapiro, and O.J. Simpson during Simpson's trial for murder at the Los Angeles County Superior Court in 1994. **Opposite top:** Ted Bundy; **Opposite center, left to right:** Ed Gein, the 1950s Wisconsin serial killer and cannibal; Richard Speck; South African serial killer, Moses Sitole after his arrest in 1995; he murdered at least 38 women; and Peter Sutcliffe, who killed 13 women in the north of England in the 1970s.

"Every society gets the kind of criminal it deserves. What is equally true is that it gets the kind of law enforcement it insists on..." ROBERT KENNEDY

Crimebusters

The sometimes deadly conflict between criminal forces and those required to uphold the law can trace back to every early civilization. Over time, as criminals—and their crimes—became more sophisticated, it became necessary for law enforcement agencies to rise to these challenges with innovative new methodologies for detection and apprehension. In the majority of cases they have proven themselves more than equal to the task.

> "When morals decline and good men do nothing, evil flourishes."
> J. EDGAR HOOVER, FBI DIRECTOR

BRANCHES OF LAW ENFORCEMENT

Around the world, the primary goal of a police force is the prevention of crime rather than its detection. When law enforcement officers are doing their job properly—implementing policies and practices that result in the best service to the public, and defining priorities like education and performance measurement—the crime rate in their communities is typically low . . . and the satisfaction rate high.

Small Towns to Big Cities

In America, as in many other countries, there is a hierarchy to law enforcement based on size of jurisdiction. Local law enforcement begins with municipal police departments, which oversee a specific village, township, or city. Next comes metropolitan police, which cover a wider area and may be responsible for multiple communities and municipalities.

County police, typically found in metropolitan regions, cover an entire county, parish, or borough and are also responsible for patrols and investigations. Full-service police

patrol the entire county, limited service looks after unincorporated districts, and restricted service provides security to county-owned properties.

A sheriff's department may also be located within a county. Sheriff's are elected officials (as opposed to policemen, who are appointed or hired) who are not police, but who have a number of different responsibilities. They uphold the county jail, are responsible for security in the courts, and enforce laws throughout the county. They may also transport criminals, run crime labs, and collect taxes.

The state police, sometimes called the highway patrol, provide law enforcement including patrols and investigations. Different departments of state government may have their own dedicated enforcement divisions, including those that oversee the state capital, college campuses, state hospitals, airports, correctional facilities, the water department, and fish and game/wildlife. In addition, the attorney general of each state has their own state bureau of

KEY STATS

In the US, as of 2020, more than 420,000 officers in more than 18,000 police departments dealt with roughly 8.25 million crimes a year and made about 10 million arrests.

investigation to call upon. For instance, in the Lone Star State, the Texas Ranger Division fulfills this role.

At a major crime scene, hostage situation, or natural disaster, multiple policing agencies may be involved, cooperating under mutual aid agreements. The complex command chain in these fraught situations by necessity must remain fluid and flexible.

The Alphabet Agencies

At the national level, there are two types of policing agencies—federal police, who possess full federal authority as given to them under the United States Code, and federal law enforcement, authorized to enforce various laws at the federal level. Each group may maintain a smaller division of the other, as with the FBI police. The agencies have jurisdiction in all states, US possessions, and US territories. Originally limited by the US Code to investigating matters within the power of the federal government, with the passing of the post-9/11 Patriot Act, those limitations have broadened. Some agencies, like the US Park Police, are granted state arrest authority.

The Department of Justice (DOJ) is responsible for the majority of federal law enforcement duties, including the Federal Bureau of Investigation (FBI), the Drug Enforcement Administration (DEA); the Bureau of Alcohol, Tobacco, Firearms, and Explosives (ATF); the US Marshals Service, and the Federal Bureau of Prisons.

The Department of Homeland Security (DHS) reports to the DOJ and oversees Immigration and Customs Enforcement, Customs and Border Protection, United States Secret Service, United States Coast Guard, and a number of other agencies.

MODERN POLICING CONCERNS

Around the globe, police forces deal with many of the same threats— domestic or foreign terrorism, civil unrest, and cyber crimes—and face similar internal challenges, including recruitment and retention, budgetary constraints, burnout and suicide, keeping pace with technology, and improving community outreach.

Police forces around the world: Opposite, top to bottom: Bicycle police, Paris France; State Troopers, Kansas USA; Policewomen, Indore India; Metropolitan Police officer, London England; **This page, top to bottom:** Tourist policeman, Luxor Egypt; An experienced officer, Stockholm Sweden; Local police discuss a situation, Lagos Nigeria.

BOW STREET RUNNERS, BOBBIES, AND SCOTLAND YARD

For many centuries the apprehension of criminals largely relied on the public. In England, for instance, up until the 18th century, the cry of "Thief!" or "Murderer!" meant that any nearby group was obliged to pursue the wrongdoer. If the criminal was captured, he or she was handed over to a constable or nightwatchman, typically an untrained local . . . and the only form of protection against crime offered by the state.

During the mid-eighteenth century, however, a new method of law enforcement arose. Consisting of trained agents, it became, in effect, London's first professional police force. Founded in 1749 by magistrate Henry Fielding (author of the classic novel *Tom Jones*), the group was known as the Bow Street Runners because they were attached to the Bow Street Magistrate's Office. The job of the original force of six was similar to that of "thief takers," rough men who apprehended petty criminals for a fee. Fielding intended to regulate and legalize his force, however, a marked contrast to the corruption and malicious arrests for which the less-scrupulous policers of London's streets were known. The "runners," who were paid with funds from the central government, served writs and traveled throughout England to apprehend criminals, especially the highwaymen who preyed on travelers.

Sir Robert's Own

Another gentleman with far-thinking notions on how a teeming metropolis might be made safer was Sir Robert Peel, member of Parliament and future two-time prime minister. In 1829, Peel, then home secretary, established the Metropolitan Police Force on Whitehall Place,

THE "YARD" IN POPULAR CULTURE

"LESTRADE AND HOLMES SPRANG UPON HIM LIKE SO MANY STAGHOUNDS."

"Scotland Yard" has always stirred the imagination of the public, whether it be Inspectors Lestrade or Gregson in the Sherlock Holmes stories, or the many crime series and movies that feature the Metropolitan Police or its Criminal Investigation Division (CID). Bobbies, still in their traditional custodial helmets, are a fixture in London. Just don't snap a selfie with them—a recent anti-terrorism law bans photos of police officers.

in London's City of Westminster. The building's rear door, which served as the public entrance, opened onto Great Scotland Yard, and thus that street name became synonymous with the Metropolitan Police, and, eventually, with any police activity in London. (Great Scotland Yard was once the site of a medieval palace that housed Scottish royalty during visits to the city.)

Sir Robert's initial force consisted of a thousand men, affectionately known as "bobbies," or less affectionately as "peelers." The bobbies were so effective in reducing the level of crime in the capital city—no small task—that by 1839 they had replaced the Bow Street Runners. By 1857 all cities in Britain were required to establish their own police departments. As a result of

this much-needed innovation, Sir Robert Peel is considered the father of modern policing.

New Scotland Yard

In 1890 the force relocated to a Gothic brick building on the Victoria Embankment—which became New Scotland Yard—and in 1967 moved to a modern 20-story office building near the Houses of Parliament. The Yard is responsible for all 32 boroughs of London except for the City of London, which is policed by its own force.

Scotland Yard possesses extensive files on all known criminals in the UK, and has a "Special Branch" that guards visiting dignitaries. The Special Branch is also responsible for maintaining communication between British law enforcement agencies and Interpol.

A CLOSER LOOK:

"Scotland Yard" is a byword for London's Metropolitan Police, but also refers to its HQ, whilst MI5 is Britain's counter-intelligence service. MI6 is their secret intelligence service—think James Bond.

Opposite, top: New Scotland Yard, headquarters of "the Met"—London's Metropolitan Police; **Opposite, bottom left:** A London bobby of the Victorian age, circa 1865; **Top:** A group portrait of the officers of a London Police Station in the 1890s (note their ceremonial swords, and service medals); **Above:** A cadre of London policewomen from 1918.

TAMING THE WILD WEST

"... in the spring of 1866, my life was threatened daily, and I was forced to go heavily armed." JESSE JAMES

During America's Colonial era, law enforcement was provided by a combination of untrained volunteers, elected sheriffs, and militia. (As early as the 1600s the first sheriff's offices were created in New York City.) In the 1700s the Carolinas established night watches to look out for escaping slaves; some of these watches evolved into actual police forces. Eventually, many cities in the Eastern states were benefiting from more regulated and systematic forms of policing.

But as pioneers and expansionists began to settle the still uncharted regions of America's West and as small communities took shape, a breed of lawless outsider sprang up on these frontiers, intending to profit from the toil of hopeful new residents. Known as bushwhackers, dry-gulchers, gun sharks, pistoleros, hustlers, owlhoots, sidewinders, cattle rustlers, stage-coach bandits, safecrackers, and train robbers, they were, in simple terms, outlaws. Many of these miscreants achieved legendary status, especially after being featured in penny dreadfuls, the cheap, popular publications of the late 1800s. These lurid stories immortalized names like Billy the Kid, Sam Bass, Belle Starr, Doc Holliday, Jesse James, Butch Cassidy, and the Sundance Kid, and gangs like the Clantons, the Cowboys, the Doolin-Daltons, the Wild Bunch, and a host of others.

Naturally, local law enforcement—constables, marshals, sherifs, deputies, and detectives numbering in the thousands—

attempted to thwart their activities. This group also included some legendary names: Wyatt Earp, Doc Holliday (who played for both sides), Bat Masterson, Wild Bill Hickok, Bill Tilghman, and Pat Garrett, who famously shot Billy the Kid. These lawmen were usually able to "clean up" larger cities, rowdy cattle towns like Dodge City and Abilene in Kansas and mining hotbeds like Tombstone in Arizona. But because most outlaws typically moved quickly from region to region—you generally don't stick around after rustling cattle or robbing the only bank for many miles—and lawmen had limited jurisdiction, there was little these peace officers could do to curtail crime on a meaningful scale.

Rising to the Challenge

Meanwhile, back East, Scotsman Allan Pinkerton, famous for foiling an assassination attempt against President Lincoln, had formed a private security and detective agency in the late 1850s. His agents safeguarded valuable railroad shipments, infiltrated unions, and were used as guards in labor disputes. Pinkertons was also known for hiring women and minorities, an uncommon practice at the time. At its height it

was the largest private law enforcement agency in the world.

Eventually overland stage companies and railroads, tired of being robbed en route, enlisted the Pinkertons to head West and act as bounty hunters. The agents infiltrated the Reno gang, which was responsible for the very first train robbery, and pursued Butch Cassidy and his Wild Bunch. They spent months, and even lost officers, chasing notorious bank robbers Jesse and Frank James. During a standoff with their widowed mother at her home in Clay County, Missouri, someone threw a bomb into the house, resulting in their mother losing an arm and the death of their young half-brother. As public opinion turned against the Pinkertons, they withdrew.

What helped halt the rampant lawlessness in the West was simply the great numbers of people who eventually settled the towns—bringing with them the trappings of civilization: schools, churches, lawyers, judges, temperance societies, and subsequently, larger police forces. The introduction of barbed wire in the 1870s was also a factor: the wide open plains, so handy for escaping on horseback, soon no longer existed.

A CLOSER LOOK:

The Pinkerton logo, the image of a large unblinking eye combined with the slogan, "We never sleep," led to detectives being called private eyes.

KEY STATS

According to historians, the period known as the Wild West occurred between the end of the Civil War, 1865, and the closing of the Frontier by the Census Bureau in 1890.

Opposite, top: The Wild Bunch, circa 1900, the notorious train-robbing gang of Butch Cassidy and the Sundance Kid. (The Sundance Kid is seated left, Butch Cassidy is seated right); **Opposite, bottom:** Jesse James; **Above left:** Allan Pinkerton (left), stands with President Abraham Lincoln, and Union General John McClernand during the Civil War Battle of Antietam in 1862; **Above right:** Portrait of Allan Pinkerton circa 1865.

CALLING IN THE FEDS

Top left: J. Edgar Hoover, the first director of the Federal Bureau of Investigation. Hoover was appointed director of the Bureau of Investigation, the FBI's predecessor, in 1924 and helped found the FBI itself in 1935. He remained director until his death; **Top right:** Some of the first newly-trained FBI agents pose with their pistols, 1935; **Above:** the famous FBI agent's shield; **Opposite bottom:** The bloody corpse of outlaw John Dillinger in the Chicago County morgue.

Federal law enforcement in the United States is more than 200 years old: the Postal Inspection Service's roots go back to 1772, while the United States Marshals Service was established in 1789, followed by the U.S. Parks Police in 1791. When it comes to apprehending felonious criminals—murderers, thieves, terrorists, drug and human traffickers, kidnappers, forgers, embezzlers, racketeers—the go-to agencies in Washington, DC, are typically the FBI, the ATF, and the DEA. When called in to help with a case, these agencies do not supplant local law enforcement and "take over" the investigation, but rather they form task forces, pooling their resources with the police in a coordinated effort to solve the crime.

The FBI: This branch of the DOJ was created in 1908, the same year that Henry Ford's first Model T rolled off the assembly line. America now spread from sea to sea, and with burgeoning urban populations, there was a sharp upswing in crime as overcrowded cities became breeding grounds for career criminals. Yet, there was no systematic means of national law enforcement beyond local, often poorly trained, police departments and a few federal agencies like the thinly spread Secret Service.

After anarchist Leon Czolgosz shot and killed President McKinley, Vice President Theodore Roosevelt entered the Oval Office. Roosevelt, one time head of the New York Police Force, determined to put his progressive principles to work and so appointed noted civic reformer Charles Bonaparte as attorney general. Bonaparte, who'd had to hire expensive Secret Service agents to investigate federal crimes, soon put together a group of 34 men—9 former S.S. agents and 25 of his own men—who would specifically conduct investigations for the DOJ. This was the start of the Federal Bureau of Investigation.

Although many of the modern FBI's functions are unique, it is similar to Britain's MI5, Israel's Mossad, or Russia's FSB in its support of national security. Primarily a domestic agency, the FBI has 56 field offices in major American cities and more than 400 resident agencies in smaller cities. It also maintains 60 Legal Attache (LEGAT) offices abroad and 15 sub-offices in US embassies and consulates that typically coordinate with foreign security services.

The ATF: The Bureau of Alcohol, Tobacco, Firearms, and Explosives, formed in 1972, is responsible for investigating and preventing the unlawful use, manufacture, and possession

THE F.B.I.'S MOST WANTED MEN

Eleven years after its founding, the Bureau of Investigation, at the request of the Army, issued a request for information on the location of one William N. Bishop, a runaway soldier. This "identification order," or IO, contained a detailed description of the man and a a recent portrait. It became the FBI's first ever "wanted" poster and set them up, permanently, in the business of catching fugitives. Bishop was captured less than five months later. So far 162 fugitives have been captured due to civilian cooperation—two while taking a tour of the FBI! The longest time spent on the list was 32 years by Victor Manuel Gerena. The oldest listee was Eugene Palmer, 80, added in May 2019.

IDENTIFICATION ORDER NO. 1217
March 12, 1934.

DIVISION OF INVESTIGATION U. S. DEPARTMENT OF JUSTICE
WASHINGTON, D. C.

Fingerprint Classification
12 9 R O
14 U 00 9

WANTED

JOHN DILLINGER, with alias,

FRANK SULLIVAN

NATIONAL MOTOR VEHICLE THEFT ACT

DESCRIPTION

Age, 31 years
Height, 5 feet 7-1/8 inches
Weight, 153 pounds
Build, medium
Hair, medium chestnut
Eyes, grey
Complexion, medium
Occupation, machinist
Marks and scars, 1/2 inch scar
    back left hand; scar middle
    upper lip; brown mole between
    eyebrows
Mustache

Photograph taken January 25, 1934

John Dillinger

CRIMINAL RECORD

As John Dillinger, #14395, received State Reformatory, Pendleton, Indiana, September 16, 1924; crime, assault and battery with intent to rob and conspiracy to commit a felony; sentences, 2 to 14 years and 10 to 20 years respectively;
As John Dillinger, #13225, received State Prison, Michigan City, Indiana, July 16, 1929; transferred from Indiana State Reformatory; paroled under Reformatory jurisdiction, May 10, 1933; parole revoked by Governor - considered as delinquent parolee;
As John Dillinger, #10587, arrested Police Department, Dayton, Ohio, September 22, 1933; charge, fugitive; turned over to Allen County, Ohio, authorities;
As John Dillinger, received County

Jail, Lima, Ohio, September 28, 1933; charge, bank robbery; escaped October 12, 1933;
As Frank Sullivan, arrested Police Department, Tucson, Arizona, January 25, 1934; charge, fugitive; turned over to Lake County, Indiana, authorities;
As John Dillinger, #14487, arrested Sheriff's Office, Crown Point, Indiana, January 30, 1934; charge, murder - bank robbery; escaped March 3, 1934.

The United States Marshal, Chicago, Illinois, holds warrant of arrest charging John Dillinger with feloniously and knowingly transporting Ford V-8 four door sedan, motor number 256447, property of Lillian Holley, Sheriff, Lake County, Indiana, from Crown Point, Indiana to Chicago, Illinois, on or about March 3, 1934.

Law enforcement agencies kindly transmit any additional information or criminal record to the nearest office of the Division of Investigation, U. S. Department of Justice.

If apprehended, please notify the Director, Division of Investigation, U. S. Department of Justice, Washington, D. C., or the Special Agent in Charge of the Office of the Division of Investigation listed on the back hereof which is nearest your city.

(over)   Issued by: J. EDGAR HOOVER, DIRECTOR.

---

of firearms and explosives; acts of arson and bombings; and the illegal trafficking and tax evasion of alcohol and tobacco products. The ATF's activities are frequently carried out with task forces made up of state and local law officers. It also operates a one-of-a-kind fire research lab in Maryland where full-size mock-ups of arson cases can be simulated.

The DEA: The Department of Drug Enforcement, founded in 1973, is tasked with combatting the trafficking and distribution of drugs in the US. It enforces the Controlled Substances Act, sharing jurisdiction with the FBI, US Immigration and Customs Enforcement, and US Customs and Border Protection. It has sole responsibility for coordinating and pursuing US-based drug investigations both domestically and abroad.

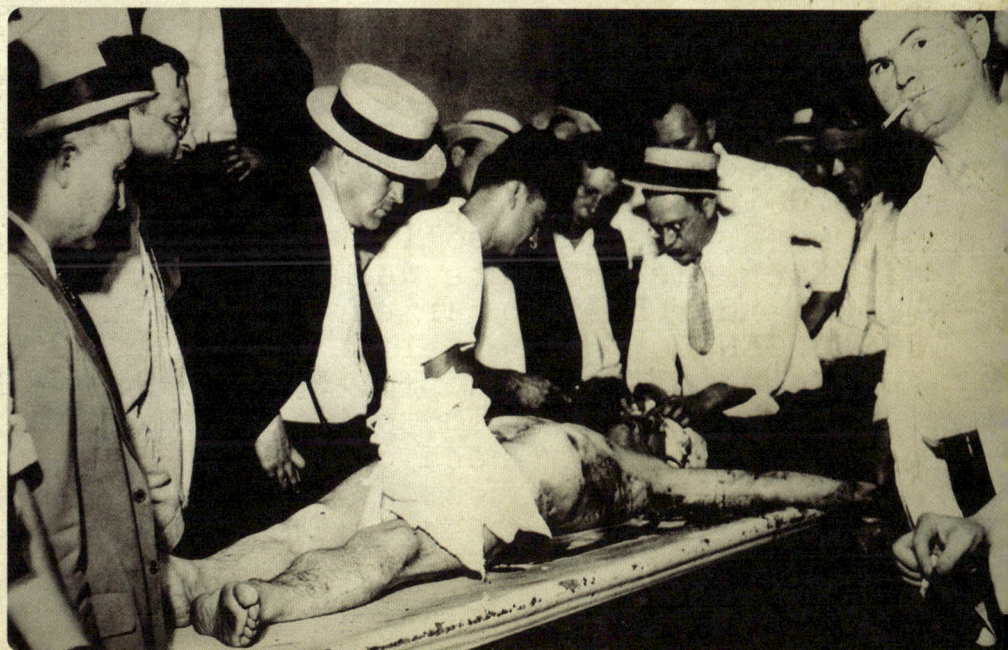

"Mine is a gruesome job, but for a scientist with a love for the mechanics of the human body, a great one." JUDY MELINEK, FORENSIC PATHOLOGIST

THE ADVENT OF FORENSIC SCIENCE

Top: The enormous FBI Fingerprint Department at the DC Armory, during the Second World War in 1944; **Above:** Forensic science has a range of formidible tools to ascertain the identities of long-dead people.

Forensic science, or criminalistics, is the application of scientific methods to criminal and civil law, especially when utilized during an ongoing investigation. The job of forensic scientists is to collect, preserve, and analyze evidence in a laboratory setting. Some scientists prefer collecting their own evidence at the crime scene, while others analyze material brought to them by the police. Some specialists analyze financial, banking, or numberical data in order to investigate financial crimes. Forensic scientists may be consultants drawn from private firms or academia, or may themselves be government employees. At court trials, they are often called as expert witnesses for the prosecution or the defense.

Scientific and surgical investigation was widely employed by London's Metropolitan Police during their pursuit of Jack the Ripper, who brutally murdered a number of women in the 1880s. Policemen conducted house-to-house inquiries throughout Whitechapel; forensic material was collected and examined. Suspects were identified, traced, and either examined more closely or eliminated. Police work follows the same pattern today. By the turn of the 20th century, the science of forensics had become largely established as an invaluable tool for criminal investigation.

Top Forensic Tools:

Toxicology: The study of the nature, effects, and detection of poisons in the human body. In 1773, Swedish chemist Carl Wilhelm Scheele devised a method for detecting arsenious oxide, simple arsenic, in corpses. In 1806, German chemist Valentin Ross learned to detect the poison in the walls of a victim's stomach. Today the three main sub-disciplines of forensic toxicology are postmortem, human performance, and forensic drug testing.

Ballistics: Henry Goddard of Scotland Yard pioneered the use of bullet comparison in 1835, when a flaw in the bullet that killed the victim led back to the manufacturing mold. A spent projectile found in a body or at a crime scene can also reveal the specific weapon used.

Anthropometry: First applied by French

policeman **Alphonse Bertillon in the 1870s,** he created a system that used anthropological measurements of a criminal's body as a means of identification.

Fingerprints: No two human beings share the same fingerprints, making this an ideal way to identify criminals in a database. The concept was first advocated by Sir William Herschel in 1858 in India, where he used thumbprints on contracts to avoid signature forgeries.

Identifying Human Blood: The Uhlenhuth test for species was invented by Paul Uhlenhuth in 1901 and can distinguish human blood from animal blood, based on characteristic proteins. This test represented a major breakthrough in forensic science.

DNA: In 1984, British geneticist Sir Alex Jeffreys pioneered DNA profiling, which uses variations in the genetic code to identify individuals. In 1985, a 15-year-old school girl named Lynda Mann was raped and murdered in Carlton Hayes psychiatric hospital. The police had no suspects but were able to obtain a semen sample. When a similar rape/murder took place nearby, the semen samples matched those in the Mann case. After DNA samples were collected from the men in the entire town, no match was made: then Colin Pitchfork's friend admitted he'd pretended to be Colin during the collection. Pitchfork, whose DNA was a match, was arrested for both crimes. Modern DNA databases offer an important forensic assist to police investigations.

Top, main image: Forensic scientists at work in a laboratory; **Above:** Dusting for fingerprints with black graphite-based powder, which is used on light surfaces. White talcum-based powder is used for dark surfaces.

INTERNATIONAL LAW ENFORCEMENT

Top: In today's world, law enforcement agencies have to work beyond national borders, and track crime globally; **Above:** The crest and flag of the CIA; **Opposite Top left:** Crest of Interpol, the International Criminal Police Organization; **Opposite top right:** The CIA Complex at Langley, Virginia; **Opposite bottom:** Lyons, France— the Headquarters of Europol, the European Union Agency for Law Enforcement Cooperation

During the 20th century, as improved modes of transportation and faster means of communication made the world more accessible, racketeering mobs, drug cartels, terrorist cells, and larcenous individuals were more easily able to commit crimes internationally. This meant that concerned countries now needed some form of law enforcement that could legally cross national boundaries in order to investigate those crimes or threats to their national security. Below are some of the major agencies currently responsible for policing the globe.

The CIA: The US Central Intelligence Agency was formed in 1947, successor to the OSS (Office of Strategic Services), which was created by President Roosevelt in 1942 and modeled on the battle-tested British Secret Intelligence Service. Unlike the FBI, the CIA has no law enforcement function; its official goal is gathering overseas intelligence that might affect US security. Also known as the Agency and the Company, the CIA exerts foreign political influence through its tactical divisions

and has been instrumental in establishing intelligence services for US allies. It is the only agency authorized to carry out covert actions at the behest of the American president. While providing support to certain foreign political groups and governments, it has been involved in regime changes, terrorist attacks, and planned assassinations of foreign leaders, for which the agency has faced severe criticism on the world stage. After the terrorist attacks of 9/11, the CIA grew in size, with a commensurately inflated budget. The agency has recently shifted its focus from counter-terrorism to counter-cyberwarfare operations.

Interpol: The International Criminal Police Organization, headquartered in Lyons, France, was conceived during the first International Criminal Police Congress in 1914 and got its start in 1923. It came under Nazi control in 1938, fell moribund, but was revived at the end of World War II. The organization, which currently has 194 member nations on six continents, provides investigative support, expertise, and training in three areas of transnational crime—terrorism, cybercrime,

and organized crime. This wide scope includes drug trafficking, political corruption, crimes against humanity, child pornography, intellectual property infringement, and white-collar crime. It further enables cooperation among national law enforcement agencies by supplying criminal databases and communication networks.

Europol: Headquartered in the Hague, Netherlands, the European Union Agency for Law Enforcement Cooperation was formed in 1998 in order to process criminal intelligence and combat terrorism and organized crime through a cooperative effort by EU member states. The agency has no executive powers and its agent are not allowed to arrest suspects without prior approval from the authorities in said member states. Its origins can be found in TREVI, a security forum created by the European community in 1976 that first dealt with terrorism and was then expanded to cover cross-border crime. Today, Europol assists in the fight against international crime: illicit drugs, human trafficking and migrant smuggling, intellectual property crime, cybercrime, euro counterfeiting, and terrorism. Additionally, they prepare threat

assessments, strategic and operational analysis, and general situation reports.

United Nations Office on Drugs and Crime: UNODC offers members of law enforcement, prosecutors, judges, and customs officials a range of training programs specifically geared to fighting organized crime in their local settings.

"All my life I wanted to be a bank robber. Carry a gun and wear a mask. Now that it's happened I guess I'm just about the best bank robber they ever had. And I sure am happy." JOHN DILLINGER

Bootleggers & Bank Robbers

Two of America's most tumultuous decades occurred consecutively: the 1920s were marked by the excesses of the Jazz Age along with a nationwide ban on alcohol called Prohibition, while the 1930s saw the Great Depression and the Midwestern Dustbowl calamity. As is often the case, major disruptions of normal life created opportunities for criminals.

WE HOLD THE 18th AMENDMENT TO BE UNCONSTITUTIONAL
THE VOLSTEAD ACT MUST BE REPEALED "IF THIS BE TREASON MAKE THE MOST OF IT"

CHALLENGING PROHIBITION

"I don't even know what street Canada is on." AL CAPONE

Top: One of many anti-Prohibition parades held across the United States in the weeks and months after the passing of the Volstead Act—the 18th Amendment to the Constitution—which saw the complete banning of alcohol nationwide; **Above, and Opposite:** Revenue agents confiscating and pouring away illicit bootleg liquor.

During the 19th century, the role of the police in America altered radically. The uncontrolled influx of immigrants and the sometimes violent effects of labor unions created the need for a more organized system of law enforcement. The first centralized city police force was established in Boston in 1838, with similar forces created in New York City, Chicago, New Orleans, and Philadelphia. By the turn of the 20th century, the majority of American cities had a structured police department.

But during the "roaring" 1920s, a decade known for its jazz-fueled energy, many city police found themselves outmatched by criminals—and civilians—intent on violating the Volstead Act. This legislation, which enforced the ratification of the 18th Amendment, prohibited the production, distribution, or transportation of alcohol. Drunkenness had become a public scourge in many parts of the country, with husbands drinking away their paychecks, and men and women becoming

so drunk that they passed out in the streets. The government, encouraged by temperance leagues and progressives, stepped in . . . and Prohibition was the result. The reformers had expected to witness an era of high morality and societal uplift, but what they actually got was a marked rise in crime and an unholy increase in violence.

"Joe sent me."

As it turned out, there were big bucks in booze. Almost immediately, the criminal element in the country began to smuggle alcoholic beverages into the US, from Canada, Mexico, or from foreign ships along the coasts—or illegally produce their own, a process called bootlegging. The powerful gang leaders who supplied liquor and beer to the masses rose from all backgrounds: Al "Scarface" Capone was Italian-American; Jack "Legs" Diamond was Irish-American, and "Dutch" Schultz was the son of Jewish immigrants. (Ironically, the crime networks they established across the "dry" country became the foundations of the

"...if you don't like action and excitement, you don't go into police work." ELLIOTT NESS

organized crime syndicates of the future.) Clubs called speakeasies that sold forbidden liquor—or homemade hooch called "moonshine" and "bathtub gin"—sprang up, but required secret passwords to get inside. Police regularly raided them, but they just as quickly reopened. That was because the criminal elements behind them were not afraid of local cops, who were often on the gang's payroll.

Meanwhile, the gangsters fought amongst themselves for control of lucrative territories, turning urban centers into bloody battlefields. Finally, in 1930, Frank J. Loesch of the Chicago

Crime Commission entreated President Hoover to break Capone's grip on his city. Elliott Ness, a 27-year-old treasury agent working for the Justice Department, was sent to Chicago to take down kingpin Capone. After reviewing lists of Prohibition agents, he recruited men he knew to be incorruptible, whom the press labeled "the Untouchables." Within six months of forming his team, Ness's raids on stills and breweries had destroyed many of Capone's bootlegging operations, resulting in a loss of $9 million. Capone was indicted on five thousand violations of the Volstead Act . . . but was ultimately imprisoned for tax evasion.

A PRESIDENTIAL COMMISSION

During Prohibition, President Herbert Hoover appointed the 1929 Wickersham Commission to investigate the procedures and practices of police departments nationwide. The Commission's findings of widespread police laxity when it came to enforcing Prohibition, contributed to the repealing of the 18th Amendment. It also spurred a movement that professionalized policing and redefined the role of the "career cop."

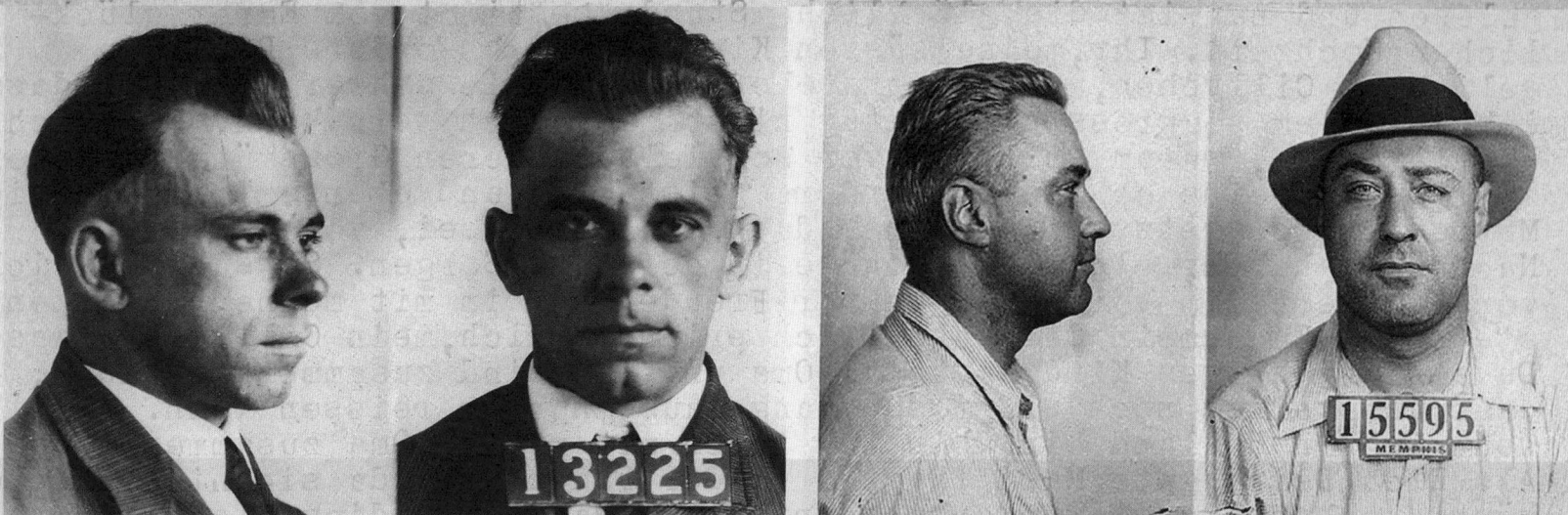

"Okay boys, let's go make a withdrawal." JOHN DILLINGER

MAYHEM IN THE MIDWEST:
DEPRESSION DESPERADOS

Above: Lester Gillis—aka "Baby Face" Nelson;
Top line mugshots: left to right—John Dillinger, "Machine Gun" Kelly, Kate "Ma" Barker and her son Fred, and "Baby Face" Nelson.
Opposite, center: The Biograph movie theater, site of Dillinger's killing by FBI agents;
Inset image: The infamous Sing Sing Prison in Ossining, upstate New York.

Before Prohibition had even ended, another national crisis erupted. In 1929 poor practices in banking, lending, and investing, including rampant speculation, caused the US Stock Market to crash, resulting in a sharp decline in stock values. This set off a nationwide economic crisis known as the Great Depression, which affected many other countries. Plants and factories closed, small businesses folded, and millions of Americans saw their nest eggs disappear, almost overnight. Breadwinners now stood on breadlines, awaiting government-issued food and other necessities.

During this period, with the status quo foundering and law enforcement preoccupied by civic unrest, banks again became fair game for American criminals. Unlike the bootlegging gangsters, many of whom had origins outside the US, these lawbreakers were home-grown, typically from rural areas in the Midwest, Southwest, or West. According to FBI Special Agent Melvin Purvis, "Most of the top-flight hoodlums of the Middle West were 100-percent American boys with no foreign background whatsoever."

The term outlaw was now applied to kidnappers, murderers, and especially bank robbers. While early Western outlaws like Jesse James rode horses to make their getaway, these criminals used cars. Hence, they were known as "auto bandits" or desperados. The federal police agencies soon labeled them "public enemies" and placed them on lists of "Most Wanted Men."

The Headline Makers

Like their Western forebears, these larger-than-life crooks sparked the imagination of the beleagured American public; newspaper exposés and crime-based magazines became popular with both teens and adults. The most infamous bank robbers included:

KATE BARKER

BARKER

5437

(1931) K5440

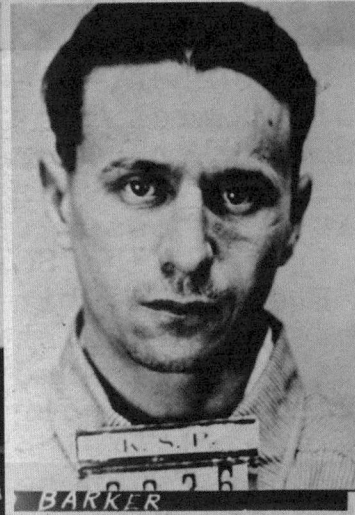

John Dillinger, the top dog when it came to American crime, was accused of robbing at least 24 banks as well as four police stations. In fact, his entire gang was listed as public enemy number one. He was incarcerated several times and escaped twice—once by using a gun made from blackened soap. Known for his dark looks, sharp-dressed style, and taste for attractive women, he was on the lam (hiding out) in Chicago when he was shot down outside a movie theater by federal agents. He'd been betrayed by Romanian brothel madam, Ana Cumpănaă, the Lady in Red, while escorting his lover, Polly Hamilton, one of Ana's "girls."

"Baby Face" Nelson (Lester Gillis), who was partners with John Dillinger, and who helped him to escape from Crown Point Prison in Indiana. He was characterized by his boyish looks ... and vicious killings.

"Machine Gun" Kelly (George Barnes), who was known for carrying a Thompson sub-machine gun, and for kidnapping oil tycoon Charles F. Urschel, who later helped to indict Kelly.

Kate "Ma" Barker, the mother of several criminals, ran the Barker-Karpis gang. The FBI described her as "the most vicious, dangerous, and resourceful criminal brain of the last decade."

Charles Arthur "Pretty Boy" Floyd, robbed more than 30 banks in Oklahoma and the Midwest but was considered a folk hero, a Robin Hood. Shot by police in 1934 after he killed a bounty hunter, more than 20,000 attended his funeral.

Improved bank security and more secure vaults, some with time locks, eventually made banks less of an easy target for criminals. Today, closed circuit cameras, silent alarms, and marked money also act as a deterrant.

THE PROSPECT OF PRISON

Due to the ruthless nature of so many Depression-era bank robbers, the threat of a long prison sentence was meant to become a major curb on crime. American prisons took on a fearsome aspect, and while the names of brutal penitentiaries and correctional facilities like Leavenworth, San Quentin, Sing-Sing, and Alcatraz were spoken of with great trepidation, the robberies continued.

MAYHEM IN THE MIDWEST: BONNIE & CLYDE

"They've been shot at before, but they do not ignore, that death is the wages of sin." BONNIE PARKER, *THE TRAIL'S END*

Above, and Top: The series of photographs the gang took of themselves, which did much to cement their legend in the eyes of the U.S. populace;

Females were no strangers to murder, but throughout history their ranks remained relatively thin and their infractions typically more of the "parlor" variety, poisonings and crimes of passion. One of the most famous female lawbreakers of the 20th century, however, was a violent bank robber called Bonnie Parker. Partnered with Clyde Barrow, she embarked on a path of such cold-blooded outlawry that she and Barrow became legendary.

Parker started life in Rowena, Texas, dropped out of high school at 15 to embark on a short-lived marriage, and thenbecame a waitress in Dallas. (A regular customer, Ted Hinton, would be part of the final posse that tracked her down.)Like many young women with dreams of the future, she kept a diary and wrote poetry. She met Clyde Barrow when she was 19, probably at a mutual friend's home in East Dallas.

Barrow was born to a poor Texas farm family, and as a teen was arrested several times for theft along with his brother Buck. He met Parker when he was 20, and they immediately clicked. Clyde was eventually jailed in Eastham Prison Farm for auto theft, but he escaped when Bonnie smuggled him a weapon. Recaptured and rejailed, he suffered repeated sexual assaults, finally killing his tormenter by crushing his skull with a pipe. Another prisoner, a lifer, took credit for the crime. Barrow had two toes lopped off in order to avoid the grueling field work, but he was released six days later when his mother's petition for parole was approved. Those familiar with Clyde said prison had changed him, turned him into a "rattlesnake."

The Barrow Gang

Beginning in 1932, Bonnie and Clyde and the other gang members held up a string

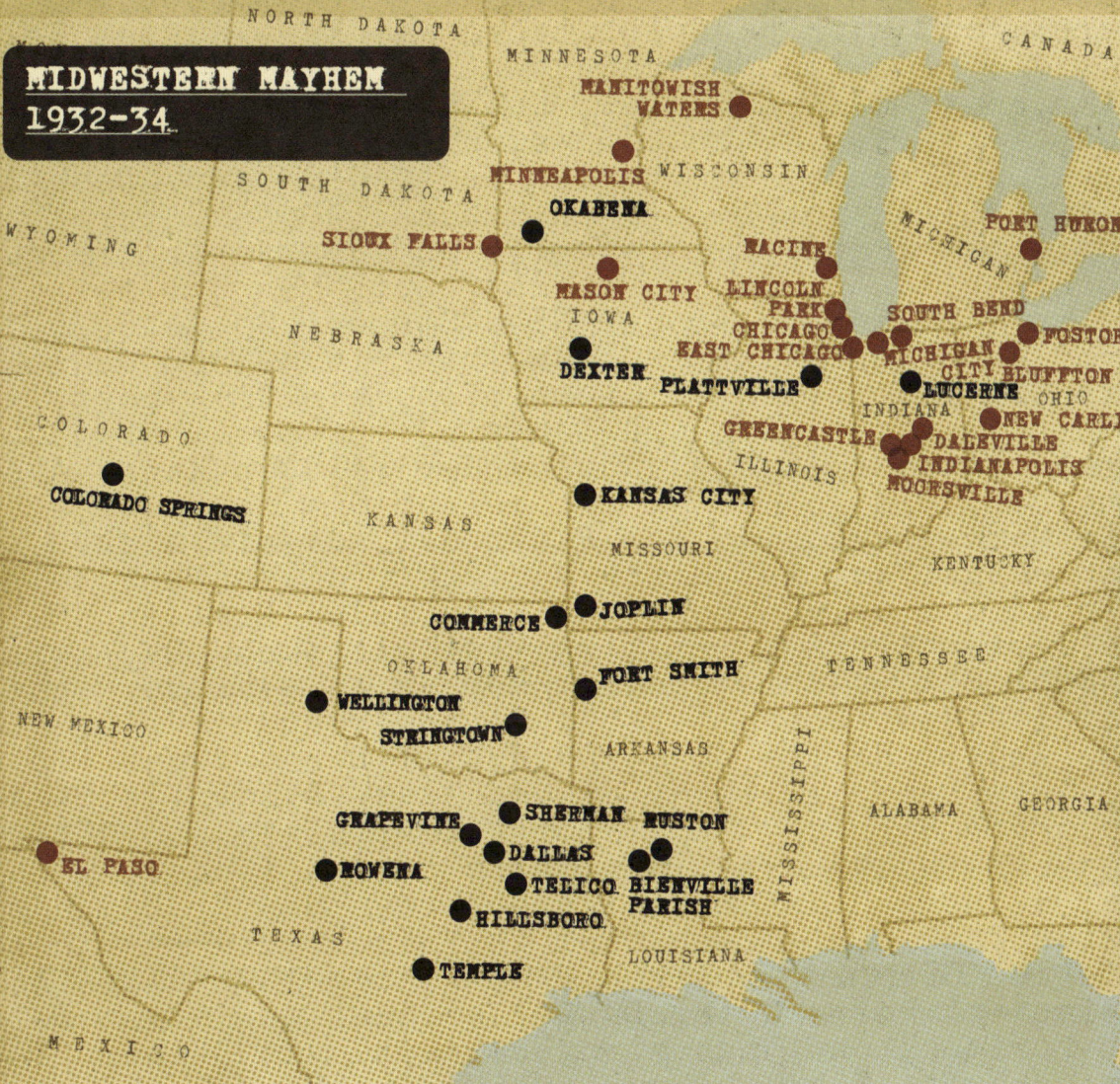

MIDWESTERN MAYHEM 1932-34.

Map locations: NORTH DAKOTA, MINNESOTA, CANADA, MANITOWISH WATERS, SOUTH DAKOTA, MINNEAPOLIS, WISCONSIN, OKABENA, WYOMING, SIOUX FALLS, RACINE, MICHIGAN, PORT HURON, NEW YORK, MASON CITY, LINCOLN PARK, SOUTH BEND, PENNSYLVANIA, IOWA, CHICAGO, MICHIGAN CITY, FOSTORIA, NEBRASKA, DEXTER, EAST CHICAGO, BLUFFTON, PLATTVILLE, LUCERNE, OHIO, INDIANA, NEW CARLISLE, GREENCASTLE, DALEVILLE, COLORADO, ILLINOIS, INDIANAPOLIS, MOORESVILLE, COLORADO SPRINGS, KANSAS CITY, KANSAS, MISSOURI, KENTUCKY, JOPLIN, COMMERCE, OKLAHOMA, FORT SMITH, TENNESSEE, WELLINGTON, STRINGTOWN, NEW MEXICO, ARKANSAS, GRAPEVINE, SHERMAN, HUSTON, MISSISSIPPI, EL PASO, ROWENA, DALLAS, ALABAMA, GEORGIA, TELICO, BIENVILLE PARISH, HILLSBORO, TEXAS, LOUISIANA, TEMPLE, MEXICO

KEY STATS

Clyde Barrow's stolen 1934 Ford Deluxe Sedan was riddled with 167 bullet holes when the police ambush ended.

of banks, gas stations, and convenience stores ranging from Texas and Louisiana in the south, Arkansas, Oklahoma, Missouri, Illinois, Indiana, Iowa and as far north as Minnesota. They killed a number of people—civilians and lawmen both. Clyde's gang included his brother Buck, Buck's wife Blanche, W.D. Jones, and Henry Methvin.

The couple did not expect to get away with their crimes and always assumed they would die in a hail of bullets. Clyde claimed he simply wanted revenge against the Texas penal system for the abuses he had suffered. The gang was hunted relentlessly, and gun battles were frequent—yet they still managed to outshoot the police, due to Clyde using a BAR, a Browning automatic rifle, a type of light machine gun. After one raid in Joplin, Missouri, that sent the gang scurrying, the police found Bonnie's diary and her camera. The resulting photos, especially Bonnie smoking a cigar and holding a pistol and

then posing with a shotgun aimed at Clyde, were published in national newspapers and turned the Barrow Gang into headliners.

The gang stayed active and on the run, despite Bonnie's leg being badly burned during a car accident, and even after Buck was shot and wounded in the head. In late July, 1933, Buck and Blanche were apprehended; Buck died of his wound, while Blanche ended up in prison. Undeterred, the gang continued the robberies and shootouts until a former Texas Ranger was brought in, Frank Hamer, a Texas Highway Patrol officer. The public's "romance" with the pair was waning and they clamored for justice. Hamer began charting their path and, aided by government wiretaps, was able to anticipate the pair's routine. On May 23, 1934, the police, with Hamer leading the posse, set up an ambush. Bonnie and Clyde were both shot to death in their car as they drove a country lane to Sailes, Louisiana.

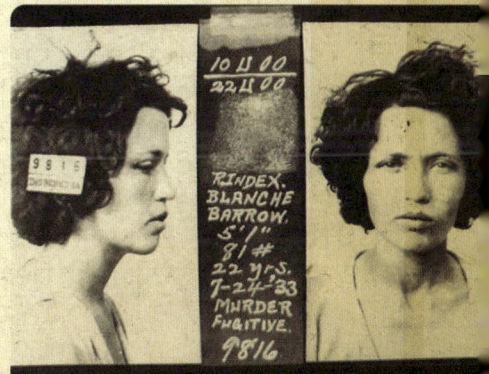

Top: Frank Hamer, the former Texas Ranger who masterminded the successful ambush of Bonnie & Clyde; **Above:** Blanche Barrow's "Murder fugitive" mugshots taken after she was captured, July 24, 1933.

"Organized crime constitutes nothing less than guerilla war against society." LYNDON B. JOHNSON

3 Chapter Three

The Rise of Organized Crime

Organized crime is defined as "criminal activities that are planned and controlled by powerful groups and carried out on a large scale." These highly centralized enterprises are set up specifically to engage in cargo theft, fraud, robbery, smuggling, trafficking, kidnapping, and extorting "protection" payments. In America such criminal organizations are called the mafia or the mob, and their members referred to as gangsters, mobsters, hoodlums, racketeers, goons, and wiseguys.

Italian emigrés into the U.S. photographed on their arrival at Ellis Island in 1905

THE MAFIA'S ORIGINS:
ITALY AND AMERICA

Sicily, a large Mediterranean island off the tip of Italy's boot, was for centuries ruled by a string of foreign invaders—including the Phoenicians, Arabs, French, and Spanish. Inevitably, the repressed residents banded together for protection and carried out their own brand of justice. The term mafiosa at that time had no criminal connotations; it simply meant those suspicious of authority. In the 19th century, however, some mafia groups evolved into private armies, extorting money from landowners for "protection," and eventually growing into violent criminal organizations.

Organized crime was no stranger to America. Street gangs had existed there since the time of the Revolution, so it is not surprising that the first serious wave of immigrants to the Northeast—English, Irish, and German—formed into gangs. This was especially true around New York's Five Points neighborhood, where the Dead Rabbits, Roach Guard, Whyos, Daybreak Boys, and Humpty Jacksons brutally battled each other, and new immigrants, for territory. Other nationalities, Jews, Poles, and Italians, also formed gangs in urban centers. Chinese immigrants in the late 1800s formed tongs, highly structured gangs involved in gambling and drug trafficking. These were matched in power by the emerging Italian organized crime network that evolved into the American Mafia . . . and which would eventually solidify its influence during Prohibition.

It was during the late nineteenth century that the major influx of Italians occurred. Many brought the traditions of the Old Country along with them, including the mafia culture. Like other immigrants, Italians came expecting opportunity and riches. Relegated to festering

MEMBERS OF BLACK HAND ARRESTED AT FAIRMONT/W.VA.

Si presento la mano Nero

ITALY, SHOWING THE CITY OF NAPLES AND THE ISLAND OF SICILY

slums like New York's Lower East Side and Chicago's South Side, however, and facing widespread discrimination, many Italian men despaired of ever elevating their families out of the poverty loop. The nascent American mafia emerged in these neighborhoods, providing jobs that teetered on the wrong side of the law. Some men became actual foot soldiers for the mob, or even enforcers, if they were willing to take lives.

The mafia eventually became linked in the eyes of the public with Americans of Italian descent. Although there *were* non-Italians in the mafia, including Irishmen, Germans, and Jews, they were considered *associates* and not actual members.

The Mark of the Black Hand

The Black Hand was an extortion racket located in America's major cities and was likely a precursor to the actual mafia. By around 1904, the name had become synonymous with the society's method of extortion: the delivery of a letter marked with a black hand, implying death or bodily harm if the recipient didn't meet the note's monetary demands. In 1910 Chicago, former Black Hander Big Jim Colosimo and his South Side Gang went to war with the Black Hand, who were threatening him. Gang violence

ripped through the already devastated slum neighborhoods, taking many lives.

The mafia proper eventually established itself in the United States and in doing so created such a successful template for theft, intimidation, corruption, extortion, drug and sex trafficking, and money laundering, that other unsavory foreign syndicates flocked to seek their fortunes in the land of the free . . . which soon became the land of the freebooter.

Top left: Members of the Black Hand, arrested in Fairmont West Virginia; **Top right:** A facsimile from an original Black Hand letter. The Italian translates as "You are presented with the black hand"; **Opposite:** A chilling reportage photograph taken in Sicily—the young victim's family scramble up the ravine to discover the murdered body of their kidnapped son. This iconic image bears an uncanny resemblance to scenes that would years later become integral to the plot of Francis Ford Coppola's *Godfather Part II*.

LA COSA NOSTRA:
THE MAFIA IN AMERICA

The Offspring of Prohibition

Ironically, the Volstead Act directly led to the establishment of organized crime syndicates in North America. Once mafia leaders sensed the looming end of profitable Prohibition, they held a national conference in Atlantic City, NJ, in 1929. Here, they solidified their bootlegging networks to become national and expanded their empires to embrace racketeering and even some legitimate businesses. Violence would be kept at a minimum to decrease visibility.

Top left: Mulberry Street in 1905, in the heart of Manhattan's "Little Italy"; **Top center:** the brutal murderer Guiseppe Morello in the early 1900s. Born in Corleone, Sicily, he was head of the Morello Family in East Harlem; **Top right**: Johnny Torrio in 1939. He ran with the Five Points Gang in New York before helping to put together the "Chicago Outfit" in the early 1920s. U.S. Treasury officials judged him "the biggest gangster in America."

The first published mention of mafia-type activities in America was in the spring of 1869, when the New Orleans Times reported that the Second District had become overrun by "well-known and notorious Sicilian murderers, counterfeiters and burglars," who had formed a co-partnership for the plunder and disturbance of the city. Giuseppe Morello was likely the first known Mafia member to come to the US, fleeing with six other Sicilians after murdering 11 wealthy landowners, and the chancellor and vice chancellor of a local province. Morello was eventually extradited back to Italy.

Perhaps the first Mafia-based killing occurred in October 1890, when New Orleans Police Superintendent David Hennessy was murdered, execution-style. Dozens of Sicilians were arrested, and 19 were eventually indicted. After the jury acquitted them (amid rumors of bribed and intimidated witnesses), the outraged citizens lynched 11 of the 19 defendants.

A second wave of New York street gang activity, from the 1890s to 1920, found Paul Kelly's Five Points Gang flexing its power in Little Italy, in the Lower East Side. Kelly recruited several young Italian hoodlums who later became famous crime bosses—Johnny Torrio, Al Capone, Lucky Luciano, and Frankie Yale. The gang was often in conflict with the Jewish Eastmans in the same neighborhood. There was also an influential Mafia family in East Harlem, while the Neapolitan Camorra was also quite active in Brooklyn. Other states were not exempt—Chicago's Italian 19th Ward became known as the "Bloody Nineteenth" due to frequent Mafia violence caused by feuds and vendettas.

Eventually, mafia bosses bribed officials—policemen, judges, public officials, even congresspeople—to look the other way so they could go about their illicit business unmolested. Sometimes there were turf wars, when one mob wanted to horn in on the action of another mob, and the resulting conflict was known as "going to the mattresses." Mob bosses would be mowed down by hitmen while dining out ("Crazy" Joe Gallo) or getting a haircut (Albert Anastasio). The seasoned "dons" who came from Sicily to New York were referred to as Mustache Petes, due to their prominent facial hair, while the American-born foot soldiers were called Young Turks. Gang members had colorful, often slightly ominous,

PREDOMINANT GANGS OF NEW YORK 1890S TO 1916

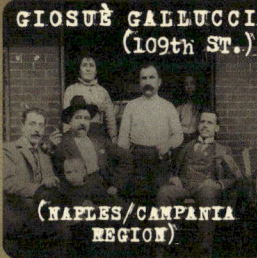

GIOSUÈ GALLUCCI (109th ST.)
(NAPLES/CAMPANIA REGION)

THE BRONX

SOUTH BRONX

LYNDHURST

NORTH BERGEN

GUTTENBERG

WEST NEW YORK

ITALIAN HARLEM

FLUSHING BAY

BELLEVILLE

ARLINGTON

KEARNEY

HUDSON

HOBOKEN

HARRISON

HUDSON RIVER

MANHATTAN

Central Park

EAST RIVER

MORELLO FAMILY (107th ST.)
(CORLEONE/PALERMO, SICILY)

CORONA

QUEENS

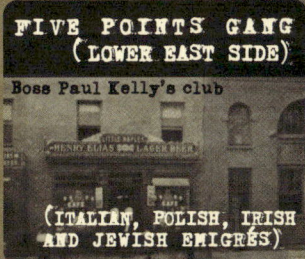

FIVE POINTS GANG (LOWER EAST SIDE)
Boss Paul Kelly's club
(ITALIAN, POLISH, IRISH AND JEWISH EMIGRÉS)

EASTMAN GANG (LOWER EAST SIDE)
(JEWISH EMIGRÉS FROM EASTERN EUROPE)

MIDDLE VILLAGE

GLENDALE

WOOD HAVEN

LOWER EAST SIDE

U.S. NAVY YARD

NEWARK BAY

JERSEY CITY

ELLIS ISLAND

Statue of Liberty

GOVERNOR'S ISLAND

THE BROOKLYN BRIDGE

BROOKLYN

NAVY STREET GANG, BROOKLYN
(COMORRA: NAPLES/CAMPANIA REGION)

BAYONNE

UPPER BAY

FLATBUSH

BROOKLYN

"I didn't kill anyone that didn't deserve killing in the first place." MICKEY COHEN, GANGSTER, BOXER, AND ENTREPRENEUR

names like Ice Pick Willie, Tick-Tock, Whack-Whack, Greasy Thumb, and Cadillac Joe.

By the 1950s, the mafia had become the preeminent organized-crime network in America. It had spread to all 48 states, controlled interests in Cuba, and was involved in criminal activities ranging from loan-sharking to prostitution, while at the same time infiltrating labor unions and industries such as construction, sanitation, and New York's garment industry.

During the late 20th century, American and Italian prosecutors started enforcing tough anti-racketeering laws and actually were able to convict top bosses. In order to avoid long sentences, some convicted mafiosos chose to break with the sacred code of omerta and testify against their brethren. By the early 2000s, after hundreds of arrests, the might of the mafia had been undermined in both nations, although it is doubtful if it will ever be completely eliminated.

Above: New York City, showing the boroughs of Manhattan, the Bronx, Queens, and Brooklyn. From the 1890s to 1916, four predominant gangs ruled parts of the City. In "Little Italy," part of the Lower East Side, both the Five Points Gang and the mainly Jewish Eastman Gang rubbed shoulders very uneasily, whilst up in East Harlem, and south across the East River in Brooklyn, Sicilian, and Neapolitan gangs were in charge. The Five Points gang employed well-known future mob bosses Lucky Luciano and Al Capone.

Top Crime Bosses of the Past Century

It is hard to imagine the power and scope of an organized crime boss—as far-reaching as that of a general, or even a president, in many cases. National borders and international laws mean little to them when it comes to engineering a score or seeking retribution. The following list of the most feared and influential bosses of the previous hundred years includes leaders of mobs as well as heads of drug cartels.

1. Lucky Luciano (1887–1962): Influential and ambitious, Italian-born Luciano helped legitimize the mob's presence in America. After joining the notorious Five Points gang, he moved up the mob ranks. He is considered the father of modern organized crime after creating the Commission (in part to stop gang wars) in 1931. He was deported to Italy in 1947.

2. Frank Costello (1891–1973) A native Italian, Costello served US prison terms for assualt and robbery. With Lucky Luciano he was involved in gambling, bootlegging, and expanding mob operations. He served as head of the Luciano crime family (later Genovese) and in 1957 the "Prime Minister" survived an assassination attempt that killed Albert Anastasia.

3. Al Capone (1899–1947) "Scarface" Capone was a powerful mafia boss and bootlegger in the 1920s. With mentor Johnny Torrio, he co-founded the Chicago Outfit (formerly the Black Hand), which oversaw smuggling and prostitution. He killed seven gang rivals in the St. Valentine's Day Massacre, and was famously imprisoned for tax evasion in 1931.

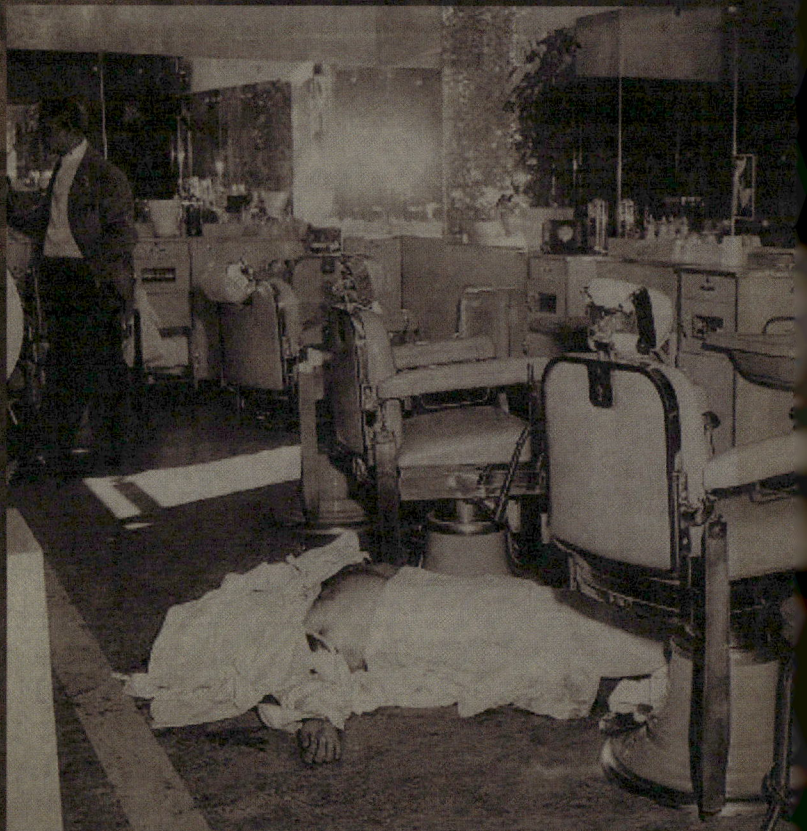

4. Albert Anastasia (1902–1957) Known as the "Earthquake" and "Mad Hatter," Italian-born Anastasia was an enforcer for Lucky Luciano and became head of his Brooklyn rackets. By 1951, he'd turned New York Harbor into a crime zone. Anastasia became head of the Mangano family, but was assassinated in his Manhattan barbershop by **Carlo Gambino** in 1957.

8. Frank Lucas (1930–2019) An African-American drug lord known for his lavish lifestyle, Lucas learned his trade under Harlem mob boss Bumpy Johnson. He broke the drug monopoly of the Italian-American mob, creating a heroin ring that dealt directly with suppliers in Southeast Asia. He was arrested and sentenced to 70 years but turned state's witness.

Below left: After one of the most audacious and sensational mob 'hits,' the bloody corpse of Albert Anastasia lays covered by towels, awaiting the arrival of FBI agents to the scene at the barbershop in the Park Sheraton Hotel, 56th Street and 7th Avenue, Manhattan. Anastasia, himself frequently labelled "the lord high executioner," was assassinated by long-time hitman Carlo Gambino, see below.

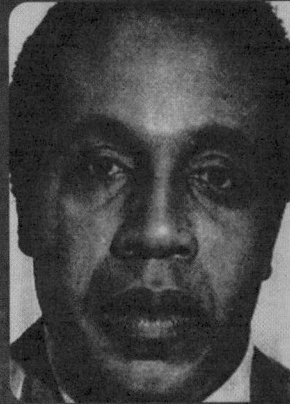

5. Carlo Gambino (1902 – 1976) The "Godfather" and "King of the Underworld" had a long and successful career as a crime boss. Inducted into the mafia as a hitman in 1921, Gambino joined Luciano's "Young Turks." After murdering Albert Anastasia, he became head of the Mangano crime family— now the Gambinos—in control of loan sharking and illegal gambling.

9. John Gotti (1940–2002): Part of the Gambino crime family, Gotti continued to distribute heroin against family ethics, invoking the anger of boss Paul Castellano. Gotti organized Castellano's murder and thus became the most powerful mob leader of the 1980s. The "Dapper Don" was brought down when his underboss, Salvatore Gravano, cooperated with the FBI.

6. Bugsy Siegel (1906–1947) Seigel was a handsome, engaging Jewish-American gangster involved in rackets, murder, and illegal gambling. A former hitman, he founded Murder, Inc., the enforcement branch of the mafia and later established the Las Vegas Strip in Nevada. In 1947 he was shot dead by a hitman in Beverly Hills.

10. Griselda Blanco (1943–2012) Blanco started with pickpocketing and prostitition in her native Colombia, but she eventually gained control of the notorious Medellín Cartel, and became the first female billionaire criminal. "The Cocaine Godmother," was involved in 200 trafficking-related murders. She was shot dead by police in 2012.

7. Whitey Bulgar (1929–2018): Known simply as "the Irishman," Bulgar exemplified the Irish mafia in America— tough-minded and relentless. Bulgar was both an organized crime boss—he led the Winter Hill Gang of Somerville, Massachusetts, just north of Boston— and also an FBI informant, providing intel on his rivals, the Italian Patriarca crime family.

11. Pablo Escobar (1949–1993) A Colombian drug trader and narcoterrorist who founded the Medellín Cartel, Escobar reigned as the "King of Cocaine" and "El Patrón." He began by selling fake lottery tickets, graduating to auto theft and kidnapping. The cocaine cartel he established in 1976 became the most successful to supply the US— transporting 70 tons a day.

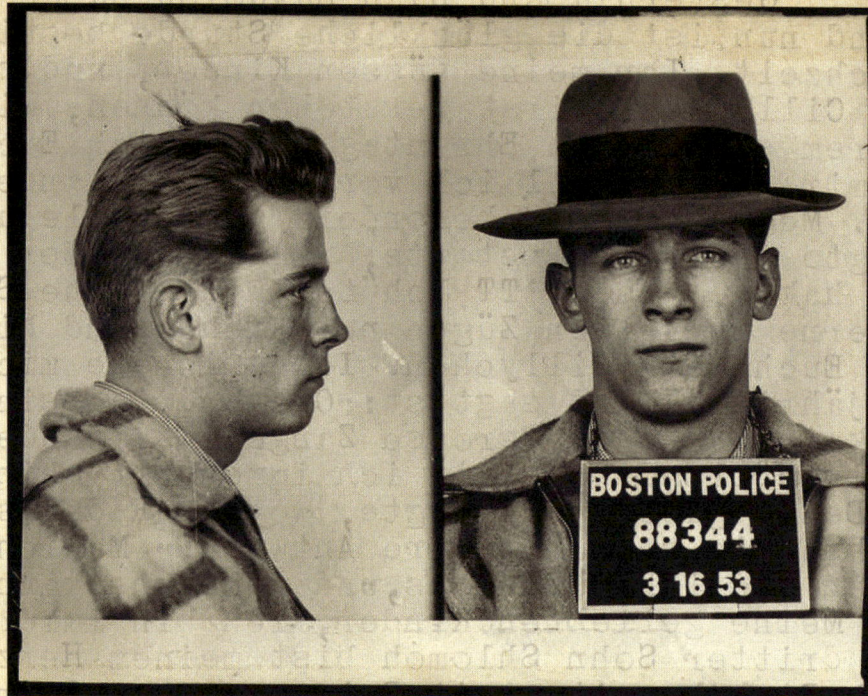

THE IRISH AND RUSSIAN MOBS

Top left: Dean O'Banion in 1921; **Top right:** Whitey Bulgar in 1953, when he was aged 24. The 2006 movie, *The Departed*, **above**, is loosely based on his story with The Winter Hill Gang of Boston. Jack Nicholson plays the Whitey Bulgar character; **Opposite left:** Russian mob enforcer Boris Nayfeld in 2018, at the Russian Baths in Brooklyn. The borough's Brighton Beach area has been a focus for Russian mobs since the 1990s; **Opposite right**: Tattoos tell each man's story of crime and punishment.

The Irish Mob

Irish mobs existed in America since the 18th century, making them the oldest form of organized crime in the country. They were found in most major cities, including New York, Boston, Philadelphia, Chicago, Cleveland, and New Orleans. Some notorious gangs included New York's Dead Rabbits, Chicago's North Siders, and Philadelphia's K&A Gang. The Irish dominated organized crime starting in the 1840s and later produced gangsters like Dean O'Banion, Owney Madden, Red Hamilton, Whitey Bulgar, and Danny Greene. Their dominance waned in the 1920s and 30s as their power was gradually usurped by the mafia. At that time, many members turned to "machine" politics, where they could legally put their fingers in the pot.

In modern times, the Westies organized crime group was responsible for racketeering, drug trafficking, and contract killing in the Hell's Kitchen neighborhood of Manhattan's West Side. In the late 1970s, they even partnered with the Gambino mafia family.

Boston's Winter Hill Gang was one of America's most successful crime syndicates, controlling the city's underworld from the 1960s into the 1990s. The members were known for fixing horse races in the Northeast. In the 1970s and 80s, the FBI office in Boston was infiltrated through corrupt agent John J. Connolly, allowing mob boss Whitey Bulger to use his status as a government informant against rival leaders.

Russian Mobs

The Russian mob, or Bratva, consists of various organized crime elements that originated in the former Soviet Union. Organized crime in Russia began during the days of czarist Empire, but it was not until the Soviet era that the elite vory v zakone ("thieves-in-law") emerged as leaders of prison groups in forced-labor camps and their code of honor became more defined. In the black market economy that

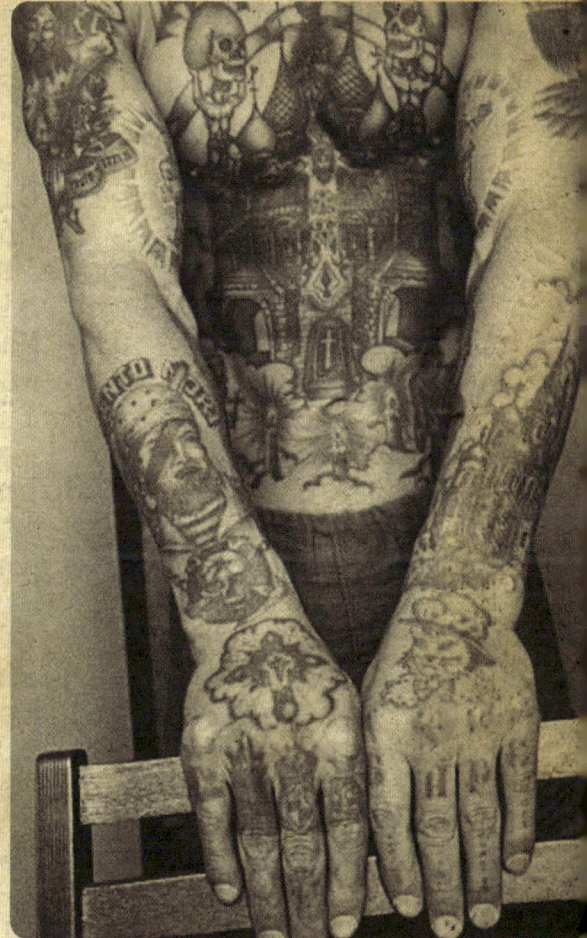

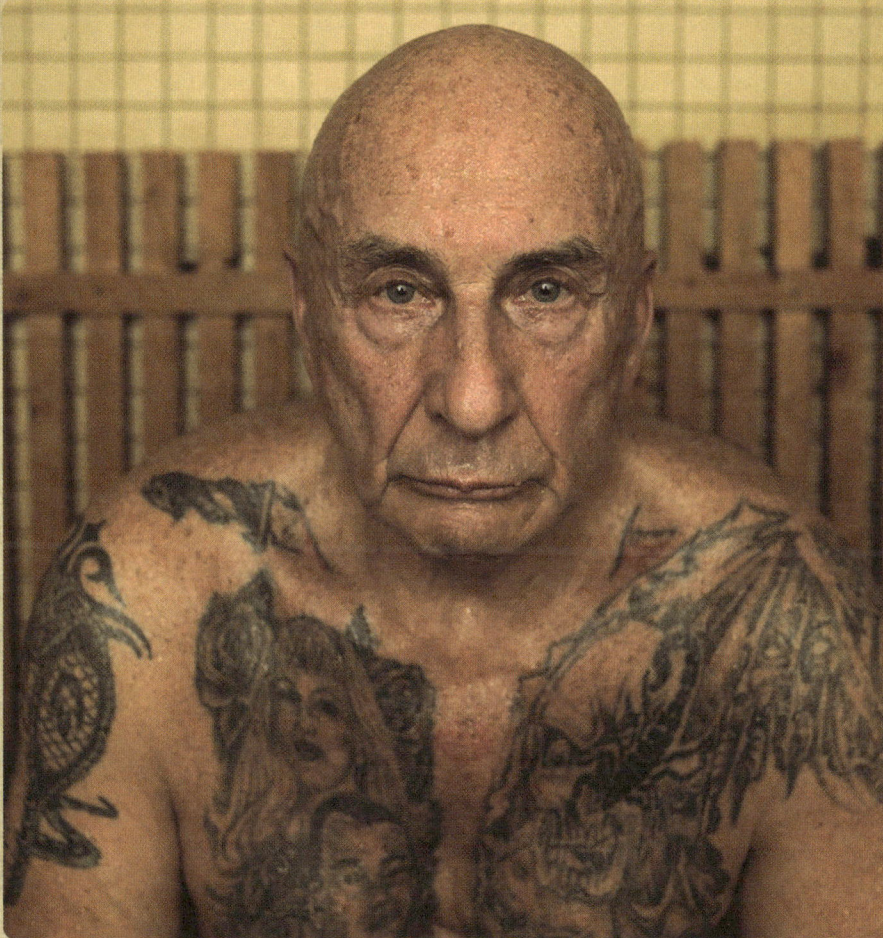

flourished after the end of World War II, the death of Stalin, and the fall of Soviet Russia, additional gangs naturally sprang up.

Members of the Russian mobs migrated to America after the fall of the Soviet Union—becoming involved in racketeering, drug trafficking, prostitution, and fraud. In the 1990s, the FBI proclaimed that Russian mobs posed the greatest threat to American security. The public became more aware of Russian criminal influence after professional hockey players Alexei Zhitnik, Vladimir Malakhov, and Alexander Mogilny were targeted for extortion. According to testimony before Congress in 1996, Mogilny evaded the threat with the help of the FBI, while Zhitnik reportedly sought help from "a more powerful criminal."

Other Eastern European Mobs

Although the term "Russian" is used generically to refer to a variety of Eurasian crime groups, actual Eastern European mobs in the US include the Armenians, Ukrainians, Lithuanians, Belarusians, and residents of the Caucasus region of the former Soviet Union (Chechens, Dagestanis, and Georgians). This includes the fearsome Odessa Mafia, the most dominant and powerful Ukrainian group, which operates out of Brighton Beach, New York. During the 1990s, they became notorious when bodies began stacking up during a turf war. Today many of the Russian mobs focus more on cybercrime and less on street crime. As the Italians learned in the 1940s and 50s, the less visibility, the better.

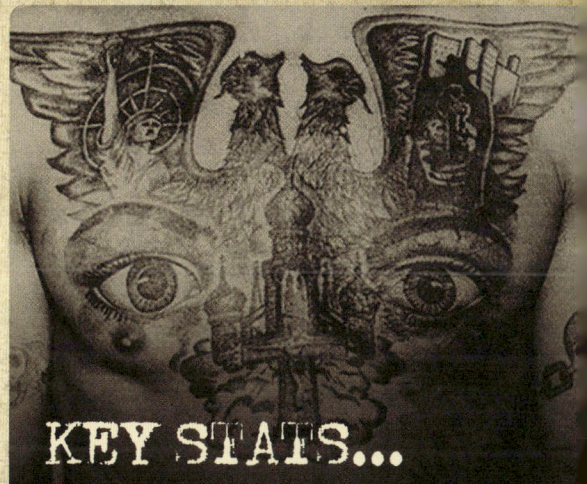

KEY STATS...

Today there are more than 6,000 organized crime groups in Russia, with 200 of them having achieved global outreach. At least 27 have been identified as operating in the United States.

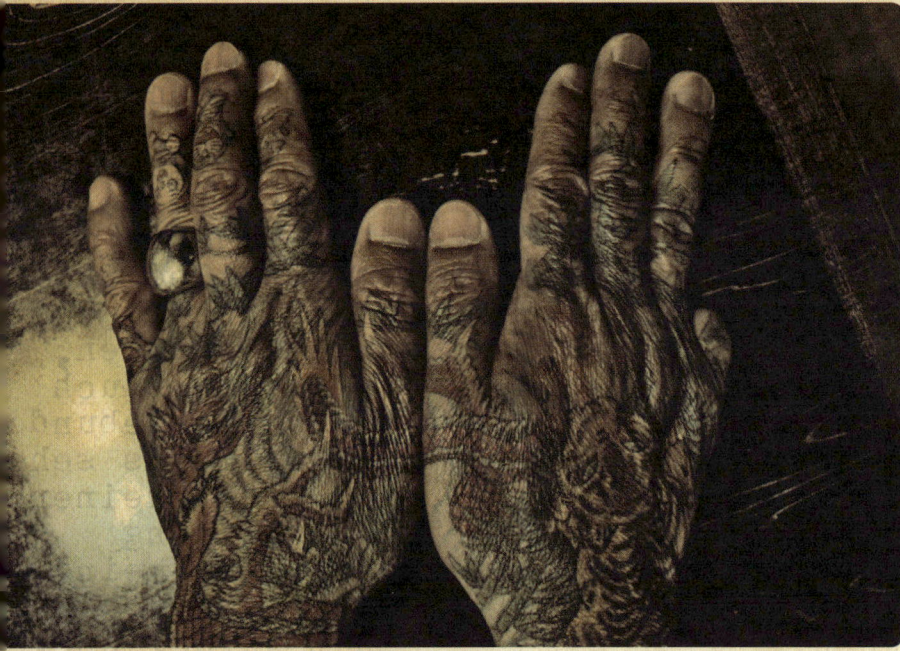

TONGS, TRIADS, AND YAKUZA
ASIAN CRIME SYNDICATES

Top left: Hands of the Yakuza; **Top right:** Tong gang members, circa 1890s; **Above:** Tong elders in 1950s San Francisco; **Opposite left:** A display of Yakuza body decoration from 1970; **Opposite top right:** Triad members photographed in China, circa 1940s; **Opposite center:** A still from the feature film *Triad* (2014), set in Hong Kong; **Opposite bottom:** A group of Yakuza women, circa 1980s.

For centuries the merchants of the world paid dearly for riches exported from Asia—spices, silks, precious gems, ivory, artwork, and, more recently, the raw materials for producing narcotics and other drugs. It is not surprising that countries like China and Japan have long histories of organized crime networks, which naturally cut themselves in on this profitable commerce.

According to Interpol, the illegal activities that modern Asian crime syndicates engage in include drug trafficking, illegal gambling, extortion, kidnapping, human smuggling, and money laundering. The impact of these crimes is so far reaching, it can often be felt on a global level.

The Tongs

Many thousands of Chinese immigrants fled to America in the 19th century to escape harsh conditions at home or they were recruited as laborers for massive construction projects like the new railroads. In either case, they often met with scorn and discrimination from the general population. In response, the Chinese community in San Francisco, which numbered 21,000 by 1890, formed a tong, which literally means "meeting hall." Among other things, this organization provided loans and settled disputes between members.

Tongs first appeared in China in 1644, when the Ming dynasty was overthrown by the Qing dynasty, and an early tong sought to restore the power of the Mings. As racial prejudice increased in 19th-century America, the tongs offered a rare support resource. Because the majority of Chinese in the US were men, tongs were also heavily involved in importing women from China, both for marriage and for prostitution; sadly, many of these women did

not leave China by choice. Tongs eventually spread to every major US city, incorporating prostitution, gambling, drug trafficking, and racketeering. The North America tongs exhibited many similaries to the Hong Kong triads, including their initiation ceremonies and paying respect to the same deities.

Triads

These transnational organized crime syndicates are based in Greater China, with outposts in countries with significant Chinese populations. Founded in the 1800s by the Han, triads were originally a branch of the secret Hung Society. The word "triad" represents the union of heaven, earth, and humanity. Triads have engaged in drug trafficking since the days of the 19th-century opium bans, but their activities were heavily suppressed under Mao Zedong. Today, China, with its widespread chemical industry, remains a source for legitimately produced chemicals that are used as "precursor" chemicals for the production of heroin, cocaine, ecstacy, and crystal methamphetamine. The country's proximity to both the Golden Triangle and the Golden Crescent as well as its many port cities, make it a valuable transit center for drug trafficking. The triads currently smuggle chemicals to American meth labs and also engage in counterfeiting and extortion. The Hong Kong triad is distinct from the mainland syndicates, engaging in more white collar crime.

Yakuza

Yakuza, also known as *gokudō*, are members of a transnational organized crime syndicate that originated in Japan and is headquartered in Kobe. The Japanese police and the media call them *bōryokudan*, while yakuza refer to themselves as *ninkyō dantai*. They have more influence in Japan than the triads, even though the triads operate more independently and

A CLOSER LOOK

The term "yakuza" comes from a card game Oicho-Kabu, where the worst hand is a combination of three cards that add up to 20, for a score of zero.

in more countries. In 1992, the Anti-Boryokudan Act reduced yakuza numbers, but as of 2020 there are still roughly 25,900 active members. Street thugs are often recruited, but members come from all economic backgrounds. The only women recognized are the wives of bosses, called "older sisters." Infractions are treated seriously: first offenders must cut off the tip of the pinky; a second offender loses the tip of the ring finger, and so on. This form of penance is waning, however, as it aids the police in identifying yakuza members.

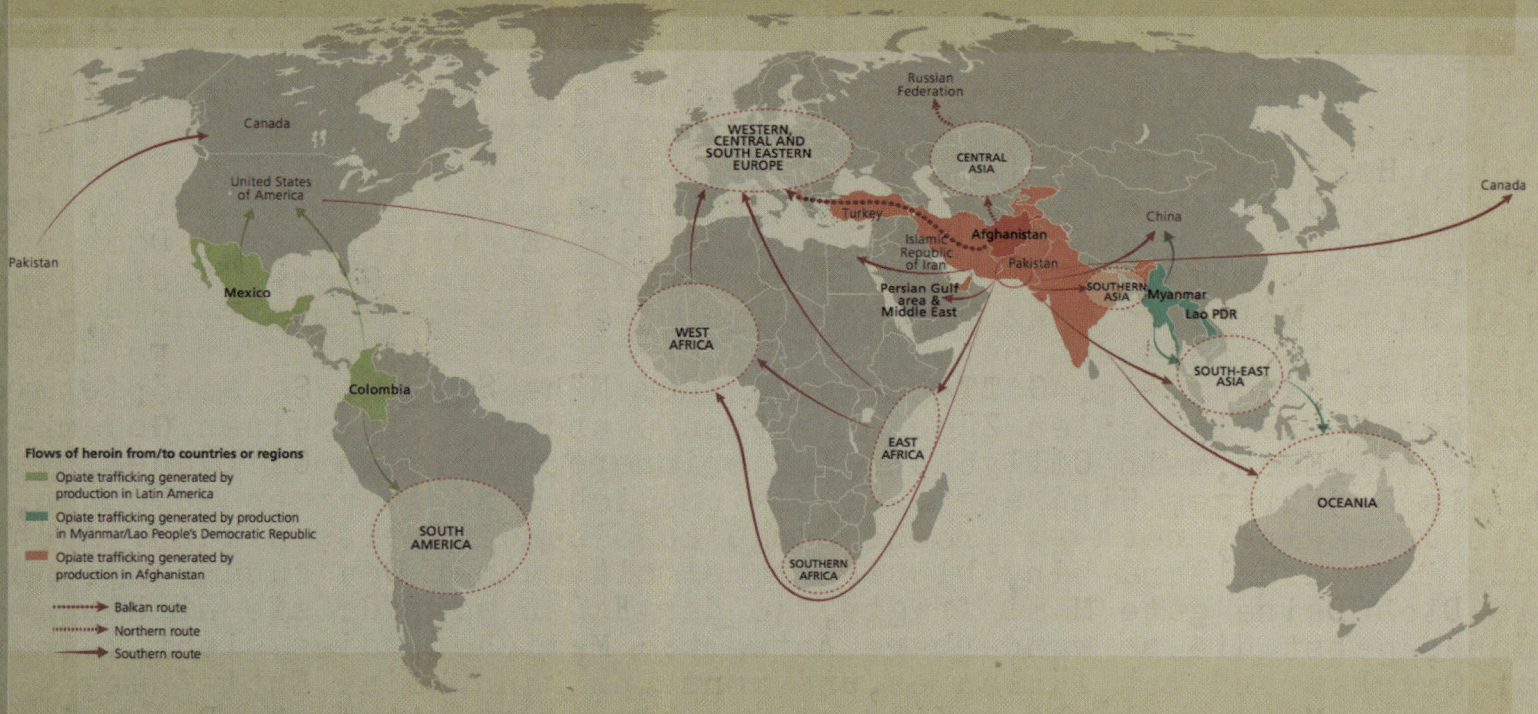

Flows of heroin from/to countries or regions

- Opiate trafficking generated by production in Latin America
- Opiate trafficking generated by production in Myanmar/Lao People's Democratic Republic
- Opiate trafficking generated by production in Afghanistan
- → Balkan route
- ⋯ Northern route
- → Southern route

HEROIN, COCAINE, METHAMPHETAMINE
DRUG CARTELS

Top: Global opiate trafficking routes. Afghanistan is the epicenter of the world's opium production; **Above:** A drug seizure displayed by Mexican police; **Opposite center:** Much of the cocaine, methamphetamine, and marijuana in the USA originates in Colombia and is handled through the Mexican drug cartels, who battle fiercely among themselves for territory and exclusive access to drug routes; **Opposite center, right:** Joachim "El Chapo" Guzman, drug lord of the Sinaloa Federation, after his arrest by the US DEA; **Opposite top, left and right:** A cocaine processing plant; **Main background image:** The jungles of Colombia, site of the majority of the world's cocaine production.

Drug cartels are large, sophisticated organizations that oversee the sourcing, processing, shipping, and distribution of illegal drugs and other controlled substances. The cartels' slick methods for moving drugs evolved from the more primitive types of smuggling once overseen by the mafia and other crime networks. Drugs have been found in fruit and vegetable shipments; fake carrots, bananas, and watermelons; canned jalapeños and tamales; exotic pet snakes; frozen sharks; even inside breast implants.

The first controlled substances to interest smugglers included marijuana, hashish, opium, heroin, and cocaine. More recent street drugs include crack cocaine, crystal methamphetamine, ecstasy or mollies, as well as various prescription opioids. The majority of these drugs are highly addictive, thus creating a very motivated customer base. Because addicts are quite willing to commit robberies or take up prostitution to support their habit, the drug trade frequently gives rise to secondary crimes.

Cartels typically erect their headquarteres in the regions where the drugs are manufactured. For the stimulant cocaine, that would be Colombia, Bolivia, and Peru. After the raw coca plant is harvested, the drug is processed in clandestine laboratories. The product is shipped worldwide, or travels through South and Central America to Mexico, where it is smuggled into the US. Heroin, a highly addictive stimulant derived from the opium poppy (via morphine), is sourced in the Golden Triangle of Southeast Asia—the Lao People's Democratic Republic, Myanmar, Thailand, and Vietnam—and more recently in the Golden Crescent in southwest Asia—Iran, Pakistan, and, in particular, Afghanistan. There, narcotics traffickers funnel money to the insurgents, and the insurgents, in turn, protect the poppy growers from government interference. Chemical drugs, like crystal meth or ecstasy, are often produced by small, rural laboratories. This "home lab" phenomenon has sent American DEA agents deep into the remote pockets where the drugs are produced, harking back to the days of Treasury agents chasing down moonshiners in the woods.

Map legend

- Cocaine traffic
- Methamphetamine precursor supply lines
- Marijuana and meth traffic
- All drug traffic
- Arellano Felix Organization
- Cartel Pacifico Sur
- Los Zetas
- Sinaloa Federation
- Carrillo Fuentes Organization
- Gulf Cartel
- Knights Templar/La Familia Michoacana
- Independent Cartel of Acapulco
- Disputed Territory

UNITED STATES

California
San Diego
Tijuana
Mexicali
Arizona
New Mexico
Douglas
Nogales
Agua Prieta
El Paso
Juarez
Texas
Chihuahua
Pacific Ocean
Nuevo Laredo
Laredo
McAllen
Reynosa
Culiacan
MEXICO
Mazatlan
Tampico
Venezuela, Brazil
from Colombia
Cancun
Merida
Gulf of Mexico
Puerto Vallarta
from Asia
Manzanillo
Lazaro Cardenas
Mexico City
Veracruz
Acapulco
from Colombia
HONDURAS
BELIZE

Major Latin American Cartels

From 1972 to the early 1990s, Colombia's Medellin cartel was one of the most powerful on earth, earning profits of $60 million per day at its peak. It also waged a violent war against the government of Colombia. But in 1992 the cartel began to crumble; especially after Colombian National Police killed its fugitive leader Pablo Escobar in 1993. Today, a resurrected version, now called *Oficina de Envigado*, controls much of Colombia's drug trade through local associates who sell cocaine to their Mexican clients, thus keeping La Oficina out of reach of the DEA.

As of 2021, the Sinaloa Federation cartel, which deals in both cocaine and heroin, remains Mexico's dominant drug cartel . . . and is quite likely the largest drug network in the world. Joachin "El Chapo" Guzman, who headed Sinaloa, was in 2009 ranked by Forbes as a billionaire and is said to have been the most influential drug lord in history, surpassing even Pablo Escobar. Currently, Ismael "El Mayo" Zambada runs the cartel.

Major Asian Cartels

The Golden Triangle networks include Burma's Khun Sa, Red Wa, Hawngleuk Militia, and Han cartels. Golden Crescent cartels include the Pakistani Afridi Network, and Afghanistan's Noorzai, Khan, Karzai, Bagcho, and Haqqani organizations.

How Drugs Are Smuggled

Once carried by pack animals to distribution centers, mass shipments of drugs in modern times are either flown to their destination (sometimes using ultralight aircraft), carried across oceans in cargo containers, or transported overland via commercial trucks, often mixed in with legitimate cargo or hidden in compartments inside the trucks. Oftentimes, tunnels between countries or frontiers are excavated to avoid border checks. Many drugs reach the US from Mexico in this manner.

"It is from the Bible that man has learned cruelty, rapine, and murder; for the belief of a cruel God makes a cruel man."

THOMAS PAINE, *THE AGE OF REASON*

4 Chapter Four

Murder Most Foul

The taking of another human life is generally viewed as the ultimate sin against society. Witness the banishment of Cain after slaying Abel. Yet that potential stigma clearly did not deter the numerous people who have resorted to murder to further a desire for money, power, or revenge . . . or to rid themselves of an unwanted family member—including their spouse or even their own child.

A modern murder site reconstruction.

"Now that it is all over, she should tell us, in the interest of science, how she did it." SIR JAMES PAGET, ST. BARTHOLOMEW'S HOSPITAL

A Gallery of Victorian POISONERS

Throughout history, poison has been used as a means for murder. During the Italian Renaissance, the politically ambitious Borgia family was known for eliminating cardinals, bishops, and nobles with arsenic, strychnine, and aconite administered in drinks and incorporated into clothing, flowers, and book pages.

Up until the late 1800s, it was difficult to detect a poison in a dead body. Arsenic actually leaves little or no trace, and coroners attributed many poisonings to natural causes, such as heart attack or apoplexy (stroke). As a result, poison became a popular and convenient way to dispose of unwanted . . . connections. The trend became so widespread that England had to establish a register of poisons: anyone purchasing a potentially lethal substance, even just to clear rats from the shed, had to furnish their name and address.

Meanwhile in America . . . in 1918 Charles Norris, New York City's first medical examiner, and Alexander Gettler, his toxicologist and forensic chemist, brought genuine evidence and reliable forensic techniques to the formidable job of apprehending poisoners.

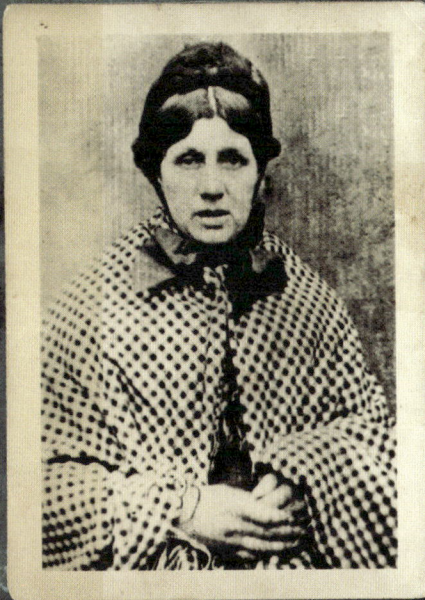

MARY ANN COTTON

Mary Ann Cotton is remembered as Britain's premier mass murderess: she used arsenic to poison three husbands, a lover, and at least 11 children, ostensibly for insurance money. At 20 she married William Mowbray and had four children. William went to sea but died suddenly while at home, as did three of their children. Mary Ann then married George Ward. After he died, Mary Ann collected the insurance money and wed James Robinson, a recent widower. She likely killed three of his children, their baby girl, and her daughter by Mowbray. After a suspicious Robinson cast her out, she married widower Frederick Cotton. She poisoned Frederick, one of two sons by his first wife, and another new baby. Mary Ann took a lover, and he died of gastric fever. When young Charles Cotton proved an encumbrance, she hastily killed him. At last, a local physician, Dr. Kilburn, became suspicious. In 1873 Mary Ann was found guilty in the death of Charles and hanged at Durham Jail.

ADELAIDE BARTLETT

When Edwin Bartlett died mysteriously in 1886, wife Adelaide was the main suspect. Although Edwin's post-mortem revealed liquid chloroform in his stomach, there was no trace in his mouth or throat. Naturally, Adelaide's defence was the question of how the chloroform got into the stomach. Adelaide was acquitted, and afterwards Sir James Paget of St. Bartholomew's Hospital remarked of the Pimlico Mystery, "Now that it is all over, she should tell us, in the interest of science, how she did it."

Florence MAYBRICK

In 1889, when James Maybrick died after a short illness, his relatives were suspicious. After locking Florence in her room, they searched the house and found a packet labelled "Arsenic. Poison for rats." The autopsy revealed traces of arsenic in Maybrick's stomach, and Florence was accused of his murder. She was sentenced to death, commuted to life imprisonment, and was released in 1904.

MADELINE SMITH

In 1855, Smith was a beautiful 21-year-old socialite living in Glasgow. While having an affair with packing clerk Pierre Emile L'Angelier, she had written him some very frank letters. With a society engagement pending, Madeline tried to get the letters back. L'Angelier refused and threatened to show her fiancé the letters unless she married *him*. She purportedly poisoned Pierre with arsenic in a cup of cocoa. At her trial the jury found the case "not proven," a verdict that was legally possible only in Scotland.

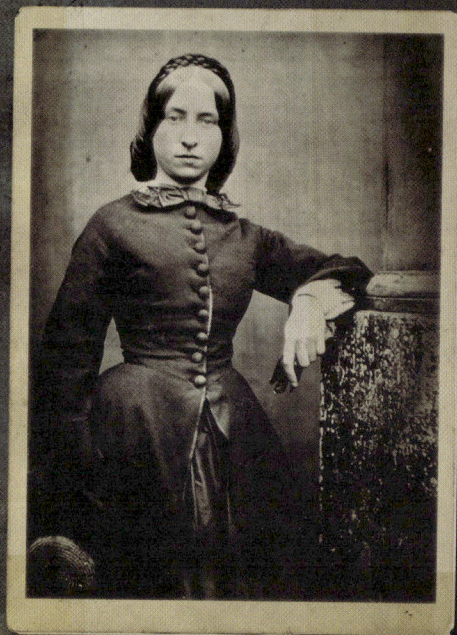

Christina Edmunds—The Chocolate Cream Killer

When prickly spinster Edmunds fell in love with her physician, Dr. Beard, she was sure that her love was returned. In truth, the married doctor was simply embarrassed. In 1871 Edmunds sent Mrs. Beard a box of chocolates poisoned with strychnine. When the wife recovered Edmunds began purchasing chocolates, lacing them with poison, then returning them to the shop to be purchased by others. A young child died as a result. Edmunds was arrested when Dr. Beard informed on her. "The Chocolate Cream Killer" served a life sentence in Broadmoor Criminal Lunatic Asylum.

THOMAS CREAM—The Lambeth Poisoner

Known as the Lambeth Poisoner, Cream was a Scottish-Canadian medical doctor and serial killer who poisoned a number of London prostitutes with strychnine. After his "helpful" attempts to frame others for his crimes raised the suspicions of Metropolitan Police detectives he was caught, and after trial executed at Newgate.

GEORGE CHAPMAN— The Borough Poisoner

The Borough Poisoner, aka Polish-born Seweryn Kłosowski, was a serial killer in late-19th century England. Also a polygamist, he married an English girl, in spite of having a wife in Poland. In addition, Chapman took at least four mistresses and killed three by poisoning with tartar-emetic: Mary Isabella Spink, Bessie Taylor, and Maud Marsh. Convicted in the death of Marsh, he was hanged in 1903. Chapman had also been a major suspect in the Jack the Ripper murders some fifteen years earlier.

DR. WILLIAM PALMER

Among England's most notorious poisoners, Palmer killed his friend John Cook with strychine for financial gain and likely murdered his wife, brother, mother-in-law, and four of his children as infants. He collected large insurance settlements for both his wife and brother. Palmer was executed by hanging in 1856.

Dr. Edward Pritchard

In 1865, this English doctor living in Glasgow poisoned his mother-in-law, J then killed his wife a month later. Dr. Paterson, the physician attending both women was highly suspicious and refused to sign the death certificates. When the bodies were exhumed, they were found to contain the poison antimony. Pritchard was hanged in 1865 before a crowd of 100,000, the last man to be publically executed in Scotland.

NAME YOUR POISON . . .

Arsenic: This naturally occurring heavy metal is tasteless and colorless, and is not detectable in the body, with death mimicking natural illness. It was the go-to poison for Victorian murderers.

Botulism toxin: Produced by anaerobic bacteria, this poison is rated as the most toxic substance: as little as 1 nanogram per kilogram can kill a person.

Chloroform: This early form of anesthestic ($CHCl3$) became popular as a poison in the 1920s.

Cyanide: Emitting the scent of bitter almonds, this poison makes the body unable to use life-sustaining oxygen. Nazi Hermann Göring killed himself with cyanide the night before his hanging.

Ethylene glycol: Antifreeze has a sweet taste, making it ideal for poisoners. It is currently the number one homicide-related poison in the US.

Opium: While not a poison, many people succumbed to overdoses of laudenum, a tincture of opium.
Ricin: A white granular substance found in castor beans, in powder or mist form it has been used in "mail attacks," including one targeting the White House, and as a bioterror weapon.

Strychnine: This crystalline alkaloid ($C21H22N2O2$) forms a white, odorless, bitter powder; it is a neurotoxin that causes asphyxia and is normally used as a pesticide.

VX: This synthetic substance with the consistency of motor oil, intended as an insecticide, is now used as a nerve agent that causes rapid asphyxiation. VX appeared in the thriller *The Rock*.

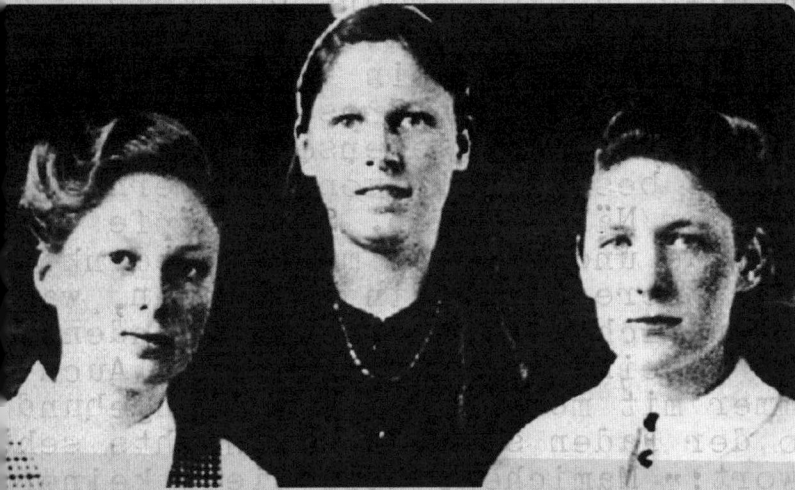

After police investigators analyze evidence from a murder scene, sometimes the necessary clues just don't appear. Here are two notable "unsolved cases" that baffled police departments then . . . and now.

UNSOLVED MURDERS

Top left: 12-year old Muriel Drinkwater (center) was murdered on the evening of June 27 in 1946; **Top right:** Her route home from school, and somewhere along which she was abducted; **Above:** The village children bring flowers to Muriel's funeral; **Opposite, main picture:** Elizabeth Short, the 22-year old victim; **Opposite, bottom left:** George Hodel, one of many suspects in the crime; **Opposite, bottom right:** The horrific crime scene pictures.

Muriel Drinkwater
Carmarthen, Wales

The "Little Red Riding Hood Murder" took place in 1946 and later featured the oldest DNA to be extracted as evidence in a murder case. Muriel Drinkwater, age 12, was the daughter of farmer John Drinkwater and wife Margaret. On June 27, 1946, the girl rode the school bus from Gowerton Grammar School to Tyle-Du Farm, and embarked along the one-mile path to the house, which curved in and out of the woods. Her mother saw her enter the woods, but not come out again. The last person to see her was Hubert Hoyles, 13, who bypassed her after buying eggs at the farm. When she did not return home, more than a dozen local men began a search.

The next day Drinkwater's body was found in the woods by a police inspector. She had been raped, bludgeoned in the head, and shot twice in the chest. Two days later the gun was found, a World War I-era Colt .45. Detectives from Scotland Yard arrived in Swansea to assist, while police visited every house within 150 square miles and interviewed 20,000 men. The police circulated a description of a person of interest, a 30-ish man with "thick fluffy hair and wearing brown corduroy trousers and a light brown sports jacket," but the suspect was never located.

In 2003 detectives re-opened the case, hoping to find DNA evidence on the gun, but too many people had handled it. The victim's clothes were believed lost, but in 2008, a team of retired detectives working cold cases found Drinkwater's blue coat, underwear, and school uniform in storage. On the back of the coat, a now-invisible semen stain was circled in yellow crayon

Scientists successfully retrieved a DNA profile, but no match was found in the national DNA database. Hubert Hoyles, who passed Muriel, was exonerated by the DNA evidence. Having long been suspected of the murder, he was happy to clear his name. Welsh true crime author Neil Milkins has theorized that notorious child killer Harold Jones was responsible for the murder, but DNA tests also cleared Jones.

The Black Dahlia
Los Angeles, California

Perhaps the most famous unsolved murder in modern history, the 1947 killing of a young waitress, struck the public imagination like few crimes before it. On January 15, the remains of Elizabeth Short, a 22-year-old aspiring actress from Massachusetts, was found in a vacant lot in Los Angeles, California. The nude body had been surgically cut in half and was so drained of blood it resembled a mannequin to onlookers.

The assailant had also cut her mouth into a wide, smiling rictus. Because there was no blood on the ground, the police assumed the body had been moved from the murder site.

The murder investigation was front page news for many months. The local newspapers began referring to the victim by a dramatic and tragic name, the Black Dahlia, a play on the recent film *The Blue Dahlia*. After months of detective work—and more than 50 false murder confessions—the LAPD admitted that the lack of eyewitnesses and hard evidence was hindering their progress.

In 2013, retired police detective Paul Dostie, author Steve Hodel, and police sniffer dog Buster, searched the home of Hodel's late father, Dr. George Hill Hodel, looking for evidence of decomposing flesh. Steve always maintained that his father killed Short, and Hodel had even referred to it in conversation, "Supposin' I did kill the Black Dahlia. They couldn't prove it now." This new investigation, however, was inconclusive.

(MORE) MAYHEM IN THE MIDWEST:

IN COLD BLOOD

Main image: The Clutter family; **Above:** Truman Capote, whose *In Cold Blood* recounted the entire bloody crime and its aftermath. It became famous as the first "non-fiction novel"

Sometimes a crime strikes at the public's heart, creating a swell of outrage and a mass cry for justice. This was the case in 1959 after the cold-blooded slaying of a Kansas farm family named Clutter. The subsequent trial not only stirred a national response and left the Midwest to a state of fear, the crime was also responsible for inspiring a book that changed the nature of nonfiction writing.

On the night of November 14, ex-convicts Richard Hickock and Perry Smith drove to an isolated farmhouse in Holcomb, a rural Kansas community where residents felt so safe they rarely locked their doors. Hickock's prison cellmate, Floyd Wells, had told him of a

prosperous farmer he'd worked for named Clutter who kept a large sums of cash in his safe. Once freed, Hickock convinced a former cellmate, Smith, to help him rob the farm. The Clutters, who were highly regarded by their neighbors, consisted of father Herb, his wife, Bonnie Mae, and two of their children who still lived at home— Nancy, 16, and Kenyon, 15.

The two thieves entered the darkened house through an unlocked door, then bound and gagged the family before searching for the money. They found little of value, certainly not a safe full of cash. The jailhouse rumors of hidden wealth had been false. Whether it was due to anger, frustration, or the need to eliminate witnesses, Smith slit Herb's throat with a knife,

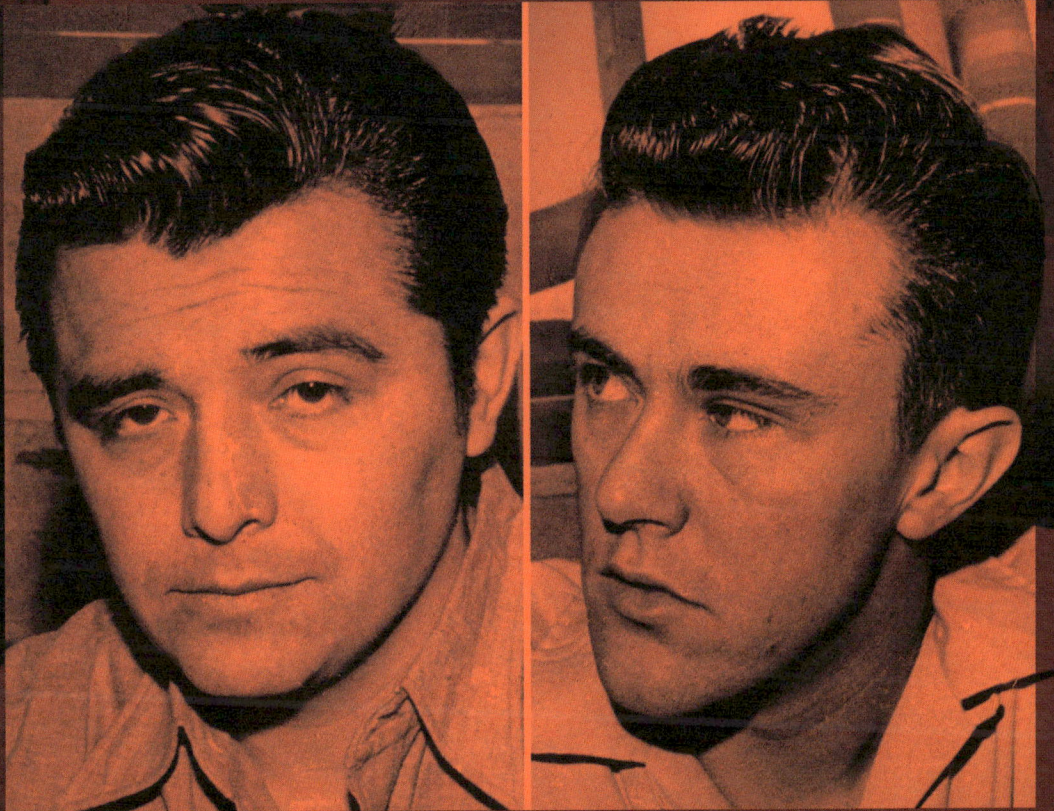

> "I didn't want to harm the man. I thought he was a very nice gentleman. Soft-spoken. I thought so right up to the moment I cut his throat."

PERRY SMITH

then both men used shotguns to dispatch all four Clutters, even the teenaged children. They headed into the night with $50, a portable radio, and a pair of binoculars.

When a schoolfriend came by the next morning seeking Nancy Clutter, she was met by the horrific sight of the murdered family. Law enforcement flocked to the scene . . . and the manhunt began. Eventually Hickock was implicated by Wells, the cellmate who had bragged about Clutter's money. The two fugitives were apprehended six weeks later and returned to Kansas to stand trial.

Meanwhile, mercurial Manhattanite author Truman Capote, author of *Breakfast at Tiffany's*, read about the murder and the search for the killers . . . and knew he had found the subject of his next book. He traveled to Holcomb with childhood friend Harper Lee, the author of *To Kill A Mockingbird*. After the capture of Hickock and Smith, Capote conducted many interviews with them. He grew quite close to the two men,

especially Perry, and compiled more than 8,000 pages of research. His aim, he said, was to treat "a real event with fictional techniques," creating a synthesis between factual reporting and a literary work of art.

At their trial, both men received the death penalty. After five years on death row in the Kansas State Penitentiary they were executed by hanging, Hickock first, then Smith. Hickock took 20 minutes to die.

Capote's book, *In Cold Blood*, **first serialized in the The New Yorker in 1965, was published** to great acclaim. It is considered by many to be the original non-fiction novel. It also inspired three feature films—*In Cold Blood* in 1967, plus two biographic pictures, *Capote* and *Infamous*, from 2005 and 2006. Yet the long process of researching and writing the book had proved grueling for the author, and he never regained his vigor. His drinking increased, he started using drugs, and his health deteriorated. In 1984 he died of liver failure.

Top left: Murderers Perry Smith (left), and Richard Hickock; **Top:** Philip Seymour Hoffman as Truman Capote in the 2005 film *Capote*; **Above:** Toby Jones, also as Truman Capote in the following year's *Infamous*. Both motion pictures deal with the Clutter murders and Truman Capote's creation of *In Cold Blood*

A CLOSER LOOK::

Although *In Cold Blood* failed to win the Pulitzer Prize as Capote had hoped, it went on to become the second-bestselling true crime book after Vincent Bugliosi's *Helter Skelter* (1974), a recounting of the Manson family murders.

Left, top: Mabel Normand, the comedic actor that William Desmond Taylor felt deeply for; **Left, center:** William Desmond Taylor, who was shot dead in his Hollywood bungalow; **Above:** Mary Miles Mintner, one of Taylor's protegées, and one of the original suspects in the killing; **Main picture:** Lana Turner (left), with Johnny Stompanato and her daughter Cheryl Crane;

Since the days of silent films, the movie business has endured a number of disturbing deaths, from the unexpected departures of icons Rudolph Valentino and Jean Harlow to the shocking suicides of screen notables like George Sanders, Marilyn Monroe, and Robin Williams. But there have been few actual homicides, where show business luminaries were involved in or victims of murder.

William Desmond Taylor was an Anglo-Irish-American film director of the silent era, who produced 51 pictures. As actor William Deane-Tanner he married a New York stage actress in 1901 and fathered a daughter, Ethel. In 1908 he disappeared, deserting his wife and daughter. After serving in the war he became a top film director (as William Desmond Taylor) and mentor to teenage star, Mary Miles Mintner. In February 1922, his body was found inside his LA bungalow, shot in the back with a pistol. Suspects included Taylor's two valets and Mintner, who had developed a crush on him. Comedic actress Mabel Normand, whom Taylor loved, feared the killer was her cocaine dealer. After the director

fruitlessly tried to help her overcome her drug habit, he had threatened to testify against the suppliers. The crime was never solved; it is possible the studios squelched the investigation to avoid negative publicity. Daughter Ethel inherited his estate.

Johnny Stompanato Jr. was an enforcer for the Cohen crime family and boyfriend to Lana Turner, the popular screen actress known for her sultry roles. After serving in the Marines, he gravitated to Hollywood, where he became an enforcer for the Cohen mob and established himself on the fringes of the film industry. Stompanato was like catnip to women—Frank Sinatra once appealed to Cohen to keep Johnny away from wife Ava Gardner—but he had a spotty record as a husband, twice divorced by 24. He met Turner in 1957 during a downturn in her career. Her daughter Cheryl Crane described him as "always coiled" with "watchful, hooded eyes." His relationship with Turner was stormy, and they fought constantly. A jealous Stompanato once stormed onto a British soundstage and pulled a gun on Turner's costar, a young Sean Connery. The future Bond disarmed him and knocked

HOLLYWOOD HOMICIDES

him down. On April 8, 1958, Turner finally told her abusive lover it was over. When teenaged Cheryl heard the enraged Stompanato threaten to kill her mother, she fatally stabbed him with a kitchen knife. The jury returned a verdict of justifiable homicide.

Dorothy Stratten was a Canadian Playboy Playmate and aspiring actress who became part of a fatal love triangle. In 1979 Stratten married Paul Snider, a Vancouver club promoter and pimp, and began working at the Playboy Club in LA. Hugh Hefner believed she could transition to acting and encouraged her to dump Snider. She appeared in several low-budget films, then in early 1980 began filming the big-budget comedy, *They All Laughed*, where she and director Peter Bogdanovich fell in love. In April, after she was introduced as Playmate of the Year, she began distancing herself from Snider. He grew increasingly erratic, however, and on August 13 bought a shotgun. The next day he invited her to his LA home to "work out" the separation. Instead, Snider shot her soon after she arrived and then turned the gun on himself. Bogdanovich collapsed upon hearing the news. When *They All Laughed* had a small, disappointing run and was withdrawn by the studio, he bought the film rights and re-released it to assure Dorothy's legacy. He ended up losing his entire fortune to that act of faith *and* the LA home where he and Stratten had lived.

Above, left: No, this is not a movie, but the real-life murder trial of Lana Turner's daughter Cheryl. This is Lana Turner on the stand, giving her performance under cross-examination. Hollywood conspiracy theorists believe that it was Lana Turner who actually wielded the knife that killed Stompanato, and that 14-year-old Cheryl took the blame because, as a minor, she would receive a lighter sentence; **Above, right:** Dorothy Stretton, the 1980 Playmate of the Year, and her lover, director Peter Bogdanovich.

SHOCKING DEATHS OF MUSIC LEGENDS

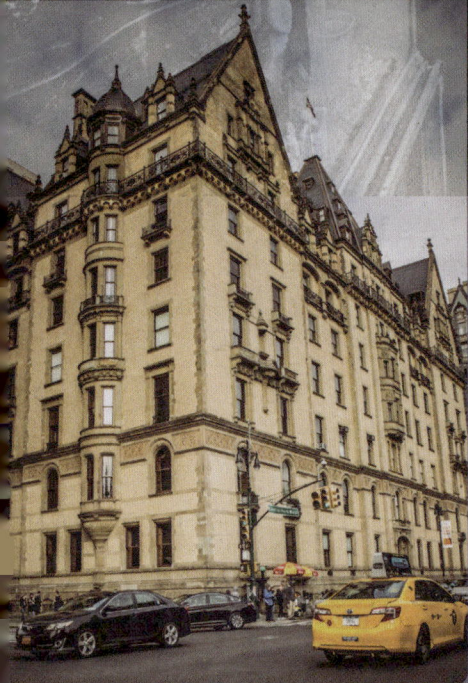

Top: John Lennon with Yoko Ono window shopping...sometime in New York City; **Above:** The Dakota Building, on the corner of 72nd St. and Central Park West, NYC; **Above right:** Mark Chapman, Lennon's assassin

It feels especially painful when a celebrity is murdered or dies unexpectedly . . . and we experience that hollow feeling of being punched in the gut. These larger-than-life figures, so insulated and protected, seem like they should be immune from physical danger. Yet celebrity deaths occur more frequently than we would like, and in many cases—such as with Princess Diana, who was pursued to her death by papparazzi—the whole world mourns with us.

John Lennon New York, NY

A founding member of the Beatles, John Lennon exerted a powerful influence as a songwriter and antiwar activist. After the mythic band broke up in 1970, he moved to New York City with wife, conceptual artist Yoko Ono. There, he and Ono had a son, Sean. Lennon said he liked the anonymity of the Big Apple, where few people accosted him in the street. Yet he was never really out of the public eye: he continued to write and perform and produce albums.

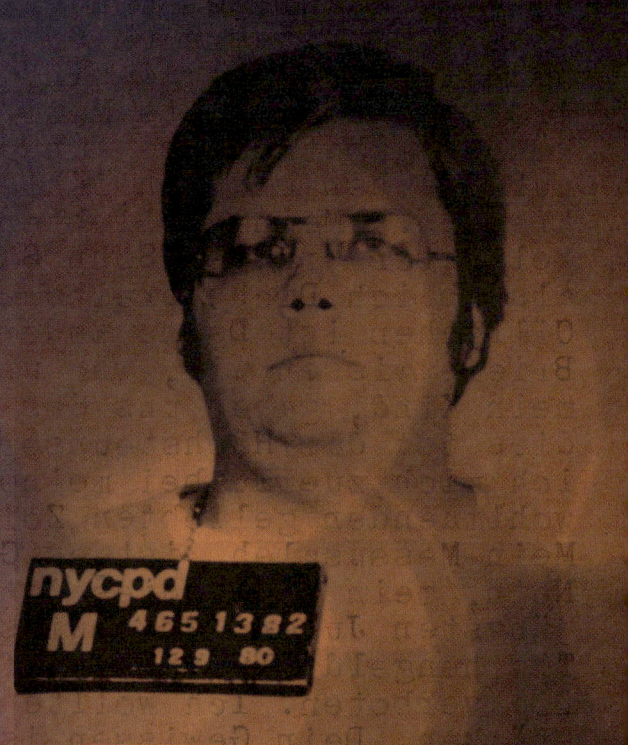

So on December 8, 1980, when Lennon was shot and killed in front of his West Side apartment building, much of the world was stunned and saddened. His assailant, Mark David Chapman, was a former fan from Hawaii who was angered by Lennon's lifestyle, his statements, and his previous remark that the Beatles were "more popular than Jesus." Chapman planned the murder for several months, intending to wait for Lennon outside his home, the famed Dakota. There is even a photo of Lennon signing Chapman's copy of *Double Fantasy* earlier that evening.

Later that night, however, when Lennon and Ono returned from a recording session, Chapman stepped out from the shadows and fired four shots into Lennon's back. Rushed to Roosevelt Hospital in a police car, he was pronounced dead on arrival. Chapman, who gave himself up to the police, was sentenced to 20 years-to-life in prison.

Selena Corpus Christi, Texas

Selena Quintanilla-Pérez was an attractive, slender, brunette singer of Mexican-American and Cherokee heritage. The Texas native's talent became clear to her father, Abraham Quintanilla Jr., when she was only six. Her father opened a Tex-Mex restaurant, Papa Gayo's, in 1981, where 10-year-old Selena and siblings Abraham and Suzette would perform. Eventually her father kitted out an old schoolbus, "Big Bertha," and took the family on tour. But it was not until the release of her first album, *Selena Y Los Dinos*, that she gained recognition. The Tejano-style songs were based on a male-dominated genre of music that incorporates Tex-Mex with German and polka influences. In order to perform the songs in Spanish, as her father insisted, she had to learn the lyrics phonetically.

In 1992, *Entre a Mi Mundo* peaked at number one on the US *Billboard* Regional Mexican Albums chart for eight months and became her "breakthrough" recording. In 1993, Live! won the Grammy for Best Mexican-American Album. Dubbed the Queen of Tejano music, Selena would sell 30 million records worldwide.

Meanwhile Selena fan Yolanda Saldiver, convinced Quintanilla to let her start a Selena fan club. Saldiver became friends with Selena and even managed the star's clothing boutiques. But Saldiver had begun embezzling large sums of money from the fan club and boutiques. In a motel room in Corpus Christi, Selena insisted Saldiver turn over bank statements and financial records. Saldiver pulled a gun from her purse and shot the singer, severing her subclavian artery. Selena crawled away for help, but was declared dead at the hospital. Saldiver surrendered to police after a nine-hour standoff; she was later found guilty and received a life sentence.

> **"I've pent up all my aggression, kept swallowing it and swallowing it."** MARK CHAPMAN

Above: Selena Quintanilla-Perez in concert; **Left:** Yolanda Saldiver, Selena's killer.

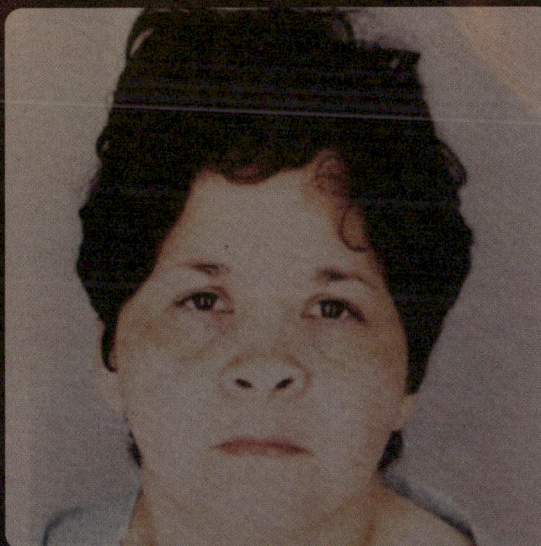

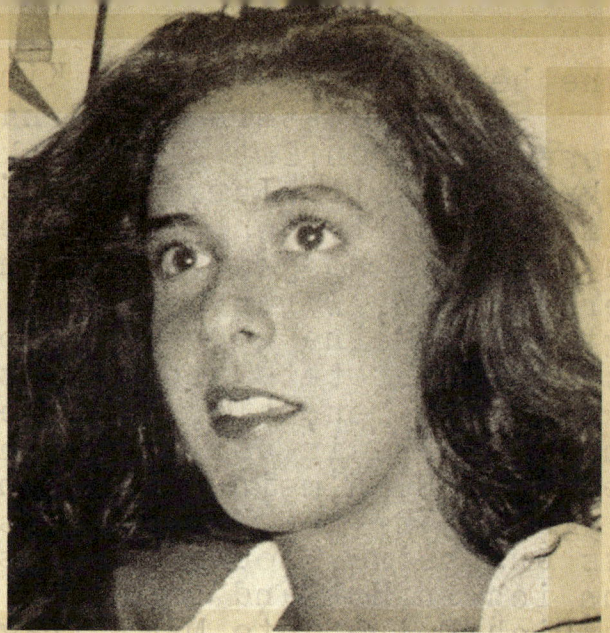

THE PREPPY MURDERER AND THE MENENDEZ BROTHERS
PRIVILEGED...AND DEADLY

Top Left: Robert Chambers, the so-called "Preppy Murderer," arrives at court for his arraignment; **Top Right:** His victim, Jennifer Levin. Chambers's defense lawyer Roger Stavis later called Levin's death "a terrible accident"; **Above:** Chambers in court. While standing trial for murder, he was also being investigated for a series of burglaries; **Opposite main picture and bottom:** The Menendez Brothers in court; **Opposite inset:** Edie Falco stars in the 2017 TV miniseries *Law & Order True Crime: The Menendez Murders.*

Robert Chambers New York, NY

This nineteen-year-old appeared to have it all. A young New York socialite with dark good looks, altheticism, and a quiet charm, Chambers enjoyed the club scene. Yet after one semester at Boston College, he was asked to leave, in part over a stolen credit card. And that was not his first foray into crime—he stole from his friends' families and from a teacher at the Browning School, possibly to fund his drug habit.

On the night of August 26, 1986, Chambers ran into Jennifer Levin at a popular hook-up spot, Dorrian's Red Hand. The two had met before, but Chambers seemed distracted. Levin engaged him, they ended up talking, and finally left the bar together after 4 AM. A few hours later, a cyclist found her body in Central Park; she had been strangled with her own denim jacket and her body bore both bite marks and bruises. Forensics showed she had put up a fight.

Bizarrely, Chambers remained near the scene, watching the police response from outside the Metropolitan Museum of Art. He was probably still high from a mixture of tequila, ecstacy, and cocaine. It was suggested that the combination created some performance issues, fueling his attack on Levin.

The police had no trouble tracing the murder to Chambers, whose face bore incriminating scratch marks. The press quickly labeled him the Preppy Murderer. In his statement, Chambers insisted Levin had initiated bondage play and rough sex, and he only pulled on her neck in retaliation. Due to lack of witnesses, the prosecution withdrew the initial charge of murder. Chambers pled down to manslaughter and served fifteen years in prison, often locked in solitary as a "dangerous prisoner." He was again arrested in 2007 for drug dealing and received a 19-year sentence.

The Menendez Brothers
Beverly Hills, California

On August 20, 1989, a prosperous Beverly Hills couple, José and Mary "Kitty" Menendez, were brutally shot in their beds. When the murder was first investigated, police suspected a mob hit because the two bodies were so disfigured after 15 rounds from two 12-gauge shotguns.

José, a Cuban immigrant, had worked his way up from menial jobs to become head of RCA

TRIALS OF THE CENTURY

"Everybody thinks we were this perfect family, but we were a disaster." LYLE MENENDEZ

Records. He and former beauty queen Kitty had two sons, Lyle, 21, and Erik, 18. Both boys were talented tennis players, egged on by a father who demanded excellence in every pursuit. Erik often feared that nothing he ever did was good enough. He eventually got in trouble for a string of burglaries. Lyle, meanwhile, received a year's suspension from Princeton for plagiarism.

The boys told police they'd been heading to the movies and only stopped at their parents' house for Erik's ID . . . when they found the bodies. Their claims of innocence were belied by their complete lack of grief—after inheriting their father's $14m fortune, they spent an estimated $700,000 within six months. Dr. Jerome Oziel, the therapist who had counseled

Erik over the burglaries, contacted him and offered to see him. Erik eventually admitted to the murders, and Oziel told his mistress, Judalon Smyth. After a fight with Oziel, Smyth contacted the police and revealed the truth. She even had audiotapes of both boys confessing. It took two years to approve two of the three tapes as admissable. Meanwhile, the trials became national sensations, full of family dysfunction and psychodrama. The boys claimed they had been emotionally abused and sexually assaulted by their father. The first trial resulted in two hung juries . . . one for each brother; the second, more sedate trial (sans TV cameras) in 1996, resulted in two convictions of first-degree murder and two sentences of life without parole.

PARENTS WHO KILL THEIR CHILDREN

"Certain monsters are sacred because often the same qualities are found in a monster and in a saint..." JACQUES ALGARRON

Above: "The Possessed" lovers, Denise Labbé and Jacques Algarron, after their arrest by French police in November 1954.

It seems unthinkable that a parent could be so affected by daily stress or personal demons that they would murder their own child. Yet some external pressure or mental instability caused these following individuals to break with reality and commit the ultimate parental sin.

Denise Labbé France

Labbé, a French government secretary, met her lover Jacques Algarron, an officer cadet, in 1954 at Rennes. Algarron was a keen follower of Nietzsche, believing himself a prime example of the German philosopher's Superman. He ordered Labbé to cheat on him so she could beg his forgiveness. Finally, he asked her to make the supreme sacrifice . . . to murder her 2 1/2-year-old daughter, Catherine. Labbe attempted it three times, finally succeeding on November 8, 1954, drowning the child in a wash basin. When the police arrested Labbé, she confessed and implicated Algarron. During the trial the couple were known as "the Possessed." She was sentenced to life with penal servitude, while he received 20 years hard labor.

Susan Smith
Union County, South Carolina

On October 25, 1994, a distraught Susan Smith told police that her car had been carjacked . . . and that the thief drove off with her two sons, three-year-old Michael and 14-month-old Alexander. The fraught tale quickly found traction in the international news cycle, and for nine days Smith was televised making heartfelt pleas for her sons' return. Meanwhile, police investigations found nothing. On November 3, Smith confessed that she had rolled her car into John D. Long Lake with the boys inside. She explained that her lover, a wealthy man named Tom Findlay, had ended their relationship, insisting he did not want children. She said she was so shaken, she acted without thinking.

Defense attorneys David Bruck and Judy Clarke brought in expert witnesses who testified that Smith, who'd had an unstable childhood—including her father's suicide, sexual assault by her stepfather, and attempts on her own life, suffered from mental health issues that affected her judgment. After a short deliberation,

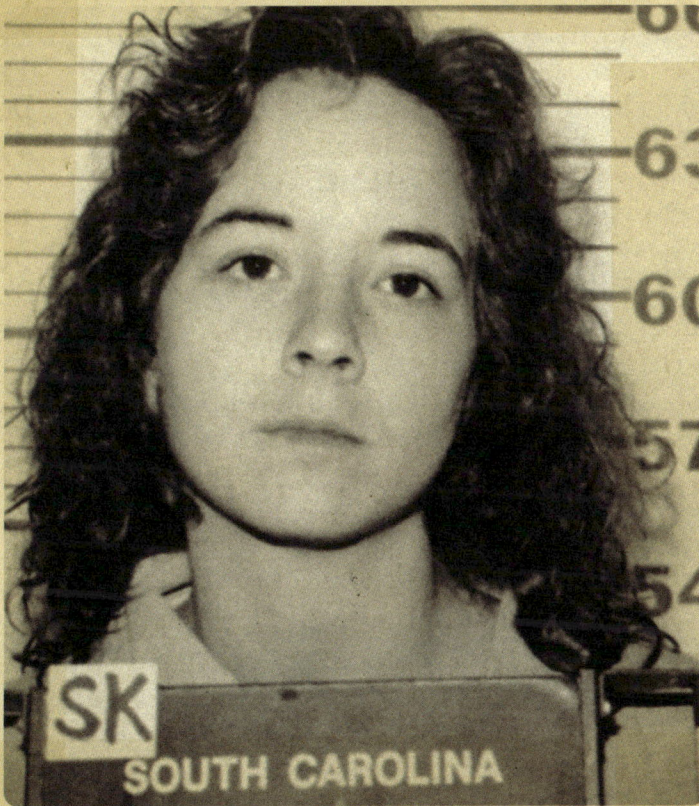

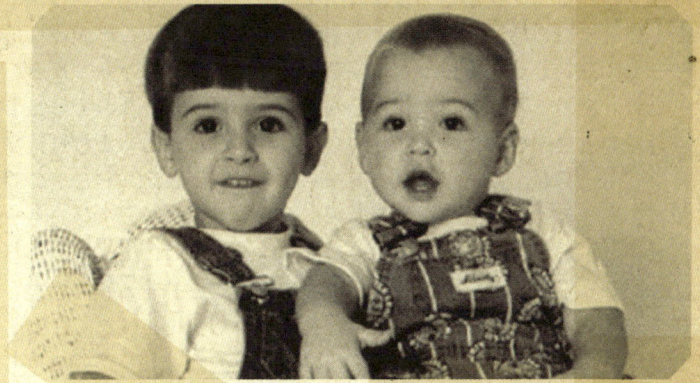

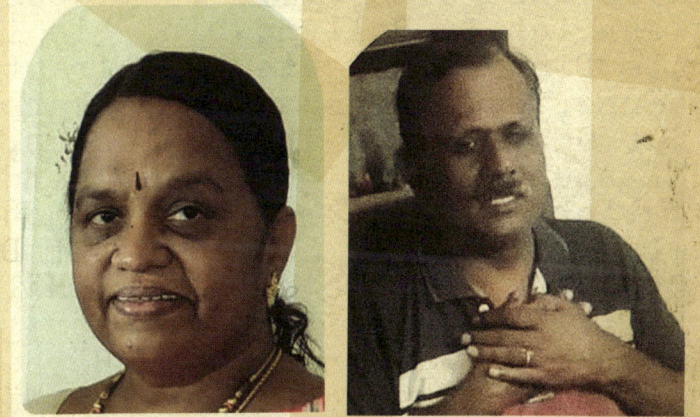

the jury found her guilty. Although the prosecutor argued for the death penalty, she was sentenced to life, with the possibility of parole in 2024.

Padmaja and Purushottam Naidu India

On January 24 of 2021, Indian police broke into a home in rural Mandanapalle, Chittoor district, Andhra Pradesh, after neighbors called to complains of "loud screams and chants" coming from the residence. There they found an academic couple, Padmaja and Purushottam Naidu, in an apparent trance. Their two adult daughters, Alekhya, 27, and Sai Divya (22), lay in a pool of blood, Alekhya on the ground floor, her sister in her bedroom. Both had been bludgeoned to death with a barbell and stabbed with a trident. Neither parent seemed aware of what had occurred.

Colleagues told police the couple were highly superstitious and held extreme religious beliefs, in spite of their academic achievements. Once out of her trance, Padmaja railed at the police for "disrupting a ritual" that was supposed to revive her dead daughters.

She claimed the police allowed demons into the house when they opened the doors and bid them return the next day to witness the resurrection of her children.

Both parents, who had been sheltering in place during the Covid pandemic with the two girls, were taken into custody. While under psychiatric care, the couple revealed that Sai Divya was murdered by her sister; Padmaja then killed Alekhya in retalliation. The parents truly believed they could revive both girls. Meanwhile, the police are still struggling to resolve the case.

Top left: Susan Smith's mugshot from November 1994. While she was incarcerated at the Camille Griffin Graham Correctional Institution, two correctional officers, Lieutenant Houston Cagle and Captain Alfred R. Rowe Jr., were charged after having sex with her; **Top:** Susan Smith's two murdered sons, Michael (left) and baby Alex; **Above center, left and right:** Padmaja and Purushottam Naidu, and, **Above:** Their two daughters, Alekya (left) and Sai Divya when they were younger. A delusional Padmaja insisted the Covid virus came from the god Shiva and claimed that she herself was Shiva.

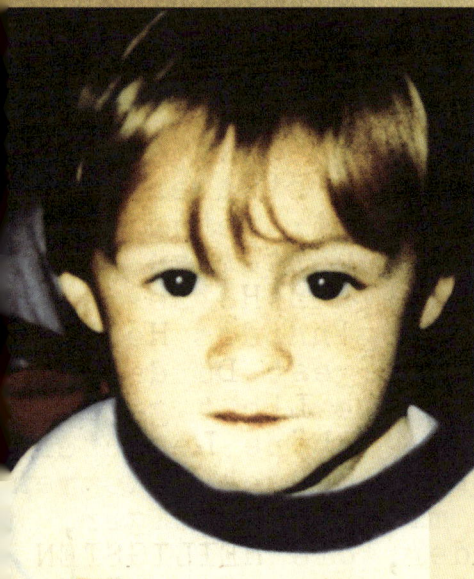

...AND CHILDREN WHO KILL

Above: Toddler James Bulger, killed by the ten-year olds Jon Venables and Robert Thompson; **Main image:** The iconic CCTV still from The Strand Shopping Centre in Bootle, Merseyside. It shows James Bulger being led away by his murderer. This image, and the chilling details of the little boy's murder, shocked an entire nation. A total of 38 people saw the two boys with the toddler, but no one realized James was in danger.

As difficult as it is to understand parents who kill their children, it may be even more perplexing to figure out why children commit murder.

Jon Venables and Robert Thompson Merseyside, England

When curiosity about how it felt to take a human life got the better of two 10-year-old English schoolboys, and they acted on this dark impulse, an entire nation reeled in horror.

On February 12, 1993 Jon Venables and Robert Thompson abducted a toddler named James Bulger by leading him away from his mother while she shopped at a mall in Bootle, Merseyside. In the hours that followed they tortured the two-year-old and eventually killed him, placing his small body across some nearby railroad tracks, where it was cut in half by a train. The remains were discovered two days later.

Closed circuit TV showed the boys selecting Bulger—they later said they'd planned to push

Name ROBERT THOMPSON
.Date 18.2.93

ame JON VENABLES
ate 20.2.93

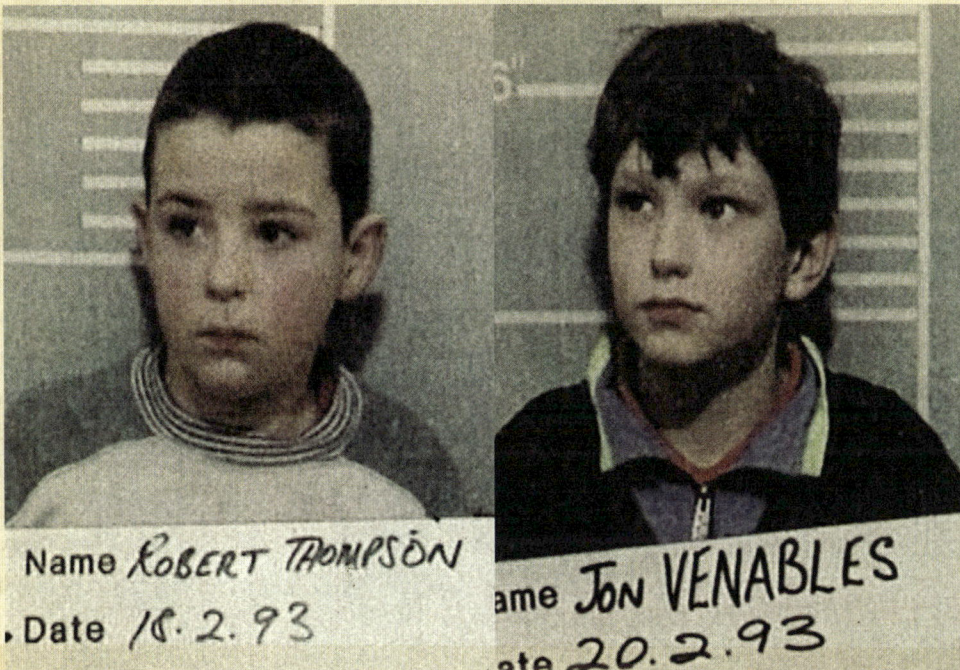

him in front of moving traffic. When they were found guilty, the youngest convicted murderers in British history, the judge declared that the boys had committed a crime of "unparalleled evil and barbarity."

Both boys received new identities after serving eight years in youth detention facilities where they received rehabilitation services. Yet the adult Venables has been arrested for possessing child porn and is currently in prison for the same offense. Thompson, once seen as the ringleader, has broken parole a few times, but has lived his life incident-free.

Lionel Tate Broward County, Florida

In 1999, 13-year-old Lionel Tate was at home with his mother, who was babysitting six-year-old Tiffany Eunick. The two children were in the basement playing, when Mrs. Tate heard a disturbance and called down for them to be quiet. Tate came upstairs and said Tiffany had stopped breathing. He claimed they had been wrestling in play. The coroner who examined the child's body had a different story. Tiffany had been stomped so forcefully her liver was lacerated, there were bruises on her legs, feet, and neck consistent with being hit by a speeding car, and she had a fractured skull and ribs and a swollen brain, as though she had "fallen from a three-story building."

Tate was convicted of first degree murder—considered by some to be an overreach. When sentencing Tate to life imprisonment, Judge Joel T. Lazarus said, "The acts of Lionel Tate were not the playful acts of a child [...] The acts of Lionel Tate were cold, callous and indescribably cruel." Eventually the life sentence was overturned and Tate received one year's house arrest and 10 years probation. Unfortunately he broke parole by threatening a pizza deliveryman with a handgun and is now serving a 30-year sentence.

Above left: Robert Thompson and Jon Venables, the killers of James Bulger in 1993. During the trial, Thompson (far left) sat detached and unmoved . . . and sucking his thumb, a habit he did not break until he was 14.; **Below:** A fourteen-year old Lionel Tate is comforted by his defense team, psychology expert Lori Butts, (left) and co-counsel Denise Bregof, after he was convicted of first degree murder in the death of six-years old Tiffany Eunick,. Sentenced to life in prison, this was overturned on appeal and Tate was given ten years' probation. **Above right:** Tate is arrested after breaking his parole. He is now serving a thirty-year sentence.

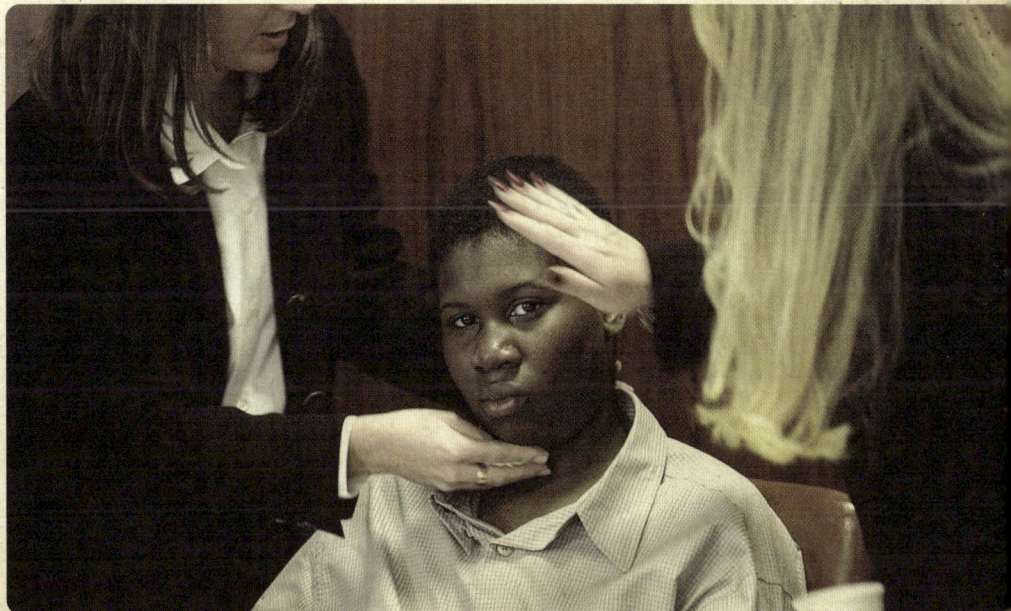

> "We just hope that someone is holding her for her child and that we can, you know, get her back with a tip." SCOTT PETERSON

HOMICIDAL HUSBANDS

Top: Christian Longo at his arraignment;
Above: Longo with the family he murdered.

In spite of maintaining a public appearance of family affection and normalcy, both these men were responsible for the gruesome deaths of their wives and children.

Christian Longo Oregon

On December 19, 2001, the body of 4-year-old Zachary Longo washed up in a marina in Waldport, Oregon. Within days the body of his sister Sadie appeared, and then the remains of his mother Mary Jane and his brother Madison were found stuffed in suitcases and floating in Yquina Bay. The man responsible for this horror was their father, business entrepreneur Christian Longo, who had fled in a plane to Cancun, Mexico, using a fake ID. The FBI immediately placed him on their 10-Most Wanted List.

To observers, the Longos appeared to be a perfect family, an attractive couple with three lively children. But the darker truth was that Christian liked expensive cars and exotic vacations. As a result he was deeply in debt and had resorted to counterfeiting checks from client companies. And still he indulged himself.

After Longo was identified by an American tourist, he was extradited to the US. At his trial, Longo insisted that Mary Jane had killed the older

children in a fit of rage over his failing finances, and that he retaliated in anger by killing her and Zachary. The jury took only four hours to sentence him to death by lethal injection. With an appeals process progressing slowly, Longo remains on death row in Oregon.

Scott Peterson Modesto, California

Like the Longos, Scott Peterson and wife Laci seemed to have a perfect life. Peterson had given up his dreams of professional golf after meeting Laci at California Polytechnic. He started working for an international fertilizer company and Laci was expecting a baby. But Scott was leading a double life, with extramarital affairs and a lavish lifestyle. Stress at his job only added more pressure. Scott wanted out . . . and he came up with a simple solution.

When the seven and a half-month pregnant Laci went missing just before Christmas in 2002, friends noticed that Scott seemed unconcerned. In November Scott had begun seeing Amber Frey, explaining that he was a recent widower. After Amber realized that Scott was the husband of the missing woman, she told the police about him claiming his wife was dead . . . weeks before she disappeared.

THE "OTHER" PETERSON MURDER

On December 9, 2001, Kathleen Peterson lay dead and bloodied at the bottom of the staircase in her Durham, North Carolina, home. Her husband, military novelist Michael Peterson, claimed she had fallen. He was charged with beating her to death, found guilty, and sent to prison for life. After serving eight years, Peterson was given a retrial hearing that introduced new factors, such as a lack of blood spatter on his shirt and mishandling of evidence. Peterson entered an Alford plea—maintaining innocence but admitting some culpability—to manslaughter. He was released with time served.

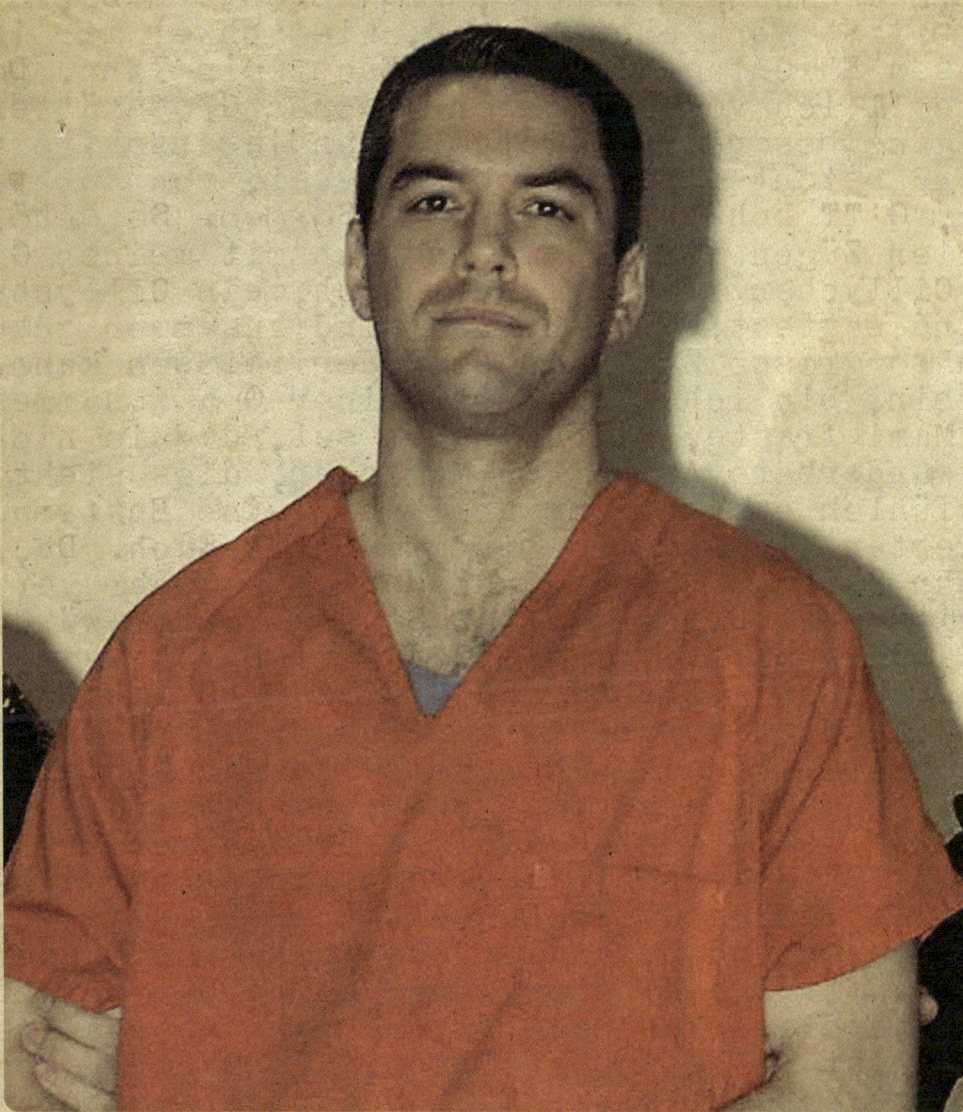

In April 2003, the remains of a baby with an umbilical cord still attached was found in a marshy area of San Francisco Bay; days later the body of a recently pregnant woman washed ashore near where the baby was found. DNA testing confirmed the identities of Laci and her baby.

Peterson was apprehended before he could escape to Mexico—a near thing—his hair had been dyed blond and his car was loaded with cash and camping gear. Peterson pleaded not guilty. Although most of the evidence was circumstantial, the jury found him guilty of first degree murder in the case of Laci, and second degree for his unborn son. After spending 15 years on San Quentin's death row, Peterson's death sentence was overturned on appeal.

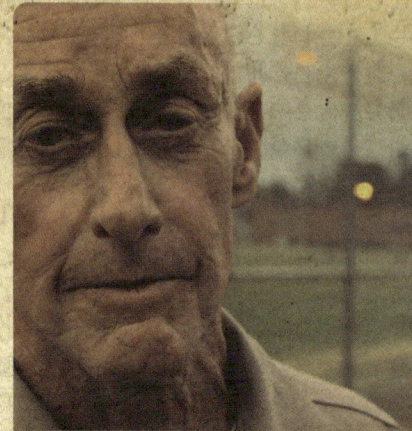

Above: Scott Peterson during a court appearance; **Left:** Laci Peterson, Peterson's wife, murdered while pregnant with their child; **Above, inset:** Military novelist Michael Peterson, found guilty of the murder of his wife Kathleen, but given a retrial after serving eight years.

JONBENÉT RAMSEY
A HIGH-PROFILE MYSTERY

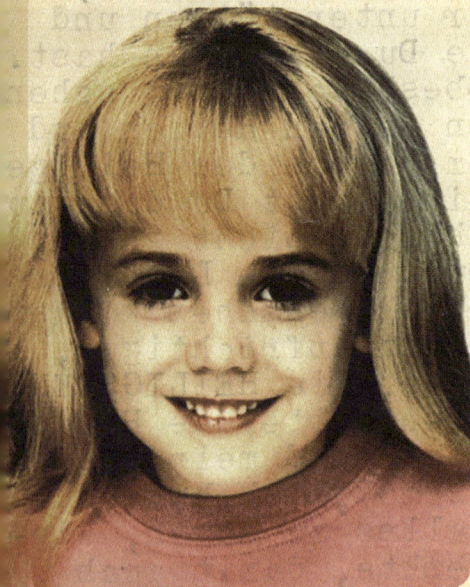

One of the most disturbing—and puzzling—murders of the late 20th century was the unsolved death of six-year-old beauty queen and model JonBenét Ramsey. Cheered by her parents, software entrepreneur John Bennett Ramsey and second wife Patsy, the delicate blond JonBenét competed in numerous pageants and won titles that included America's Royale Miss, Little Miss Colorado, and National Tiny Miss Beauty.

Above: JonBenét Ramsay, the tragic little girl whose murder sparked a national media sensation.

Then tragedy struck. On the morning of December 26, 1996, Patsy found a ransom note on the kitchen staircase of their Boulder, Colorado, home. She then realized her daughter was missing from her bedroom. When the police searched the house looking for signs of forced entry, one officer saw a bolted door in the basement, but did not open it. Hours later, during a second search, her father found JonBenét's body behind that same locked door, a nylon cord twisted around her neck. The cause of death was listed as strangulation along with a skull fracture. There was no evidence of rape, but the coroner did find a vaginal injury. Both Ramseys were questioned intensively, and their nine-year-old son Burke was also interviewed. Nothing conclusive was established, however.

The murder of the petite beauty queen became a media sensation and generated hundreds of tips and 1,600 persons of interest. The parents were placed in the glare of the spotlight, first as suspects, then—over a year later, in 1998—charged by a grand jury with endangering their young daughter by allowing her to perform wearing provocative make-up and clothing, possibly attracting the attention of pedophiles. But Boulder County DA Alex Hunter refused to prosecute.

Ten long years later, in 2008, based on new methods in DNA sampling and testing, the Ramseys were excluded from the investigation. John and Patsy were publicly exonerated by the new Boulder County DA Mary Lacy.

Procedural Problems

After the initial investigation, a number of errors came to light. The Boulder police, with no homicide department, stumbled badly on that first day. Assuming JonBenét had been abducted, the officers preserved only her bedroom as a crime scene. By the time her body was discovered in the basement, any evidence throughout the house had been compromised by investigators and family friends. Forensics did find traces of male DNA on her underclothes, but it has never been matched, even after hundreds of tests. Furthermore, evidence was lost or contaminated, and the police mistakenly shared details of the case with the family.

Subsequent independent investigators favored the intruder scenario—several windows in the house had been opened slightly to accommodate electric cords for the outdoor Christmas lights and a basement window was left unlocked. But still no results were forthcoming. Meanwhile, the media continues to rake up the mysterious murder with regular frequency. More than 15 books have been written about the case, some of them positing new theories about the girl's death.

Opposite, main image: May 24, 2000— Patsy Ramsey defends herself at a press conference where she and husband John, (right), announced they had passed a polygraph test that sought to determine if they had killed their daughter, JonBenét; **Top right:** January 1997—sensationalism on *People* magazine's front page; **Above center:** October 13, 1999—Boulder DA Alex Hunter announces that the grand jury in the JonBenét Ramsey murder did not have enough evidence to warrant an indictment; **Right:** August 29, 2006—New Boulder County DA Mary Lacy explains to the assembled TV and press the dropped charges against John Mark Karr;

On *Today*'s set as Bryant says bye-bye

JANUARY 13, 1997

People weekly

Winona Ryder, free spirit

Heartbreak in Colorado

MURDER OF A LITTLE BEAUTY

The brutal killing of pageant princess JonBenét Ramsey, 6, shocks the nation— and raises troubling questions

JonBenét wearing a beauty contest sash

Mr. Ramsey,

Listen carefully! We are a group of individuals that represent a small foreign faction. We do respect your bussiness but not the country that it serves. At this time we have your daughter in our posession. She is safe and unharmed and if you want her to see 1997, you must follow our instructions to the letter.

You will withdraw $118,000.00 from your account. $100,000 will be in $100 bills and the remaining $18,000 in $20 bills. Make sure that you bring an adequate size attache to the bank. When you get home you will put the money in a brown paper bag. I will call you between 8 and 10 am tomorrow to instruct you on delivery. The delivery will be exhausting so I advise you to be rested. If we monitor you getting the money early, we might call you early to arrange an earlier delivery of the

THE RANSOM NOTE

The rambling, two-and-a-half-page ransom letter, found by JonBenét's mom Patsy, baffled police. Dad John pointed out the demand was for $118,000, close to the amount of a work bonus he'd earlier received, indicating the murderer was someone the family knew. The note itself was bizarre—the FBI had rarely seen one so long, plus it was written at the scene on the Ramseys' own notepaper. Investigators conjectured that one of the parents had unwittingly killed the girl, then written the note to cover their tracks. Handwriting experts testified, however, that neither parent could have penned the note.

Key Stats

The police possibly targeted the Ramseys because, according to FBI statistics, there is a 12-to-1 probability that it's a family member or caregiver who is involved in the homicide of a child.

"**People live for love. They kill for love. They die for love.**"

HELEN FISHER, ANTHROPOLOGIST & AUTHOR

5 Chapter Five

Romance Gone Wrong

Not every love affair leads to a happily ever after. Sometimes violent emotions like jealousy or envy intrude; sometimes greed or the lust for material objects trumps affection or loyalty. Whatever the impediments to enduring coupled bliss, the outcome is sometimes tragic, even fatal. Perhaps there is truth in that old saying, that "love and hate are just opposite sides of the same coin."

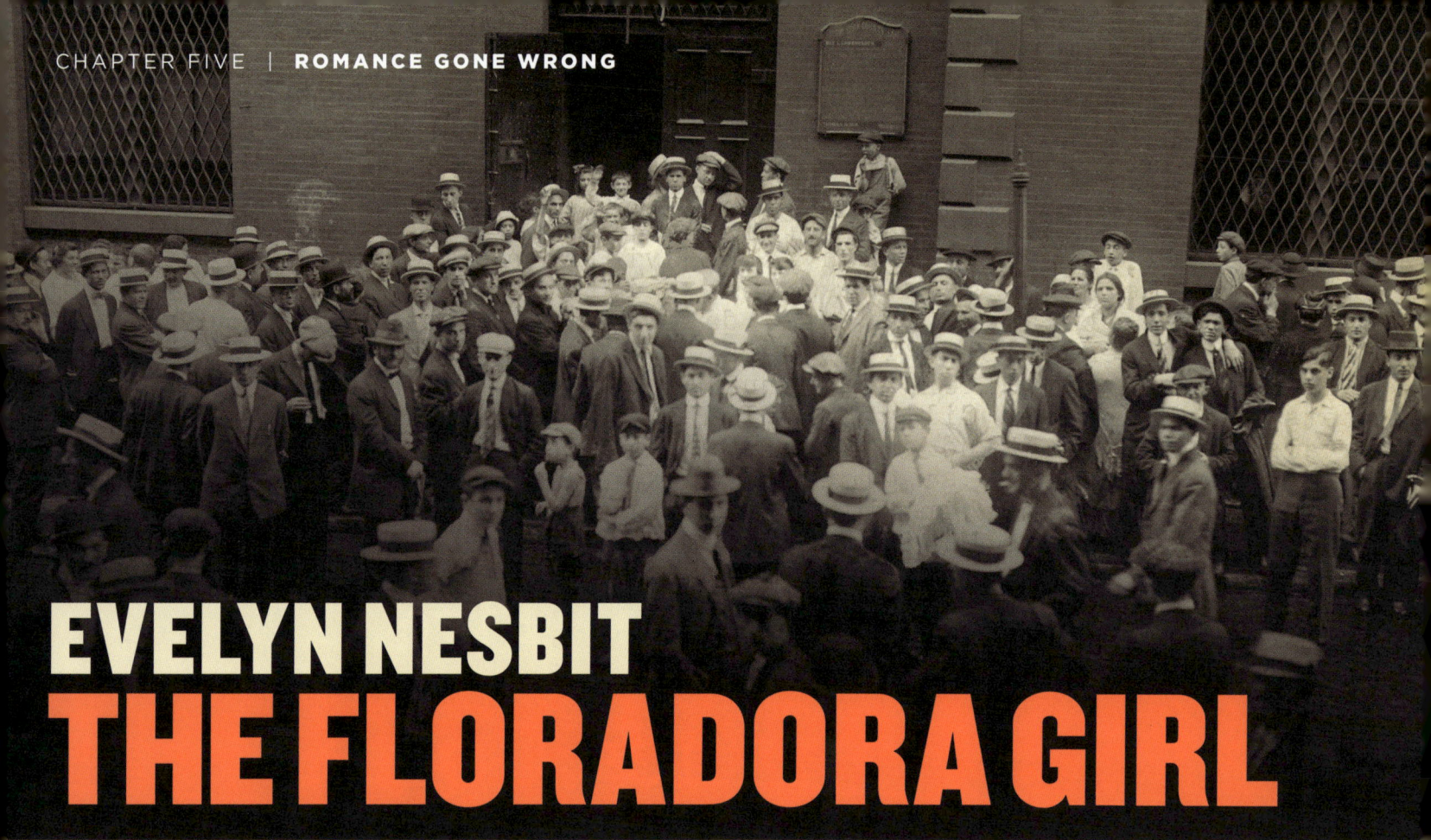

EVELYN NESBIT
THE FLORADORA GIRL

Main image: Crowds gathered outside the court buildings in New York during Harry Thaw's trial. circa 1907; **Center:** The murder victim— architect Stanford White, circa 1900; **Above:** Harry Thaw and Evelyn Nesbit. Thaw shot White three times in the head on the rooftop theater of Madison Square Garden.

At the turn of the 20th century young American women were beginning to come into their own. No longer bound to the narrow choice of marriage or dependent spinsterhood, they were finding employment in factories, offices, and retail shops. They began to display a sense of independence and freedom in their dress and in their manners.

Personifying all that modern femininity was the Gibson Girl, the inspired creation of illustrator Charles Dana Gibson. Evelyn Nesbit, a beautiful young model who posed for Gibson, seemed to typify this beau ideal of being stylish and at ease. It was not surprising that men flocked to Nesbit, with her piquant features and dark, flowing hair.

Nesbit was born in Natrona, Pennsylvania, and as a child showed interest in music and dance. The death of her lawyer father left her family penniless, and after several hard years, Evelyn and her mother and brother found work pulling 12-hour shifts in Wanamaker's Department Store. It was here that a woman artist noticed Evelyn's delicate beauty and asked her to pose for a fee. From that point on, Evelyn focused on becoming an artist's model, a choice that led her to New York, where she excelled as a live model for artists and advertising photographers. She soon moved from modeling to the stage, first as a chorus line dancer, a "Floradora Girl," and then as a featured actress, playing a gypsy in *The Wild Rose*.

A Wealthy Benefactor

Famed architect Stanford White was married with a son, but he maintained an independent social life. He saw Nesbit performing and decided to take her under his wing. Nesbit thought him old—he was 46—but was overwhelmed by his wealth. He introduced her to many influential people, including potential rivals like actor John Barrymore. But it was White who took her virginity, possibly drugging and raping her. She retained him as her lover, yet also realized that her reputation had been tarnished . . . and that suitors would be few. When Nesbit married Harry K. Thaw, the son of a coal and railroad tycoon, in 1905 she knew his history of mental illness and abusive behavior. What she could not know was the simmering

TRIALS OF THE CENTURY

resentment he felt against White for his assault on Evelyn.

On the night of June 25, 1906, Thaw and Evelyn visited the rooftop theater at Madison Square Garden to see the premiere of *Mam'zelle Champagne*. White came late and sat at his customary table. During the show's finale, Thaw drew a pistol and from two feet away shot White three times in the head. "You ruined my wife," Thaw shouted. White died instantly.

The murder, with its subtext of sex and scandal among the elite, became the talk of the nation, and reporters dubbed the court case the "Trial of the Century." White was a celebrated architect, and his passing was lamented, while Nesbit was blamed for her questionable morals

and her "unmaidenly" testimony on the stand. Thaw's mother pleaded that he not be labeled clinically insane. The compromise was a charge of temporary insanity, or what was then called a "brainstorm." Nesbit was a bit more blunt: "Harry was a madman."

In 1908 Harry was incarcerated in the Matteawan Home for the Criminally Insane in Beacon, New York. In 1910, Evelyn traveled to Berlin, Germany, where she gave birth to a child, Russell William Thaw. She maintained the boy was Harry's child, conceived during a conjugal visit to Matteawan. Thaw vehemently denied paternity. Nesbit went on to appear in a number of silent movies, including six filmed with her son Russell. The public just could never get enough of her.

Above left: a classic alluring photograph of Evelyn Nesbit, "the Floradora Girl"; **Top:** A studied portrait of Harry Thaw, son of a tycoon; **Above:** Nesbit (with distinctive headgear) and son Russell.

The CRIPPEN CASE

Michigander Hawley Harvey Crippen was a doctor of homeopathy at the turn of the 20th century who worked selling Munyon's Remedies, a line of patent medicines. In 1893 he married second wife Cora Turner in Jersey City, New Jersey, and they relocated to London seven years later.

Crippen continued peddling homeopathic medicines, while Cora sought work as a music hall performer under the name Belle Elmore. Sadly, her singing talent did not match her level of aspiration. The daughter of a Russian-Polish father and a German mother, she had been born Kunigunde Mackamotzki and reputedly possessed a foul and overbearing temperament.

In 1900 Crippen began working as a manager at Drouet's Institute for the Deaf, where he fell in love with his young typist, Ethel Le Neve. In 1905 Crippen and Belle moved to a large flat at 39 Hilldrop Crescent, Holloway—perhaps affording Crippen his own space in order to avoid the domineering Belle, who was also conducting her own adulterous affairs.

On January 31, 1910, Belle held a dinner party for acquaintances Paul and Clara Martinetti. The foursome seemed to be enjoying the meal, and when Paul asked to use the toilet, Crippen told him where it was. But Belle berated her husband for not escorting him in person. The Martinettis, who left around 1 a.m., were the last outsiders to see Belle alive. When concerned neighbors asked about her absence, Crippen told them she was visiting America. He later told them she was sick, and then that she had died.

On the Run

Unwisely, it would turn out, Ethel began to appear wearing Belle's jewelry. Less than a month after Belle's disappearance she moved in with Crippen, arousing suspicion among their friends, who passed their suspicions on to the police. When Chief Inspector Walter Dew came to the house asking questions, Crippen improvised: Belle had run off with an American, Bruce Miller. Crippen promised to track her down via advertisements.

Realizing the law was closing in, Crippen and Le Neve prepared to flee. A now clean-shaven Crippen and a "boy" who looked a lot like Ethel traveled to Brussels, where they bought passage to Canada aboard the SS Montrose. When Dew discovered Crippen and Ethel were missing, he took the opportunity to search the house. Under a brick floor in the cellar, the police found a dismembered female torso, possibly Belle's. The hunt for the runaways now became urgent.

Aboard the *Montrose*, Crippen and his "son" were arousing suspicion. They appeared a bit too affectionate—to the point where the captain wired Scotland Yard, using the newly installed wireless telegraph, courtesy of Guglielmo Marconi. Dew boarded a faster boat, the SS Laurentic, and managed to beat the *Montrose* to Quebec. The couple were identified as Crippen and Le Neve and promptly taken into custody. Crippen reportedly said, "Thank God it's over. The suspense has been too great."

Back in England, Crippen appeared at the Old Bailey in a trial that lasted only four days; still enough time to work up the press. The most incriminating evidence was a large amount of scopalamine found in the remains, a toxic substance Crippen had purchased locally. A fragment of the top of a pajama set belonging to Crippen was also found among the remains. The jury found the doctor guilty after less than an hour of deliberation. Le Neve was acquitted as an accessory. Crippen was hanged at Pentonville Prison on November 23, 1910.

Top: The infamous "mild mannered murderer", Dr. Hawley Crippen; **Center:** Crippen's "son", his lover Ethel Le Neve; **Bottom:** Crippen's wife Cora, an aspirant music hall star working under the stage name of Belle Elmore; **Background image:** Crippen and Le Neve''s trial for murder at the Old Bailey, London.

Top: Inspector Dew and Crippen, in disguise, disembark *SS Montrose* in Canada. Four weeks later, Crippen is in chains in Pentonville Prison, Holloway; **Bottom:** Crippen and Ethel LeNeve in the Old Bailey dock as the charges are read—Crippen is charged with murder, Le Neve as an accessory to murder. They are tried separately; **Above right:** The *coup de grace* is administered to Crippen in the death room at Pentonville by Hangman John Ellis. Crime novelist Raymond Chandler expressed disbelief that Crippen would carelessly bury the torso in his basement, after successfully getting rid of the head and limbs.

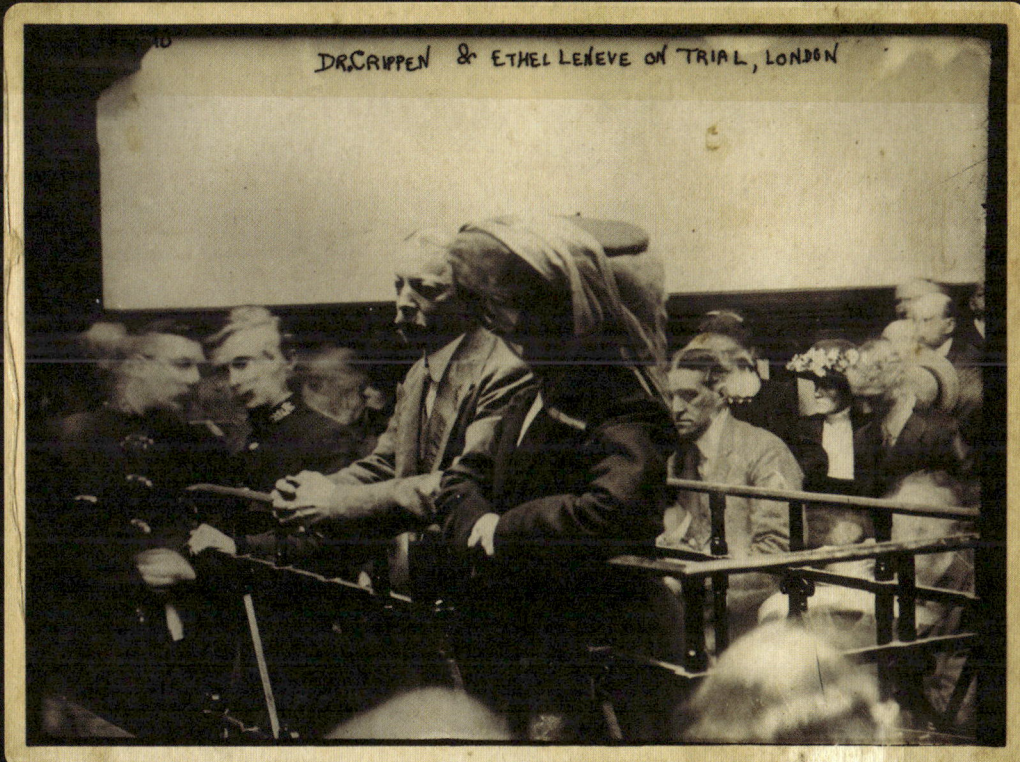

DR. CRIPPEN & ETHEL LENEVE ON TRIAL, LONDON

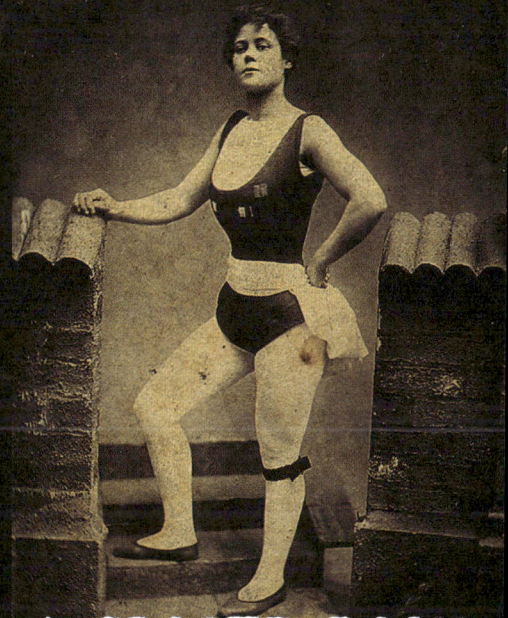

A CLOSER LOOK

Police first learned of Belle Elmore's disappearance from her friend, music hall entertainer and strongwoman Kate Williams, aka "Vulcana."

When a lover or spouse discovers that a third party is intruding in their relationship, sparks often fly. Deadly sparks in many cases, as emotions can run so high that violence is inevitable.

DEADLY LOVE TRIANGLES

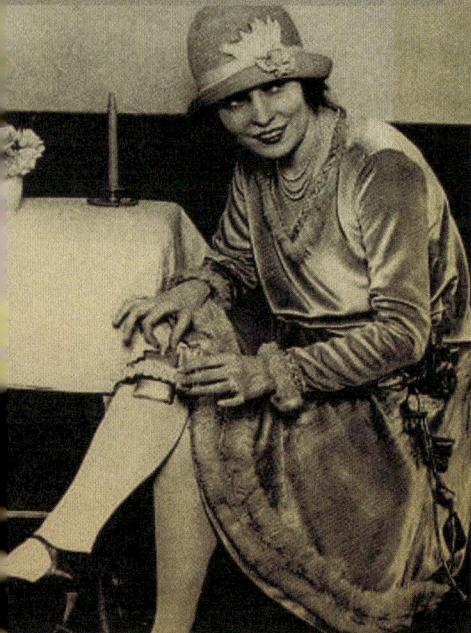

Above: George Remus, millionaire chemist-turned-lawyer-turned-bootlegger. Some say he was the model for F. Scott Fitzgerald's "Great Gatsby.";
Top: Imogene Holmes, Remus's second wife. After falling for undercover agent Franklin Dodge, the pair hatched a plot to embezzle George's money, then murder him.

Imogene and George Remus

German-American George Remus was a lawyer and a gangster, known as the "King of the Bootleggers." His second marriage was to his legal secretary, divorcée Imogene Holmes. While Remus spent two years in prison for violating the Volstead Act, Imogene began an affair with an undercover prohibition agent, Franklin Dodge, and conspired with him to have an assassin kill her husband. The assassin, meanwhile, told Remus of their plan. Imogene filed for divorce, and on October 6, 1927, was on her way to court to finalize the split. Remus got behind the cab carrying Holmes and her daughter and had his driver chase them through Cincinnati's Eden Park. When his car forced the cab off the road, Remus leaped out and fatally shot Imogene in the abdomen, horrifying those in the park. In court, Remus pleaded transitory insanity, reiterating his distress at his wife's betrayal. It took the jury only 19 minutes to acquit him.

Sheila and Max Garvie

Beautiful Sheila Garvie and husband Max, a prosperous Scottish farmer, lived in Kincardineshire. In 1964 Garvie founded a nudist club on the farm grounds—or Kinky Cottage as the locals called it. There were few moral restrictions, with orgies a regular feature. Sheila was not keen at first, but Max convinced her to join in. Sheila eventually took a lover, Brian Tevendale. Then in May 1968 Max Garvie disappeared. In August Sheila told her mother she suspected a jealous Tevendale had killed Max. Her mother informed the police, and Sheila and Brian were arrested. Shortly afterward, Garvie's body was found in an underground drain, bludgeoned and shot. Sheila and Brian were convicted of the crime, one of the most sensationalized murders in Scottish criminal history. Both were sentenced to life imprisonment but released in 1978.

Pamela and Gregg Smart

When FSU senior Pamela Wojas married fellow New Hampshire native Gregg Smart, they bonded over their love of heavy metal music. Yet their marriage showed cracks early on. Back in New Hampshire, she found work as media coordinator at Winnacunnet High School, where she met and connected with sophomore Billy Flynn at a drug-awareness program. On May 1, 1990, Pamela returned home to find her condo trashed and her husband dead. Police investigators soon accused Pamela of seducing

Right: Sheila and Max Garvie in the 1960s; **Next right:** Brian Tevendale, Sheila Garvie's lover and co-conspirator in the murder of her husband Max.

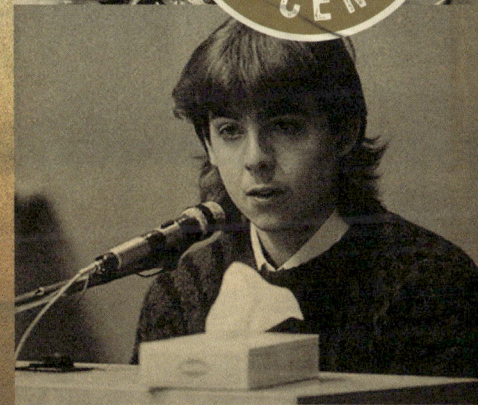

TRIALS OF THE CENTURY

Flynn and coercing him to kill her husband, believing Flynn's three buddies acted as accomplices. Smart claimed she had no part in the murder, but she incriminated herself while talking to one of the buddies. Her trial was the first in the US to allow TV cameras into the courtroom She was convicted as an accessory to murder and is serving a life sentence.

Els Clottemans Death in the Clouds

Perhaps the most bizarre case of jealous revenge took place thousands of feet in the air. Belgian school teacher Els Clottemans and her married friend Els Van Doren were both skydivers. Clotteman somehow found herself in a love triangle with fellow skydiver Marcel Somers and Van Doren. On November 18, 2006, their club performed a group dive over Flanders. After they unlinked hands, Van Doren's chute failed to open, as did her reserve chute. She plummeted more than two miles to her death. Van Doren's helmet camera filmed her tugging at the chute release. When Clottemans attempted suicide before her second police statement, she was arrested for sabotaging her friend's parachutes. She received a sentence of 30 years.

Top: Pamela Smart with her new husband Gregg in happier times; **Above:** Billy Flynn, Pamela Smart's teenage lover, and the killer of her husband. The character played by Nicole Kidman in the black comedy, *To Die For*, is loosely based on Pamela Smart. **Below:** The skydivers Els Van Doren, and **bottom**, Els Clottemans. They were both sexually involved with Marcel Somers, a fellow skydiver. Clottemans got rid of Van Doren by sabotaging her parachutes.

It is certainly not illegal to marry for money—people have been doing so for many centuries. By when it comes to cold-bloodedly murdering one's partner to gain an inheritance or insurance settlement, the law is ruthless and unforgiving.

BLACK WIDOWS

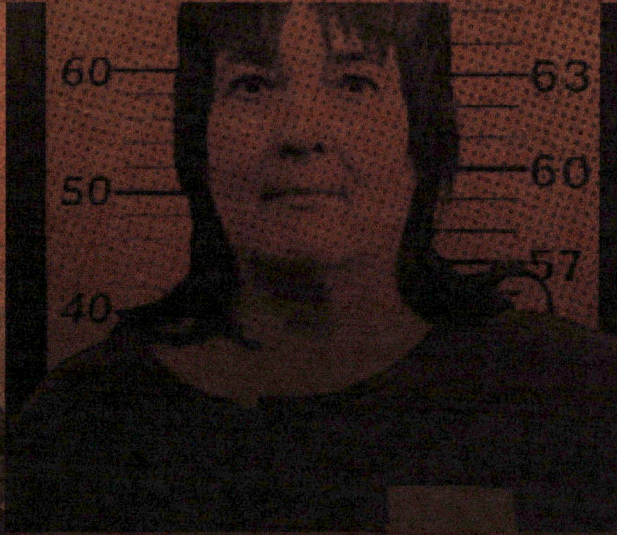

WOMEN WHO MURDER THEIR SPOUSES

Above: Catherine and Margaret Flanagan— Murdering sisters who hanged together; **Top:** "Canadian Black Widow" Evelyn Dick, who murdered and dismembered her husband; **Top right:** Jill Coit—turned in by her own son after murdering two of her husbands; **Opposite, main image:** Betty Lou Beets mugshot. She died by lethal injection in 2000; **Opposite, inset:** Chisako Kakehi of Japan. As of June 2021 awaiting execution by hanging in Japan for serially poisoning her husbands. Her final appeal has just failed.

Catherine and Margaret Flanagan Liverpool, England

These Irish sisters moved to Liverpool in the late 1800s to become landladies. They housed Catherine's son, John; lodger Thomas Higgins and his 6-year-old daughter Mary; and Patrick Jennings with his 14-year-old daughter Margaret. The sisters still worried about finances, though, and concocted a plan to collect money from the local burial society. The first victim they poisoned was Catherine's son John, followed by Mary Higgins. Next came Margaret Jennings, then Margaret Flanagan's new husband, Thomas Higgins himself. Higgins's brother Patrick investigated the deaths and brought the sisters to justice; they were hanged together.

Evelyn Dick Ontario, Canada

Known as the "Torso Murderer," Evelyn Dick was an Ontario, Canada, woman charged with killing her estranged Russian husband after the remains of his sawn-off head and limbs were found among the furnace ashes in her yard. After a famously sensational trial she was acquitted and freed . . . until a suitcase containing the remains of her infant son, Peter, was found in her attic. She served 11 years and was paroled and given a new identity.

Betty Lou Beets North Carolina

As a child, North Carolinian Beets lost her hearing to measles and suffered sexual abuse by her father. At 15 she married Robert Franklin Branson, a short-lived, abusive union. Beets then married Billy York Lane, who broke her nose during an argument. She responded by shooting and wounding him. Her marriage to Ronnie Threlkold ended when she tried to run him over. In 1979, she married Doyle Wayne Baker, followed in 1982, by Jimmy Don Beets. In August 1983 Betty Lou warned her son to leave the house because she intended to shoot his stepfather. He returned and helped her bury the body. In 1985,

MORE CANDIDATES

Chisako Kakehi of Japan killed eight men for their insurance money.

Judy Buenoano of Florida poisoned her husband and son for insurance money, and also murdered her first husband and a previous boyfriend. She became the first woman to be executed in Florida since 1848.

Betty Newmar of Ohio had five husbands who all died unnaturally, four from gunshot wounds, the fifth from possible arsenic poisoning.

WIFE KILLERS

The term Bluebeard refers to men who marry and kill one wife after the other. The name comes from a 1697 fairytale by Charles Perrault about a violent nobleman who has the habit of murdering his wives. Gilles de Rais, a 15th century child killer, was said to inspire the fairytale. Henri Landru, called the Bluebeard of Gambais, was a French serial killer who murdered and plundered the assets of at least seven women in the 1900s by luring them with "lonely hearts" ads promising marriage.

the police located the remains of Beets and Baker in her yard. In February 2000 Betty Lou died by lethal injection in Texas' Huntsville Unit.

Jill Coit

This Louisiana native married twice as a teen, but did not wait for her divorce papers before marrying prosperous William Coit. He was shot by an "intruder" shortly after filing for divorce from her. Three more marriages followed, including her lawyer from the Coit murder. Her next mark, the "big fish," was wealthy Gerry Boggs. Learning she was still married, he had their marriage annulled; she sued to keep the $100,000 he'd invested in her business. After another brief failed marriage, she and boyfriend Michael Backus murdered Boggs. Her own son turned her in for killing Boggs and Coit. In 1995, she and Backus received life sentences.

Incest, sadism, child abuse, rape, murder . . . British police have rarely encountered such a collection of sociopathic traits as those found in Fred West, who was described as the "epitome of evil." And who, in spite of being "dim" and scarcely literate, managed to attract two wives and impregnate numerous lovers. In second wife Rose he found his ideal counterpart: a woman who enjoyed sexual perversion as much as he did.

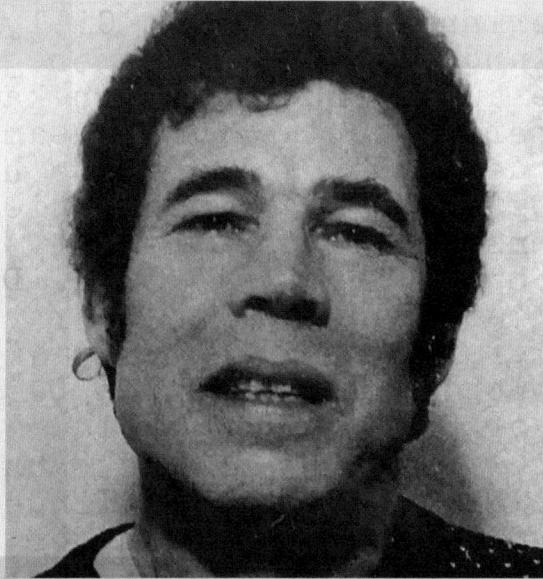

FRED & ROSEMARY WEST
GRIM AND GRISLY

Top: Fred and Rosemary West mugshots, 1994;
Above: The Wests during the height of their killing spree in the 1970s.

West was born to a struggling farm family in Much Marcle, Herefordshire. His father sexually abused his sisters, and Fred, a momma's boy, claims his own mother introduced him to sex. At school he was mocked for his thick accent and scruffy appearance. His technique with girls was to accost them and grope them. After suffering head injuries in a motorcycle accident, Fred began experiencing episodes of rage. In 1961 when he raped and impregnated his 13-year-old sister, he was banished from the house.

In November 1962 Fred married sometime girlfriend Rena Costello, a Scot who was pregnant by an Asian bus driver. After Charmaine was born, Fred and Rena had their own child, Anna Marie. A neighbor reported that Fred kept the girls prisoner with bars on the bottom of a bunk bed. At some point, Fred had three woman at his command: Rena, Isa McNeill and Anne McFall, whom he'd met in Glasgow. Rena grew tired of West's abuse and called a lover to rescue her, but had to leave her children behind. McFall, who was carrying West's child, urged him to marry her, but in July 1967 she disappeared.

A Partner in Crime

In 1969, West met 15-year-old Rose Letts at a bus station. Letts thoughts he was homeless, but he pestered her until she went out with him. She was soon prostituting herself on his behalf. They eventually had a child, Heather. Charmaine meanwhile taunted Rose, comparing her unfavorably with Rena. Rose likely killed Charmaine just before West was released from prison for tire theft. The body was stored in the coal cellar until West could bury it. Rena,

"Keep quiet or you'll end up buried under the patio like Heather ..." FRED WEST

concerned over her daughters' welfare, asked to meet with West . . . and no one saw her alive after that.

West and Rose married and moved to a house on Cromwell Street, Gloucester, later known as the "House of Horrors." Rose returned to prostitution, giving birth to seven children, some of whom were fathered by clients. Fred indulged his taste for killing now . . . and Rose was a willing accomplice. Among those they killed were Lynda Gough, 19; Carol Ann Cooper, 15; Juanita Mott, 18; and Alison Chambers, 16, while Fred murdered his 18-year-old lodger Shirley Robinson. West also repeatedly raped his daughter, Anna Marie. Heather complained to friends about the abuse and looked for work away from home. When she disappeared, West told her siblings she had taken a job in Torquay. In

1992, the Wests's daughter Louise, 13, admitted to a girl friend she'd been raped, and the girl's mother reported it. The police immediately placed the children into foster care.

None of the abused siblings would testify against their parents, but the police probe continued—and opened the gates of hell. After West admitted to strangling Heather, in a "fit of anger," the police dug up the garden. They discovered three sets of dismembered remains, along with five bodies in the cellar and another under a ground-floor room. Fred also confessed to killing Rena and Charmaine. He was ultimately charged with 12 murders, Rose with nine. On January 1, 1995, Fred asphyxiated himself in his cell, depressed that Rose had turned away from him. Rose was sentenced to life in prison without any chance of parole.

Top: No.25 Cromwell Street—the "House of Horrors"—and the 13 victims buried on the property. Between them, Fred and Rosemary West murdered these girls and women (including two of their own children) in the house; **Above:** In 1996, after the Wests' convictions, the house (and the adjoining house) was demolished and all debris removed to discourage ghoulish souvenir hunters; the lot is now a pleasant, grassy access path;

Main image: O.J. Simpson, one of the most well-known men in America. This still is from a Hertz Car Rental ad that Simpson appeared in. For years he was the face of Hertz; **Below:** The two victims of the double murder: Simpson's wife, Nicole, and her friend Ron Goldman, both brutally stabbed to death.

DEATH IN BRENTWOOD

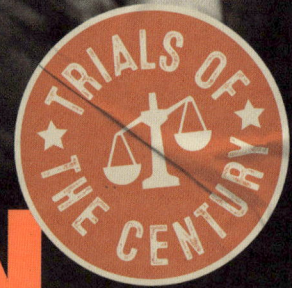

On June 12, 1994, Nicole Brown Simpson, the ex-wife of athlete O.J. Simpson and mother of his two daughters, was brutally stabbed to death outside her Brentwood home along with her friend Ron Goldman. The double homicide sent shockwaves through Los Angeles, and soon through the world. O.J., a legendary football player, actor, spokesman, and sports commentator, was one of the most recognizable people in America. The public's surprise was compounded when it appeared that O.J. himself was the main suspect.

Police targeted the former athlete at once. Not only did he have a history of violence with Nicole, his blood was found at the murder scene, and Nicole and Ron's blood, hair, and fibers were found in Simpson's car and home. A bloody glove belonging to Simpson was also found in Nicole's house, its mate outside his house.

Simpson agreed to turn himself in to the authorities, but then took off with his friend A.C. Cowlings in his white Ford Bronco. He was carrying a disguise, his passport, and roughly $9,000 in cash. His car was spotted and followed, but Simpson threatened to kill himself rather than surrender. The media filmed the low-speed car chase along California freeways, and most of the nation watched in disbelief. Eventually O.J. returned to his home in Brentwood and surrendered to police. His trial was scheduled to begin in early 1995.

A Trail of DNA

Simpson hired a "dream team" of defense lawyers that included Johnnie Cochran, F. Lee Bailey, Alan Dershowitz, and Robert Kardashian. Simpson's team protested he had been framed for the murder by racist LA cops, including police detective Mark Fuhrman, who

had a history of bigotry. The district attorneys, led by a determined Marcia Clark, believed they had a very strong case. Simpson had left his DNA in "a trail of blood" that led from the crime scene, to his car, to his bedroom. Simpson also had no alibi for the time of the murders. Cochran, however, was able to create "reasonable doubt" in the jury over the DNA findings. This was possibly because DNA was still a new type of evidence. Then, when the prosecution asked O.J. try on the bloody gloves he supposedly used in the attack, they proved too small. This resulted in Cochran admonishing the jury: "If it doesn't fit, you must acquit."

Just before the verdict, the LA police were placed on alert, fearing that a guilty verdict might cause race riots similar to those of 1992. They needn't have worried. After three hours of deliberations, the jury acquitted Simpson. Most blacks in America believed that Simpson had been framed; most white people polled thought he had killed Nicole and Ron. As for O.J., he swore to find the killer. Meanwhile, both Nicole's and Ron's families sued Simpson in civil court and were awarded damages of $33.5 million.

A Touch of Karma?

On September 13, 2007, O.J. Simpson led a group of men into a hotel room at the Palace Station Hotel in Las Vegas and robbed collectibles dealer Bruce Fromong at gunpoint. Simpson was arrested three days later; he claimed the items in question had been stolen from him and he was simply taking them back, but denied breaking into the room or holding a gun. Exactly 13 years after his acquittal for the Brentwood murders he was found guilty and sentenced to 33 years. He was released in October 2017.

Top: O.J. Simpson during his trial for murder at the Los Angeles County Superior Court. Robert Shapiro (center), was Simpson's original Lead Defense Counsel, but Johnnie Cochran (left), took over when the trial was completely appropriated by questions of race;
Left center: The famous demonstration that the murder gloves were "too small", leading Cochrane to assert: "If it doesn't fit, you must acquit."
Above: 13 years after his famous acquittal, Simpson is back on trial, this time for robbery.

"You learn what you need to kill and take care of the details. It's like changing a tire—the first time you're careful, by the 30th time, you can't remember where you left the lug wrench."

TED BUNDY

6 Chapter Six

The Mind of a Serial Killer

A serial murderer is someone who unlawfully kills two or more people in separate events that occur at different times. Their crimes are often characterized by a "cooling down" period. Although the term serial murder was coined in the 1970s by Robert Ressler, a behavioral investigator with the FBI, the pathology that expresses itself as a compulsion to repeatedly kill people, frequently total strangers, can be traced back many centuries.

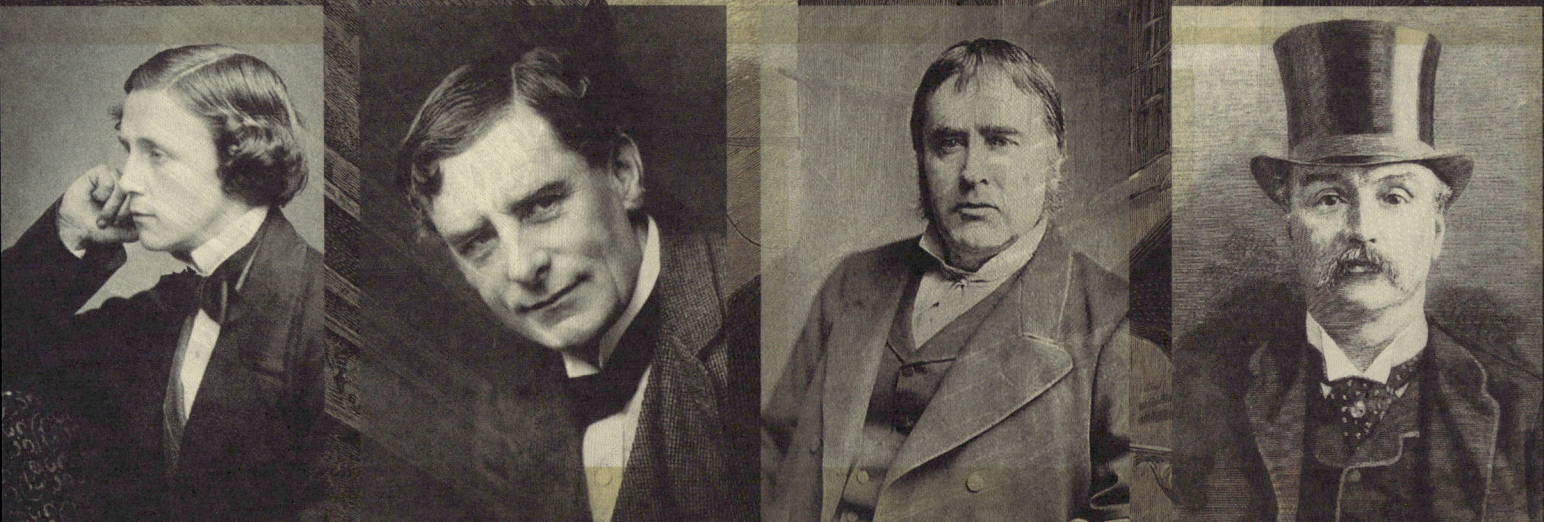

JACK THE RIPPER AND HIS VICTIMS

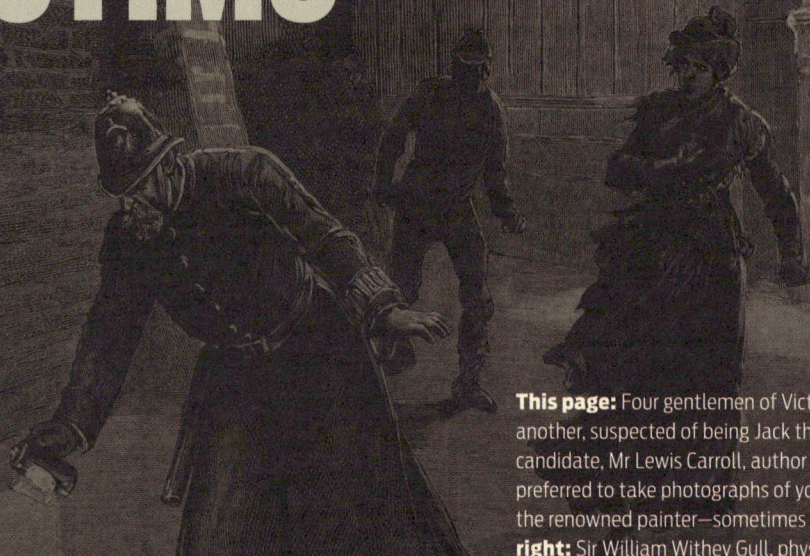

This page: Four gentlemen of Victorian society who were, at one time or another, suspected of being Jack the Ripper. **Top left:** A somewhat unlikely candidate, Mr Lewis Carroll, author of *Alice's Adventures in Wonderland*. He preferred to take photographs of young girls; **Center left:** Mr Walter Sickert, the renowned painter—sometimes of Camden Town prostitutes; **Center right:** Sir William Withey Gull, physician and surgeon to Queen Victoria,

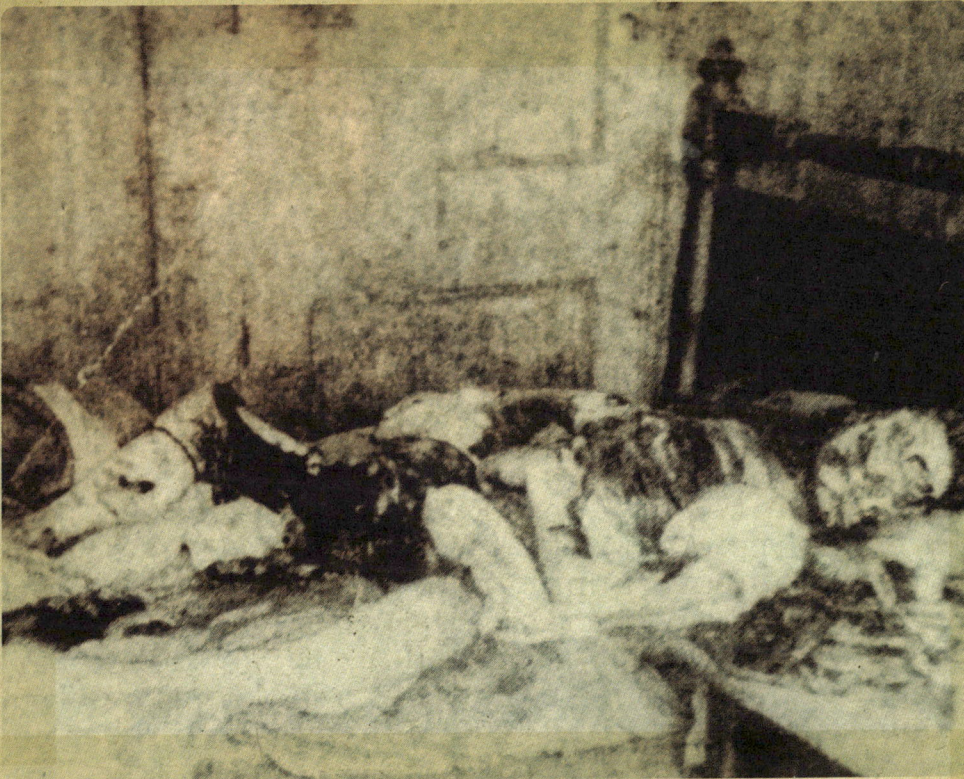

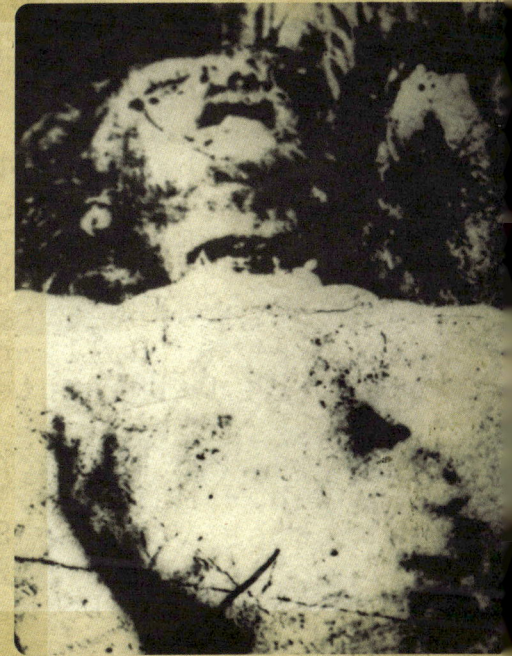

Whitechapel in the late 1800s was an impoverished warren of narrow streets in London's East End, located near the docks where the laboring classes worked. At night, prostitutes frequented the dimly lit street corners and offered their wares to passersby. Most people of respectable breeding never set foot inside the district.

On August 31, 1888, streetwalker Mary Ann Nichols was found murdered in a most gruesome manner— her throat was cut and her body mutilated in such a way to indicate a killer with some knowledge of anatomy. The police quickly searched the area, to no avail. Scotland Yard also took up the hunt.

On September 8, another prostitute, Annie Chapman was killed in the same manner. People in the better neighborhoods began to take note. Add to intro: women in the better neighborhoods began to fear because of the press. The women of Whitechapel began to take more care. Jack the Ripper, as the popular press labeled the phantom, struck three more times, killing Elizabeth Stride (found September 30), Catherine Eddowes (found September 30), and Mary Jane Kelly (found November 9). At least a dozen murders were attributed to Jack from 1888 to 1891, but these five are considered canonical by modern crime historians.

Suspects Among the Famed

More than 160 men were accused, and suspects included such luminaries as writer Lewis Carroll, painter Walter Sickert, physician Sir William Gull, and even a member of the royal family. Dozens of people wrote letters falsely claiming to be the Ripper, which complicated the investigation. Inspector Frederick Abberline and his team had at least determined the Ripper's pattern: after singling out his prey, he offered her money for sex, and then slit her throat in a dark alley. But Abberline had no forensic science to aid him like modern investigators, only anthropometry—a means identifying criminals using certain facial features, such as brow thickness or jaw shape. Almost four years later, in 1892, due to a lack of leads or fresh crimes, the most famous police investigation of the age was officially closed.

But Jack's saga was not finished . . . his brutal methods and ability to evade detection sparked the imaginations of many writers in the decades that followed, who generated countless books on every aspect of the murders. And in Whitechapel today, Jack the Ripper tours that revisit the murder sites continue to be popular.

JACK'S FOREBEARS

Many people assume Jack was the first true serial killer, but earlier cultures were no stranger to the pathology. Procrustes of Greece—possibly only a legend—waylaid travelers and hacked off their limbs, while, in Rome, a group of matrons poisoned countless men under the guise of medicating them. Locusta of Gaul was personal poisoner to Nero's family and likely killed off Emperor Claudius and his son Britannicus. Chinese Han prince Lui Pengli and his retinue of outlaws would ride out and kill people for sport, seizing their goods; as grandson to the emperor he was merely banished when caught. Queen Anula, who ruled Sri Lanka, killed four of her husbands and her son. Gilles de Reis, a 15th-century military hero, was the first serial killer of the Modern Era—he would kidnap young children, then torture them to death.

"I was born with the devil in me..." H.H. HOLMES

THE MASTER OF "MURDER CASTLE"

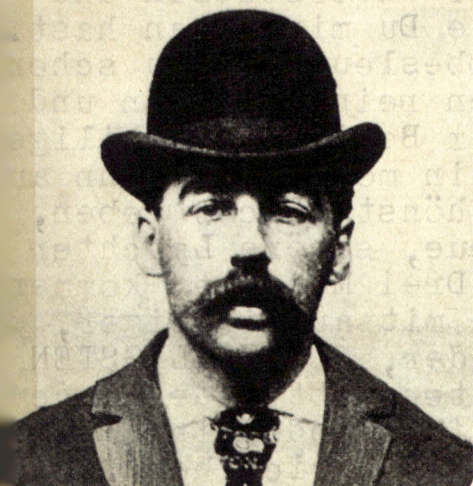

Above: Henry Howard Holmes, the ghoulish master of "Murder Castle"; **Top, left and right, and inset, opposite:** The World's Columbian Exposition—"The World's Fair," Chicago 1893.

The dazzling World's Columbian Exposition, called the White City in the press, brought millions of visitors to Chicago in 1893, among them naive young farm girls or working women who wanted a taste of adventure. Many of these girls saw advertisements for a hotel conveniently close to the grounds of the great fair and decided to stay there. A number of them were never seen again.

New Hampshire native Herman Webster Mudgett, alias Henry Howard Holmes, was from a devout Methodist family. He trained as a pharmacist, but was also a con artist and trigamist. At 17, he married Clara Lovering who was carrying his child, then in late 1886 he married Myrta Belknap in Minneapolis, with whom he had another child, Lucy Theodate. In 1894 he wed Georgiana Yoke in Denver, while still married to both Clara and Myrta.

It was in 1886 that Holmes came to Chicago, leaving Myrta and Lucy at their family home in Willamette, and found work at Elizabeth S. Holton's drugstore in Englewood. He worked hard and eventually bought the store and then an empty lot across the street. Holmes saw the upcoming world's fair as the means to indulge in his taste for murder, so he built a house especially for that purpose on the lot—an ornate three-story building, with commercial storefronts at ground level, his "special" rooms on the second floor, and hotel accommodations on the top floor. The sound-proofed torture rooms were geared for subduing and killing young women, with chutes and secret corridors that allowed their bodies to be transported to the basement, where they would be placed in quicklime or acid vats. Holmes had different construction firms work on the building so none knew specifically what the other group was doing.

The Slaughter Begins

Holmes's first victim was possibly his mistress Julia Smythe, the wife of a tenant, who gained custody of her daughter when her husband moved out. She and young Pearl disappeared on Christmas Eve, 1891. Another two women connected to Holmes, Emeline Cigrande and Edna Van Tassel, also disappeared. After Holmes convinced his stenographer, Minnie Williams, to sign over her property in Texas to him, she and her visiting sister vanished in 1893. He even killed his male assistant—his "creature"—Benjamin Pitezel for the insurance money, then went on the run with three of Pitezel's five children, whom he eventually killed in horrifying fashion, gassing the two girls and poisoning the little boy. As for the missing female "guests" at the hotel, it was impossible to calculate how many victims there were, but after Holmes was arrested for the death of Pitezel, he confessed to 27 murders. He was hanged on May 7, 1896, nine days before his 35th birthday.

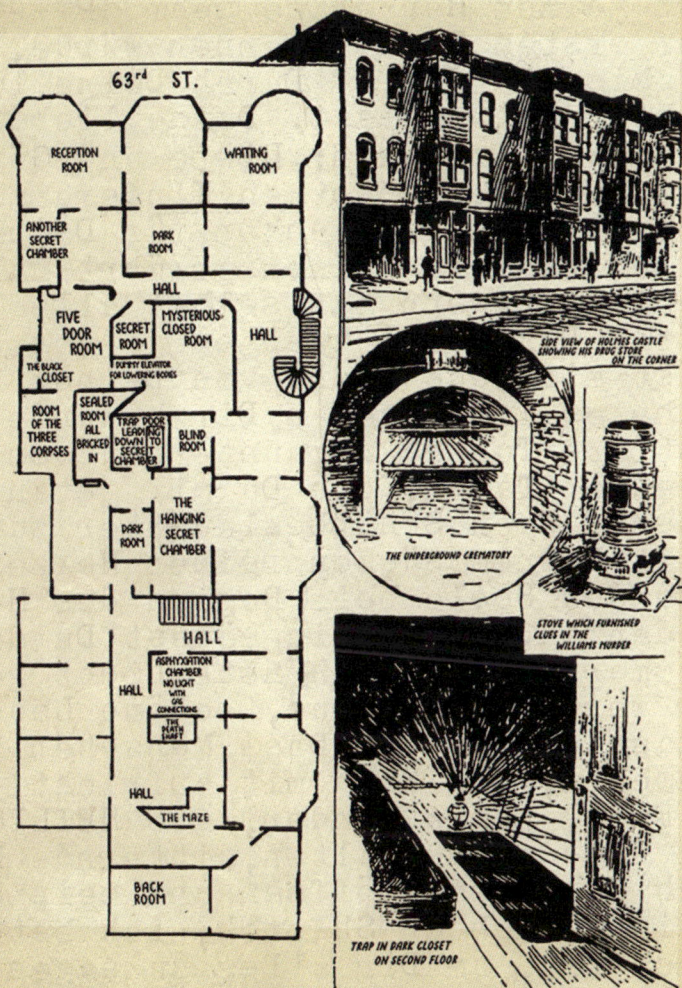

Above: A plan of H.H. Holmes's "Murder Castle," published in the *Chicago Tribune*, August 18, 1895; Top right: "Murder Castle," on 63rd Street, Chicago. Erik Larson's bestseller, *The Devil in the White City*, juxtaposes the beauty and cultural influences of the Chicago Exposition with the bestial nature of Holmes's many crimes.

ANOTHER TRAGEDY

The World's Columbian Exposition proved to be a huge success. In addition to the many educational or cultural pavilions, with their Beaux-Arts plaster facades resembling white marble, it featured the first Ferris wheel, a collection of entertainments on Midway Avenue (thus the term midway for a circus sideshow), and Buffalo Bill's Wild West Show just outside the gates. The night before the elaborate closing celebration, Chicago mayor Carter Harrison, who had just delivered the closing address, answered his front door. Eugene Patrick Prendergast, a disgruntled, unbalanced man who'd been seeking a city job shot Harrison and killed him. The closing festivities were cancelled, and eventually, most of the dreamlike White City burned down in July 1984. It was as if, in the end, Holmes had cast his evil spell over the whole exposition.

Born in Yorkshire, John Reginald Christie would become one of Britain's most sinister serial killers. As a boy he had good brain and did well at math, but was abused by his father and bullied by his mother and sisters. A hypochondriac, he associated sex with death and violent aggression and found himself sexually impotent, unless he was completely in control. His teenage friends labeled him "Can't-Do-It-Christie."

He found work as an assistant movie projectionist, then served as a signalman during World War I. He was temporarily blinded by mustard gas and also claimed to be mute for three years. In 1920 he married Ethel Waddington, but had issues in bed and often visited prostitutes. The couple separated after four years, and Christie moved to London. Here, he was convicted and jailed for numerous petty offenses—stealing postal orders, assaulting a prostitute, stealing a priest's car.

In November 1933, Christie and Ethel reconciled and moved to the ground floor flat at 10 Rillington Place in Notting Hill. Yet Christie still needed to visit prostitutes in order to release his increasing sexual rage, including a desire for necrophilia. At the start of World War II, Christie became a policeman at the Harrow Road station and began an affair with a woman who worked there . . . until her husband thrashed him.

Top left: Dickie Attenborough as John Christie and Judy Geeson as Beryl Evans in Richard Fleischer's 1971 film *10 Rillington Place*; **Above center:** Tim Roth and Samantha Morton in the BBC TV Drama *Rillington Place*, 2016; **Above:** the unfortunate real life Ethel Christie; **Top right:** The Rillington Place crime scene, showing the wrapped remains of a victim; **Center:** The real John Christie.

Living Out His Fantasies

Christie's admitted first murder was Ruth Fuerst, whom he strangled in 1943 during sex. To kill work colleague Muriel Amelia Eady, he knocked her out with domestic gas, choked her to death, and then raped her. Both Eady and Fuerst were buried in the communal garden at 10 Rillington Place.

In 1950, Christie appeared in court as principal witness for the Crown to testify against a fellow tenant, Timothy Evans, accused of killing his wife and baby. In spite of Evans's voiced suspicions that Christie was the actual murderer, he was found guilty of killing the child, and hanged. (When Christie's crimes came to light, it seemed logical to conjecture that Christie *had* killed the mother and daughter. The only other conclusion—that two murderers lived in the same building—seemed unlikely.

CHRISTIE: 10 RILLINGTON PLACE

NOTTING HILL, LONDON 1953: SOME GRUESOME DISCOVERIES AND A GROSS MISCARRIAGE OF JUSTICE

When Christie's criminal record came out during the Evans trial, he lost his banking job. In December 1952 he informed his current employer, British Road Transport Services, that he was moving north. His wife had already moved there, he told people after she disappeared. In reality he murdered her in bed on December 14, then sold her wedding ring and watch, most of their furniture, and forged her signature to empty her bank account. In the late winter of 1953, his flat became a killing field, where he murdered Kathleen Maloney, a prostitute; Rita Nelson, who was pregnant; and Hectorina MacLennan, a friend.

When Christie moved out of Rillington Place in 1953, it didn't take long for the new tenant to discover the bodies hidden in the

kitchen alcove. He notified the police, setting off a national manhunt. Christie offered to surrender if his story headlined in the *News of the World*, but he fled before the interview. Now wandering around London and sleeping in parks, Christie was finally arrested near Putney Bridge after a policeman questioned his identity.

He confessed to putting the bodies in the alcove and to killing Beryl Evans, but not her baby. At his trial for murdering Ethel he pleaded insanity, but the jury found him guilty. He was hanged in Pentonville Prison on the same gallows where Timothy Evans had died. The miscarriage of justice in the Evans case sparked public outrage and contributed to Britain suspending the death penalty in 1965.

Top left: Detectives arrest Timothy Evans for the murders of his wife Beryl, and their baby Geraldine; **Top right, and above:** The grim location attracted hundreds of sightseers. Scenes in the 1971 film used the actual address, but after filming wrapped, the local council demol[ished] the entire street

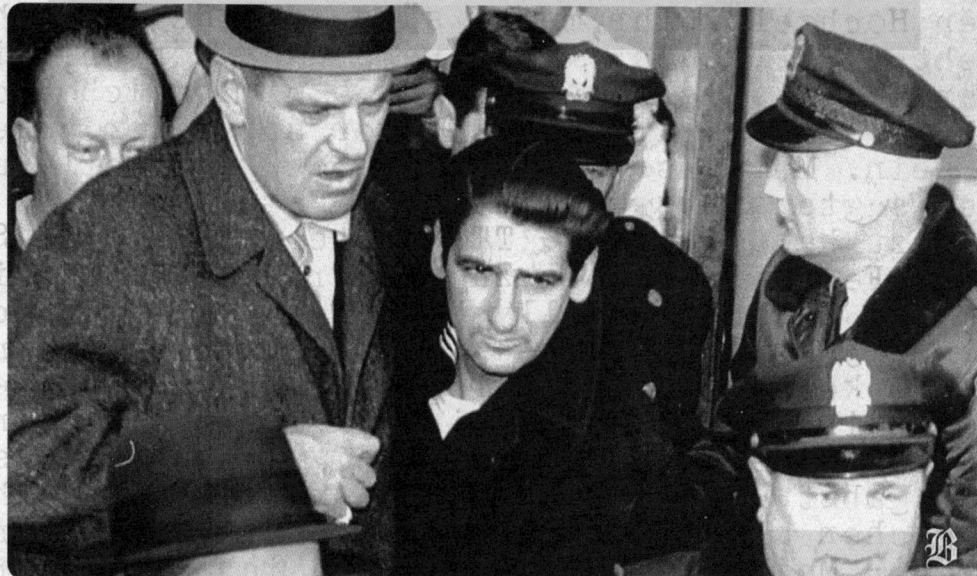

ALBERT DESALVO
THE BOSTON STRANGLER

Top left: Boston in the early 1960s; **Above, and top right:** Albert DeSalvo, The Boston Strangler. As well as committing multiple rapes in and around Boston in the early 1960s, he confessed to murdering 13 women. Despite DeSalvo recanting his confessions, recent DNA analysis confirms him as the murderer.

Albert DeSalvo was born September 3, 1931, in Chelsea, Massachusetts. His father was a violent alcoholic who often beat his wife in front of their children, bending her fingers back until they broke and once knocking out all her teeth. The boy, a known animal abuser, was only 12 when he was first arrested for battery and robbery. After two stints in the Lyman School for Boys, DeSalvo joined the army. He completed two tours and received an honorable discharge.

DeSalvo was living in Malden, Massachusetts, at the time of the Boston Strangler murders—a string of killings that occurred between June 1962 and January 1964, with 13 victims aged 19 to 85. Most of the women were attacked in their own homes, sexually assaulted, then strangled with an item of clothing. The eldest victim died of a heart attack. In fall of 1964, a rash of sexual assaults occurred in the Boston region. The perpetrator was dubbed the "Measuring Man," or the "Green Man." One victim said he tied her to the bed, raped her,

then said, "I'm sorry" before he left. The victims described this intruder in enough detail that the police were able to identify DeSalvo.

An Unexpected Confession

Even when the police had DeSalvo in custody for the Green Man rapes, they made no connection between him and the Strangler. But then DeSalvo confessed to another prisoner, George Nassar, that he was the Boston Strangler, and Nassar told his lawyer, the noted attorney F. Lee Bailey. The police at first proved skeptical, but then Albert supplied details of the crimes. Even under hypnosis he maintained his assertion. Yet there was no physical evidence that linked him to any of the murders.

In court, DeSalvo was tried for robbery and sexual offenses, and was represented by Bailey. The lawyer cited his client's Boston Strangler confessions to prove that DeSalvo was insane, but the judge would not admit them. After a 1967 plea bargain, where Bailey kept the death penalty off the table, DeSalvo

BOSTON STRANGLER MURDER LOCATIONS JUNE 1962–JAN.64

1. **Anna Slesers, 55.** June 14, 1962.
   77 Gainsborough Street, Boston
2. **Mary Mullen, 85.** June 28, 1962.
   1435 Commonwealth Avenue, Boston
3. **Nina Nichols, 85.** June 30, 1962.
   1490 Commonwealth Avenue, Boston
4. **Helen Blake, 65.** June 30, 1962.
   73 New hall Street, Lynn
5. **Ida Irga, 75.** August 19, 1962.
   7 Grove Street, Boston
6. **Jane Sullivan, 67.** August 21, 1962.
   435 Columbia Road, Boston
7. **Sophie Clark, 20.** December 5, 1962.
   315 Huntington Avenue, Boston
8. **Pat Bissette, 23.** December 31, 1962.
   515 Park Drive, Boston
9. **Mary Brown, 69.** March 6, 1963.
   319 Park Street, Lawrence
10. **Beverly Samans, 23.** May 6, 1963.
    4 University Road, Cambridge
11. **Evelyn Corbin, 57.** September 8, 1963.
    224 Lafayette Street, Salem
12. **Joann Graff, 23.** November 23, 1963.
    54 Essex Street, Lawrence
13. **Mary Sullivan, 19.** January 4, 1964.
    44 Charles Street, Boston

was nevertheless given a life sentence. Bailey had hoped his client would end up in a mental hospital where his desire to kill could possibly be understood.

As with some high-profile cases, the verdict was controversial. Critics thought Nassar, a psychopathic killer, made a far better match with the Strangler's profile. DeSalvo, they argued, simply wanted to be "famous," so it was conceivable Nassar gave him the details of the murders to gain recognition. Others felt DeSalvo killed only some of the victims, and that there was another murderer still on the loose.

In February 1967 DeSalvo and two other inmates escaped from Bridgewater State Hospital, resulting in a statewide manhunt. He eventually turned himself in to his lawyer in Lynn, and was thereafter held in a maximum-security prison, Walpole. He died there on November 25, 1973, stabbed to death in the prison infirmary. Robert Wilson, of the notorious Winter Hill Gang, stood trial for his death but it resulted in a hung jury.

Left: DeSalvo was defended by F. Lee Bailey, a high-profile defense lawyer who would go on to defend, among others, Patty Hearst (see pages 172-173) and O.J. Simpson (see pages 82-83); **Above:** Actor Tony Curtis was effective and chilling as DeSalvo in the 1968 film *The Boston Strangler;* ***Map:** Lawrence, site of two of the Strangler murders, is located some miles further north than is shown on the map. Boston was a key port by the early 18th century, populated by many English (and later, Irish) emigrés who named many of the townships around Massachusetts Bay with place names from the old country. The original Boston is an old spa town in Lincolnshire, England.

> ## "Ted was the very definition of heartless evil..."
> POLLY NELSON, BUNDY DEFENSE LAWYER

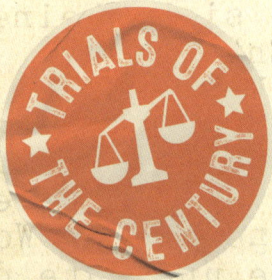

TRIALS OF THE CENTURY

"TOTAL POSSESSION"

Top: Ted Bundy, the handsome psychopath; **Above:** Carol DaRonch, who survived an attack by Bundy, gives testimony; **Opposite, left:** 16 of Bundy's victims. He confessed to killing 36 women in multiple states. The tally may be closer to 100. **Opposite insets, top to bottom:** Electric chair execution, c. 1925; Newspaper story announcing the use of the new "execution by electricity" method in New York State; **Bottom:** The body of Ted Bundy after his execution in the Raiford electric chair.

Theodore Robert Bundy was perhaps the best-known serial killer to emerge in America near the end of the 20th century. With crimes that included rape, murder, and necrophilia, he represented a trifecta of sexually deviant vice.

Bundy was born in Burlington, Vermont, to Eleanor Cowell, an unwed mother of 22. He was raised as the child of his maternal grandparents to hide Eleanor's shame. Ted was never sure of the identity of his biological father. He did well in school, but was shy and had few friends. Eventually his darker nature emerged: he liked to stare into strangers' windows at night and often stole from those who possessed something he wanted.

In 1972 he graduated from the University of Washington with a BA in psychology; while there he'd fallen in love with Stephanie Brooks, a pretty, dark-haired student from a wealthy California family. When she broke up with him,

he was devastated. Most of his subsequent victims resembled her, especially the dark hair. Ted worked hard to eradicate his shyness and after gaining more confidence, was soon involved in social and political activities. To observers, he seemed a handsome and charismatic young man.

The Carnage Begins

Bundy likely began raping and killing his victims around 1974, when young women in the Seattle area and nearby Oregon began to disappear. Some of the women were last seen with a dark-haired young man named Ted. (Bundy often lured women into his car by pretending to be injured. They almost always came to his aid. The same ruse was used by serial killer Jame Gumb in *The Silence of the Lambs*.) After knocking the victims unconscious, Bundy brought them to a secondary location to rape and strangle them. He sometimes revisited the bodies *in situ*, grooming and performing sex acts with them. A few times he broke into homes and

94

"OLD SPARKY"

Execution by electrocution, or "riding the lightning," was conceived in 1881 by Buffalo dentist Alfred P. Southwick. The electric chair was considered a more humane alternative to hanging, though many found it barbaric. Its first victim was murderer William Kemmler in New York's Auburn Prison. With the introduction of lethal injection, the electric chair has declined in use.

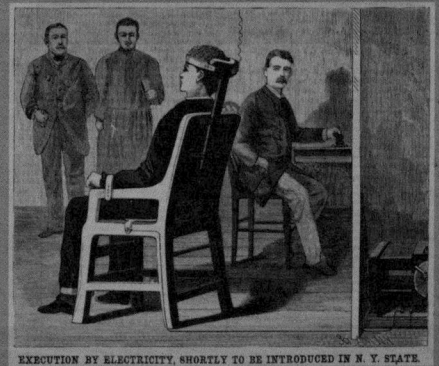

EXECUTION BY ELECTRICITY, SHORTLY TO BE INTRODUCED IN N. Y. STATE.

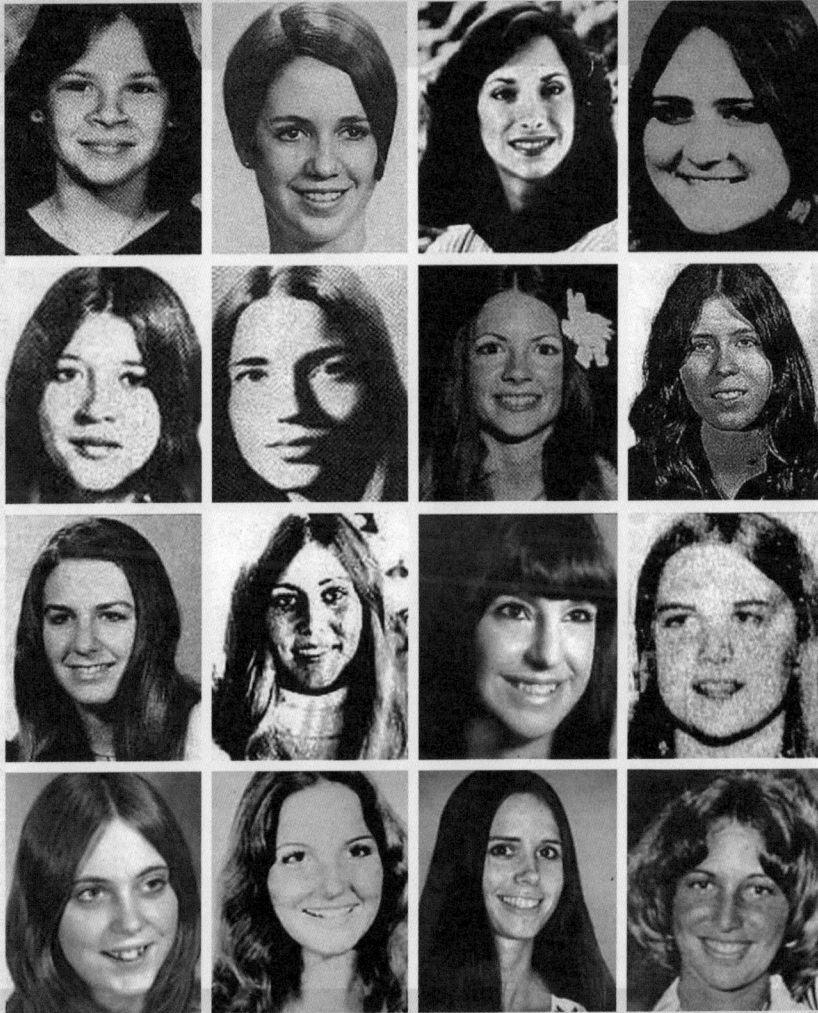

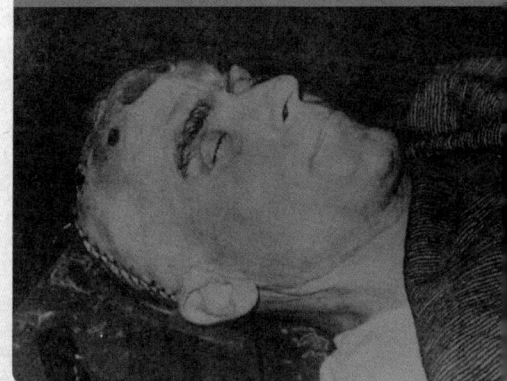

bludgeoned women while they slept. At least 12 victims were decapitated, and several heads were kept in his apartment as mementos.

That fall Bundy moved to the University of Utah for law school, and young women again began disappearing. After being pulled over by the police and seen to be carrying burgling tools, he was linked to the abduction of Carol DaRonch, one of his few victims to escape. He received a one-to-15 year sentence.

In 1977, after being indicted in the death of a Colorado women, he chose to act as his own lawyer; during a visit to the law library he jumped from a window and escaped. Eight days later he was back inside. He then starved himself to fit through a small hole he'd made in his cell ceiling and was not missed for 15 hours. He ended up in Tallahassee, Florida, where on the evening of January 14, 1978, he entered the Chi Omega

sorority house at at Florida State University and brutally attacked four coeds with a piece of firewood, killing two of them. In February, he killed 12-year-old Kimberly Leach. The police apprehended him shortly thereafter. But it was too late for his three victims.

He first stood trial for the coed killings, the bite marks left on one of the sorority sisters linking him inexorably to the crime, followed by the Leach trial. All told he received three guilty verdicts and three death sentences. During the appeals process, Bundy agreed to talk about his crimes, and admitted the powerful need to possess things that others owned. Sexual assault, he said, was "total possession." His appeals failed, and he was sent to the electric chair at Raiford on January 24, 1989. Attendees outside the prison cheered as the white hearse bearing his body drove past them.

TED KACZYNSKI
THE UNABOMBER

"The Industrial Revolution and its consequences have been a disaster for the human race…" THE OPENING LINE OF KACZYNSKI'S ESSAY *INDUSTRIAL SOCIETY AND ITS FUTURE*

Above: Professor Henry Murray. His "brutalizing" psychological study is seen by some as the trigger for Ted Kaczynski's mental trauma during and after his Harvard years; **Top, left:** A young Kaczynski at Harvard; **Top, right:** a cleaned-up Kaczynski is paraded after his capture;

Theodore John Kaczynski started life as a math prodigy and later became an academic but in 1971 ended up living rough in Montana and unleashing his anger at the spread of technology with deadly letter bombs. He became the subject of the FBI's longest and most expensive manhunt up to that time. The media took his nickname from his FBI case identification, UNABOM—University and Airline Bomber.

A native Chicagoan, Kaczynski came from a Polish-American working-class background. He recalled being traumatized as a toddler by his hospitalization for severe hives, when he was kept in isolation. Ever after, he empathized with animals kept in cages. His mother suspected he might be on what is now the autism spectrum. He excelled academically in high school and played trombone in the marching band, but other students viewed him as a "walking brain." He ended up skipping grades and graduating at 15. Sent off to Harvard without a lot of world experience, he grew into a reserved young man.

In his second year at Harvard, Ted participated in a "brutalizing" psychological study overseen by Professor Henry A. Murray. Subjects would write essays expressing their beliefs, then be filmed while an individual belittled their work with abusive attacks. Electrodes monitored the subjects' reactions to these attacks, which were replayed for the subjects over and over. In the course of three years, Kaczynski endured more than 200 hours of humiliation.

He completed his graduate studies at the University of Michigan, receiving a doctorate in mathematics. After a brief period of sexual confusion, where Ted considered gender transition and then found himself full of rage at his psychiatrist, he accepted a job as acting assistant professor at UC, Berkeley. By 1968 he was on the tenure track. But in June 1969 he suddenly resigned and in 1971 moved to a remote cabin he'd built in Lincoln, Montana. He lived offgrid without running water or electricity, using a bicycle for transportation. In Montana, at that time, this was not considered unusual. But when he started to read social and political philosophy, he developed strong anti-government, anti-technology sentiments; Jacque Ellus's *The Technological Society* became his manifesto.

INDUSTRIAL SOCIETY AND ITS FUTURE
by FC

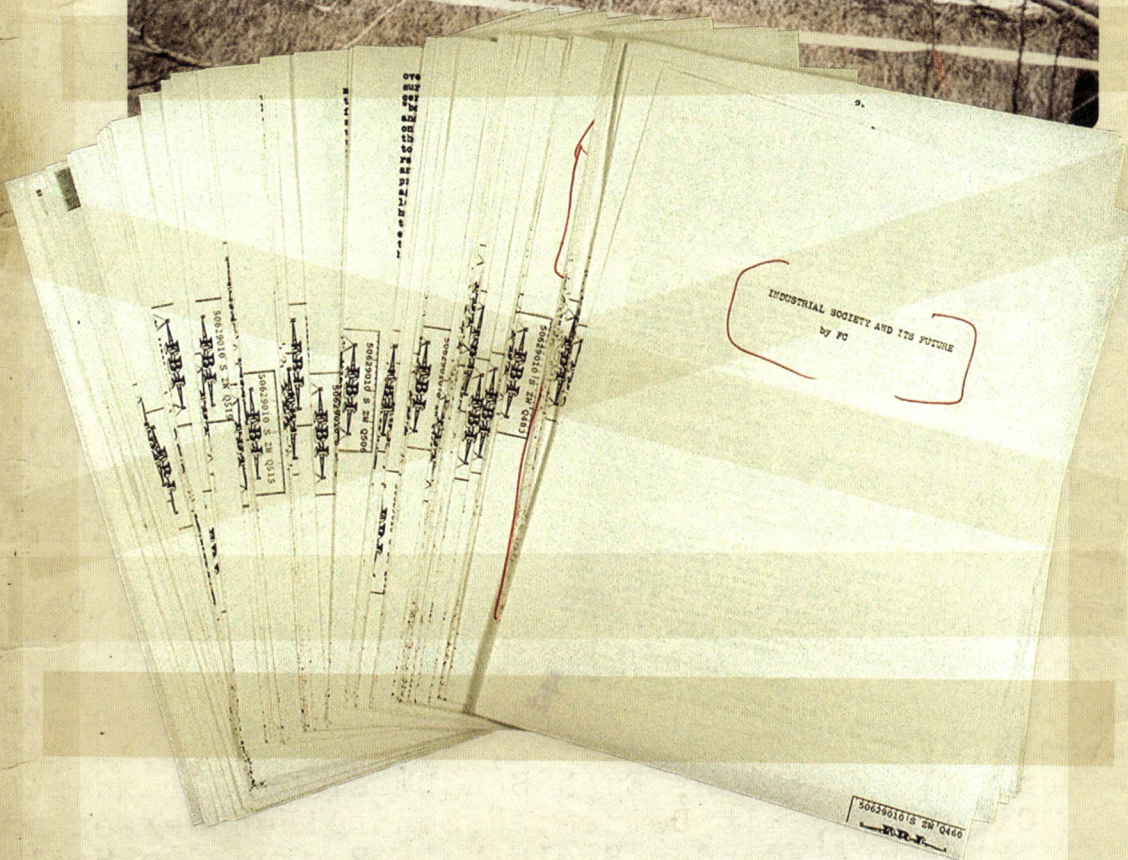

Too Close for Comfort

When road construction began to encroach on his beloved wilderness, Ted decided to seek revenge. He began mailing or hand delivering increasingly sophisticated bombs. The first recipient was Buckley Crist, a materials engineer at Northwestern University, who asked a security guard to examine a package he'd never sent that was "returned" to him. When it detonated, the man received minor injuries. In 1979 a plane bomb on a Boeing 727 failed to go off, but experts said it would have "obliterated the plane." Between 1978 and 1995, Kaczynski's bombs killed three people and injured 23 more. Components of the bombs were marked FC, for Freedom Club. Ted was careful that no fingerprints were left on any parts and also added false clues. The frustrated FBI could not seem to get a handle on him.

In 1995, hoping to draw him out, the FBI asked the *Washington Post* to publish an essay he'd sent the press along with his goals—*Industrial Society and Its Future*. David Kaczynski recognized his brother's prose style and contacted the Agency. Ted Kacszynski was finally arrested in 1996, but dismissed his lawyers, who were pushing an insanity plea to avoid a death sentence. In 1998, Ted agreed to a plea bargain, admitting guilt on all charges and accepting eight consecutive life sentences with no chance of parole.

Above: Kaczynski targeted universities, academics, computer store personnel, public relations experts, a timber industry lobbyist . . . and people named Wood, supposedly because he wanted to emphasize his "theme" of nature. The three people murdered were, top to bottom: Hugh Scrutton, Tom Mosser, and Gilbert Murray; **Top left:** Kaczynski's offgrid cabin in Montana; **Center:** the 35,000-word essay published in the *Washington Post*.

97

A criminal profile is like a police sketch, but with personality and social characteristics augmenting the physical description.

PROFILING:
PORTRAITS OF PSYCHOPATHS

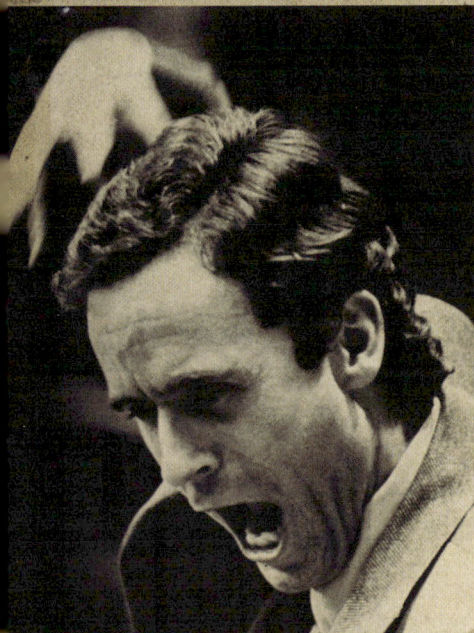

Above: Ted Bundy displays his "grandiosity" during one of his several trials—he conducted his own defense; **Top:** A dark "rogue's gallery," from left: Jeffery Dahmer, David Berkowitz, Fred West (UK), Gary Ridgway, the USA.'s second-worst serial killer, Aileen Wuornos, Rosemary West (UK), and Richard Buono;

A profile can provide tangibles like age, race, geographic location, and economic level, and intangibles such as motivations, triggers, antisocial attitudes, psychopathologies, and behavioral aberrations. In essence, profiling is where law enforcement and psychology intersect.

A Six-step Process

A relatively new field—the FBI's own system dates back to the 1980s—profiling relies on analyzing evidence gathered at a crime scene as well as statements given by witnesses. There is a six-step process used to complete the portrait, and each step is critical to the whole.

STEP 1   Input

This involves the gathering and organizing of information: investigation reports, crime scene photos, details about the neighborhood, the medical examiner's report, a pre-murder timeline of the victim's movement, and a background profile of the victim.

STEP 2
Constructing a Decision Process Model

Here, the characteristics of the homicide are set down. Was the killing serial or single murder? Was the homicide the primary motive of the killer or incidental to another crime? Was the victim at high-risk, like a homeless person or a prostitute, or at low-risk, like a businessperson or professional. Was the victim killed at the discovery site or elsewhere?

STEP 3
Crime Assessment

Does the crime scene indicate an organized or a disorganized offender, or a mix of the two? This classification is credited to FBI agent and profiler Roy Hazelwood and is the centerpiece of the agency's approach. Criteria include whether the body was posed by the killer, whether a sexual assault was performed before or after death, and whether cannibalism

or mutilation was practiced. *Organized offenders* are bright, sociable, and plan carefully, leaving behind few clues. Many dispose of the body away from the crime scene. They typically know right from wrong, but show no remorse. *Disorganized offenders* do not plan their crimes; they are likely to leave fingerprints or blood and rarely attempt to remove the body. They might be young, under the influence of drink or drugs, or mentally ill. Social skills and intelligence are below average; family dysfunction may be a factor.

STEP 4 Criminal Profile

This report offered to local investigators includes possible personality, physical, and social characteristics of the offender. It also lists objects the killer might possess, such as pornography.

STEP 5 Investigation

Local police now incorporate the profile into their own investigative procedures, narrowing the list of suspects and implementing strategies that are likely to lead to an arrest. The Atlanta child murders of the 1980s were the first time FBI profilers assisted local police, resulting in the conviction of Wayne Bertram Williams.

STEP 6 Apprehension

The proof-of-performance step, capturing the killer, is followed by assessing the accuracy of the profile when compared to the actual offender. The results are then added to an FBI database at Quantico.

TRAITS OF A SERIAL KILLER

Below are some characteristics of serial killers compiled by law enforcement. The FBI notes, however, that there are many mistaken beliefs about serial killers. They are not limited to white males—but span all ethnic groups. They are not always dysfunctional loners—many are married—or motivated only by sex—other potential triggers include anger, thrill seeking, financial gain, and a desire for attention.

- Lack of empathy ■ Manipulation
- Lack of remorse ■ Addictive personality ■ Impulsivity ■ Lust for power ■ Grandiosity ■ Sensation seeking ■ Narcissism ■ Head trauma
- Peeping-tom activities in youth
- Superficial charm ■ The MacDonald Triad: bed-wetting, fire starting, and animal cruelty.

Yet more psychopaths. Top left: Looking full of psychotic hate in his restraints, Richard Ramirez, "the Night Stalker" of the Greater Los Angeles area, then later, San Francisco; **Top right:** Ted Bundy, defense counsel; **Center, top to bottom:** Edmund Kemper, Arthur Shawcross, and Wayne Williams—the Atlanta child-killer.

From 1976 to 1977, a series of random "lovers' lane" slayings had much of New York City holding its breath in fear. Letters from the killer alluding to Beelzebub and drinking blood added a new level of disquiet.

"I was literally singing to myself on the way home, after the killing…" DAVID BERKOWITZ

DAVID BERKOWITZ
SON OF SAM

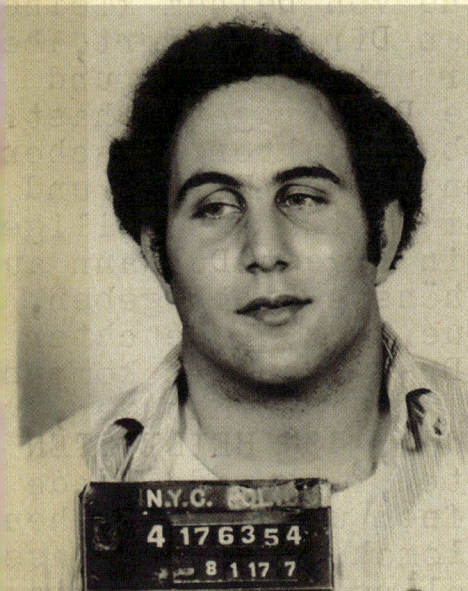

Above: "Son of Sam" mugshot; **Opposite top:** David Berkowitz is arrested and brought in, August 10, 1977; **Opposite center and bottom:** The crime scene of the Moscowitz and Violante shootings. Stacey Moscowitz died, Robert Violante survived but lost an eye.

New York City native David Berkowitz (born Richard David Falco) was the son of a waitress whose second husband insisted she give up their child days after his birth. The baby was adopted by Pearl and Nathan Berkowitz of the Bronx, a middle-aged Jewish couple who owned a hardware store. As a youth David was already committing petty theft and starting fires. At 17 he joined the Army and after his discharge tracked down his birth mother, learning with dismay of his father's callous abandonment. Psychologists felt this discovery was the "primary crisis" that shaped his adult life.

In December 1975, while working as a postal employee, he bungled his first murder attempt—a Christmas Eve stabbing of two women in Co-op City. On July 29, 1976 he used a handgun for his attack on two women sitting in a car in Pelham Bay. He killed Donna Lauria and wounded her friend Jody Valenti. The survivor identified a white male of medium height, slightly overweight, with dark curly hair. Not long after, a couple in a car saw their windshield explode before they drove frantically away. Carl Denaro suffered a serious head injury but recovered. Berkowitz wounded two women on a porch in Floral Park, then targeted another couple in a car in Forest Hills, killing Christine Freund and wounding her fiancee, John Diehl. On March 8, 1977, Columbia student Virginia Voskerichian was gunned down a block from the Freund shooting.

By matching the large .44 Special caliber bullets used to kill both women, police determined they were fired from the same gun, indicating a possible serial murderer. The press immediately labeled the suspect the .44 Caliber Killer.

On April 17, Berkowitz killed another couple in a car near the Lauria-Valenti shooting. A letter written in block capitals and found near the bodies mentioned the "Son of Sam" influence. The press adopted the name "Son of Sam" killer. Two more couples in cars were targeted, Sal Lupo

1977, April 17
Bronx

SURIANI & ESAU

6

1976, July 29
Pelham Bay,
Bronx

LAURIA & VALENTI

1

BRONX

1976, October 23, Queens

DENARO & KEENAN

2

1977, June 26 Bayside, Queens

LUPO & PLACIDO

7

MANHATTAN

LaGuardia

QUEENS

3

1977, March 8 Queens

VOSKERICHIAN

1976, November 27, Brooklyn

DEMASI & LOMINO

5

4

1977, January 30, Queens

FREUND & DIEL

Kennedy

BROOKLYN

STATEN ISLAND

8

1977, July 31 Brooklyn

MOSCOWITZ & VIOLANTE

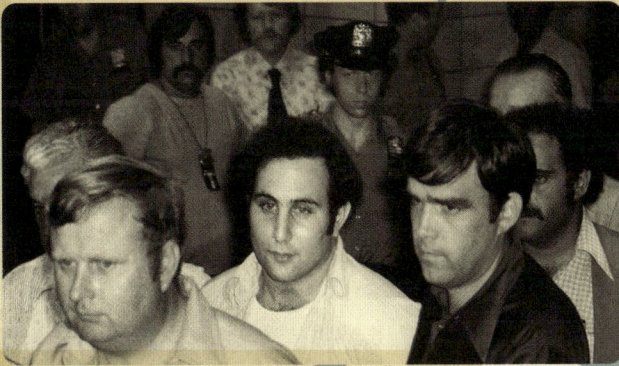

SON OF SAM SHOOTINGS, NEW YORK CITY 1976–77.

Coney Island

Rockaway Beach

and Judy Placido, and Robert Violante and Stacy Moscowitz; Moscowitz died. Near the site of the latter murder, Cacilia Davis watched a stocky man inspecting a parking ticket on his car. As she ran home, she heard shots in the street behind her. After she reported the incident, the police traced Berkowitz's car and found a gun and ammunition inside. When accosted, Berkowitz reportedly said, "I'm Sam."

He was arrested on August 10, 1977, and assessed as competent to stand trial. He confessed to the attacks and initially claimed to be obeying the orders of a "demon" dog that belonged to his neighbor, Sam, and which demanded the blood of pretty young girls. He later claimed he was part of a Satanic cult that performed ritual murder. The police found no cult, but some crime investigators believe there was a Satanic conspiracy. Berkowitz has spent his life sentence in a series of New York State prisons, including Attica.

Some serial killers leave such an indelible impression on the public that it can be hard to wipe the memory clean of their image or their deeds. For many, John Wayne Gacy had that effect.

AS POGO THE CLOWN

JOHN WAYNE GACY
"KILLER CLOWN"

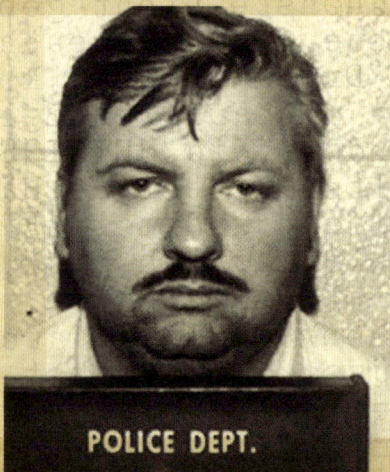

POLICE DEPT.

Born in Chicago, Gacy grew up with an alcoholic father who beat his children and his wife. Because he suffered from a congenital heart condition, Gacy's play with other children was restricted. The realization he was gay caused him even more torment.

After managing a fast-food restaurant in the 1960s, he taught himself the skills needed to start his own contracting business, PDM. Throughout the decade he was active in local politics and the Jaycees. He even married and had two children. Then in 1968 he was convicted of sodomizing a teenage boy. A psychological evaluation indicated he suffered

from an antisocial personality disorder. His wife sued for divorce, and he never saw her or his children again. He was sentenced to 10 years, but served only 18 months before relocating to Chicago.

Gacy murdered his first victim in 1972, 16-year-old Timothy Jack McCoy, whom Gacy had picked up at the Greyhound terminal. Gacy claimed he thought the boy meant to stab him and struck in self defense. But as the boy lay dying, Gacy felt an incredible thrill. He killed again in 1974, an unidentified victim . . . and continued killing through 1978, even though he was married to second wife, Carole, for much of that time. She

"Clowns can get away with murder..."

JOHN GACY, A COMMENT TO POLICE

said she often saw him escorting young men into the garage of their ranch house in Norwood Park Township.

In late 1975 Gacy joined the Chicago region's Jolly Joker clown club. He enjoyed performing in clown attire and makeup, entertaining at children's parties and fundraisers. His two alter egos were Pogo, a happy clown, and Patches, a more serious clown.

The Final Victim

After his divorce from Carole in 1976, Gacy began "cruising" for young men in earnest, killing the majority of his victims between then and 1978. He would lure the target to his house, put handcuffs on him as part of a "magic trick," then torture and rape the captive before strangling or asphyxiating him. He then buried the bodies in the crawlspace, spreading quicklime to speed up decomposition.

On December 11, 1978, Gacy was discussing a contracting job at a pharmacy, when a young male employee caught his eye. He offered the boy work, and so Robert Peist put off his family birthday dinner to talk to him. Gacy took Peist to his house, where he raped and then suffocated him. When Peist's family filed a missing person report, the pharmacist recalled Gacy talking to the boy. A police search of Gacy's home yielded nothing but they put him under surveillance. PDM employee Michael Rossi finally admitted spreading ten bags of quicklime under Gacy's house. During the second search police scoured the crawlspace—and at last found human remains. Gacy was immediately arrested and made a formal confession on December 22. Police found 26 victims under the house and three buried on the property. Gacy had also dropped another four into the Des Plaines River.

When the public learned of Gacy's clown fixation, they were deeply unnerved. The combination of leering clown, an image many adults and children find creepy, with serial killer, was doubly repulsive. The press, meanwhile, labeled him the Killer Clown. On February 6, 1980, Gacy stood trial for 33 murders. The defense argued he was beset by multiple personalities, but the jury found him guilty on all counts and recommended the death penalty. He was executed by lethal injection on May 10, 1994.

Above: Ten of the young men murdered by the Killer Clown; **Main Image:** The crawlspace under Gacy's garage, where police found the remains of 23 young men. The pegs with numbers indicate separate human remains; **Opposite, main image:** Gacy as Pogo the Clown, and **below,** his police mugshot.

"I stood there amazed. I found it all hard to believe, that I, Des Nilsen, had actually done all that…"

DENNIS NILSEN
BODIES IN BIN BAGS

Above: Dennis Nilsen after his arrest; **Main image opposite:** The reconstruction of Nilsen's kitchen at 23 Cranley Gardens, in Scotland Yard's Black Museum. On the stove is the infamous cooking pot in which Nilsen boiled his victims' heads.

Born in Aberdeenshire, Scotland, Dennis Nilsen was the son of a Norwegian soldier who rarely visited his Scottish wife. Elizabeth Nilsen finally divorced him after the birth of their third child. Dennis, or Des, was a quiet boy who as a teenager realized he was gay, an insight he kept to himself. He did note that the boys who attracted him resembled his favorite sibling, Sylvia.

Nilsen enlisted in the army, intent on becoming a chef, and enjoyed his three years of training. In 1964 he was assigned to the Royal Fusiliers in West Germany. He fell in with a "boozy lot" and after a night of drinking woke up in the flat of a young German man. Nothing had occurred between them, but Nilson began to fantasize about sex with a slender youth who was totally passive, or unconscious . . . or even dead.

While serving in the Middle Eastern State of Aden, Des was kidnapped by an Arab taxi driver who beat him and placed him in his trunk. When the trunk was opened, Nilsen used the jack handle to beat the driver until he passed out. This near-death experience later became part of

his fantasies, along with visions of dead soldiers and the haunting image of men dying at sea in Géricault's painting The Raft of the Medusa.

He joined the police force in 1973, but missed the camaraderie of the army. He finally found meaningful work as a civil servant at a job center in London's West End. Visits to gay bars led to casual but unsatisfying relationships. For a time he lived with 20-year-old David Gallichan on Melrose Avenue in Cricklewood, but Gallichan left the relationship in 1977. Now truly alone, Nilsen feared he was unfit to live with.

The Avenue of Death

Nilsen killed his first victim, 14-year-old Stephen Holmes, on December 30, 1978. He invited the boy to his house with the promise of drinks and music. (The lure of drinks or a place to sleep often worked with Nilsen's victims, mostly homeless runaways.) He choked the sleeping teen with a necktie, then drowned him in a bucket. After bathing the body, he masturbated over it, and stashed it under the floorboards. In his own words, he had "started down the avenue of death" with "a new kind of flatmate."

From 1978 to 1983, Nilsen killed at least 12 men and boys, and attempted to kill seven more. At the Melrose flat, he burned the bodies in a garden bonfire. At his attic flat in Cranley Gardens, North London, he flushed the flesh and small bones down the toilet. When the drains backed up, Nilsen himself complained. The plumber on call found a nasty surprise—human tissue. When the police questioned Des, he kept asking why they were interested in his drains. "Where is the rest of the body?" they demanded. Des calmly explained it was in two trash bags in his wardrobe. He was immediately arrested.

Nilsen admitted killing "15 or 16" people, but had trouble recalling their names. When a severed arm was located in his tea chest, its fingerprints matched those of Stephen Neil Sinclair, Nilson's last victim. On February 11, 1983, the police finally charged Nilson. He was tried on six counts of murder and two of attempted murder, with conflicting testimony on whether he was sane or suffered from a personality disorder. The jury found him guilty on all counts, and he was sentenced to life with a minimum 25 years. In May 2018 he died of a pulmonary embolism while still in prison.

A CLOSER LOOK

Actor David Tennant, who bears a noticeable resemblence to Nilsen, played the serial killer in the 2020 miniseries *Des*.

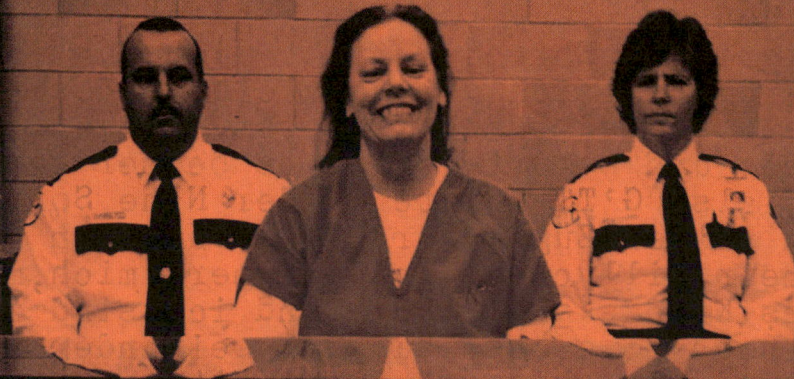

"I got really tired of it all. I was angry about the johns…"

AILEEN WUORNOS
HIGHWAY HOMICIDES

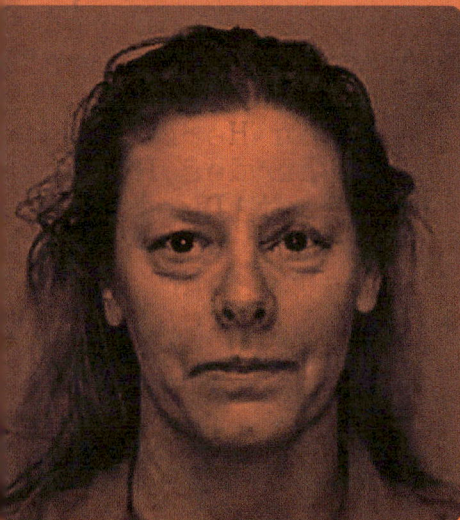

Top, and above: Aileen Wuornos in custody.

Aileen Wuornos was born on February 29, 1956, in Rochester, Michigan, and from the start got dealt a bad hand. Her father was a child molester who killed himself in prison. Her teenage mother took off, leaving Aileen and her brother in the care of her maternal grandfather, a child beater, and grandmother, an alcoholic. By age 11, she was offering men sex in return for money, beer, and cigarettes. She had a baby at 14, which she gave up for adoption. In the early 1980s, after her brother died of cancer, she moved to Florida as a full-time sex worker. Within a decade she had a police record for illegal possession of a firearm, forgery, assault, and robbery. Law enforcement records noted "Attitude: POOR."

In 1986, Wuornos met hotel maid Tyria Moore at a Daytona Beach bar, and the two women felt an instant attraction. This was only Aileen's second lesbian relationship—her "professional" clients continued to be middle-aged men. When Wuornos began murdering and robbing her "johns" in 1989, Moore was unaware. Once she became suspicious, she moved back with her family in Pennsylvania. After Wuornos was identified and arrested—items stolen from her victims were traced to the pawnshop where she sold them—police used legal threats against Moore to gain a confession from Aileen for all seven murders.

At her trial for murdering first victim Richard Mallory, Wuornos pleaded self defense, insisting her client was going to rob her and rape her. The jury did not buy it. They found her guilty and recommended the death sentence. In spite of appeals citing her wretched childhood and psychological issues—and Mallory's earlier imprisonment for violent rape—on October 9, 2002, Wuornos was executed by lethal injection at Florida State Prison.

Seven Victims

Across five counties in 1989-90, Aileen Wuornos touted for paid sex from motorists on Florida's highways, frequently posing as a hitchhiker. She shot and killed the seven men below at point-blank range, before robbing the bodies and abandoning their cars. One of the victims, 55-years old Peter Siems, was never found, though his car was located in Orange Springs.

David Spears was a 43-year-old construction worker whose nude body was found on June 1, 1990, with six bullet wounds in the torso.

Richard Mallory, a shop owner, was killed in 1989. A Volusia County deputy discovered his body, which had been shot several times in the chest.

Troy Burress, 50, was a salesman found in Marion County on August 4, 1990, shortly after being reported missing. The decomposing body showed two gunshots to the torso.

Charles Carskaddon, 40, was discovered in Pasco County a few days after Spears. A part-time rodeo worker, he'd taken nine shots to chest and stomach.

Peter Siems, 65, left central Florida for New Jersey in June of 1990. His abandoned car was found on July 4 in Orange Springs. His body was never located.

Charles "Dick" Humphreys was a retired Air Force major, a police chief, and child-abuse investigator. His body was found in Marion County on September 12, 1990 with gunshots to the head and torso.

Walter Antonio, 62, was found, partially nude, in Dixie County on November 19, 1990. He had bullet wounds to his back and head. Days later his car was found in Brevard County.

Above: Wuornos on death row; **Right:** Charlize Theron obscured her natural beauty with prosthetics and makeup to play Wuornos in the 2003 film, *Monster*, (**above right**) for which she won the Academy Award for Best Actress.

DEADLY AS THE MALE

Female serial killers have always existed. Hungarian countess Elizabeth Báthory murdered hundreds of young girls in the 1500s, while a majority of Victorian serial poisoners were women. Criminologist Eric W. Hickey, who in 1985 published the first paper on female serial killers, believed their methods were generally less violent—mostly relying on poison or asphyxiation—but it was their motives that truly differentiated them from males. "Men kill for sexual pleasure and control," he wrote, "women kill for financial gain." Even though Wuornos shot her victims, robbery was her motive.

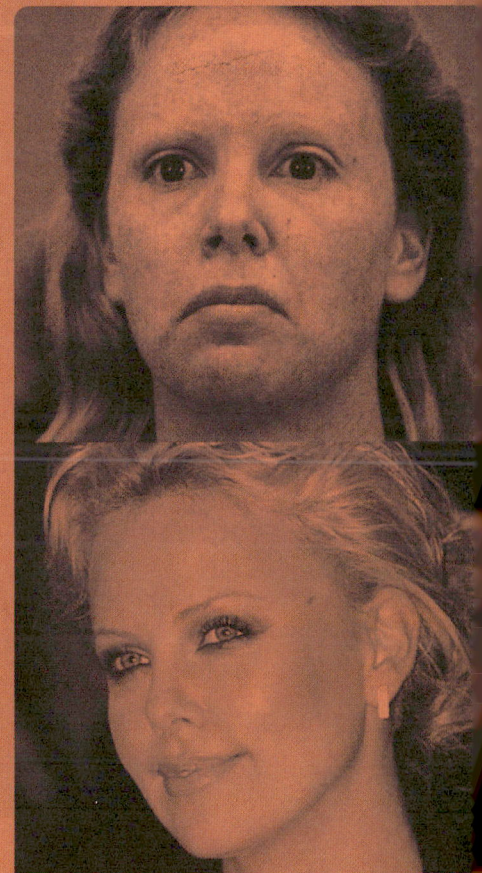

Some sociopaths acquire such a taste for murder that their need to kill consumes them. With victims numbering well into double digits, these four serial killers include that rarity, a female.

HIGH BODY COUNTS

Above: The endless acres of steers waiting to become meat at the Chicago Stockyards in 1890.

Belle Gunness Chicago

Belle Gunness was 22 in 1881 when, as Brynhild Storset, she emigrated from Norway, settling in Chicago where her sister lived. In a city of sprawling stockyards, she found work cutting up carcasses in a butcher shop. She married Mads Sorenson in 1884 and had several children. When two babies died in their home, and Belle collected the insurance, neighbors noted that she had not been pregnant either time. After she took out two consecutive life insurance policies on Mads, he died of a cerebral hemorrhage the day the policy coverage overlapped. She bought a pig farm with the proceeds. Second husband Peter Gunness and his infant daughter both died mysteriously. In 1905 she began placing newspaper ads seeking marriage, using her farm as an inducement. Henry Gurholt of Wisconsin was the first to answer ... and he soon disappeared. John Moe of Minnesota likewise vanished. There is no way to know exactly how many lonely men Belle robbed and killed. But when the Gunness farmhouse burned in 1908 with Belle and her three children inside, searchers found numerous butchered body parts in the pig

pens. Her handyman and sometime lover, Ray Lamphere, confessed that she had murdered many of her suitors. She'd also ordered Lamphere to set fire to the house with the children inside. The woman burned in the fire, he said, was *not* Belle. Gunness may have been responsible for as many as 40 deaths.

Samuel Little
Crimes across the USA

America's most prolific serial killer, Little was born June 7, 1940, and raised by his grandmother in Lorain, Ohio. Even as a child, he fantasized about strangling women. He moved to Florida in the late 60s, but continued to travel ... and was arrested in eight states for various crimes. In 1982, he was arraigned in Mississippi for murdering Melinda Rose LáPree, but not indicted. In 2012, DNA testing implicated him in the deaths of three LA women. Even though he was tied to 93 murders in many states, he was tried for the three in California and found guilty. Little believed he would never be caught because no one would miss his victims—poor black women, many of them addicts. After his sentencing, the FBI continued to interview him about his crimes, believing it

was important to seek justice for every victim. Those women he preyed on were no longer the "forgotten ones." Little died in prison at age 80.

Harold Shipman Manchester, England

Harold "Fred" Shipman was a doctor who did not subscribe to the medical pledge to "do no harm." No, this healer was in reality a killer, a serial killer of possibly hundreds. Born in Nottingham, England, Shipman had been coddled by his mother and developed a lifelong air of superiority. From 1977 to 1998, while working as a general practitioner in the Hyde area of Greater Manchester, "Doctor Death" murdered dozens of patients with an overdose of morphine. These were not mercy killings; none of the patients were terminal or in terrible pain. Investigators

believed he simply liked playing God. In 1998, after his patient death rate drew suspicion, he was arrested. The autopsy of a recent patient showed evidence of a morphine overdose. In 2000, Shipman received 15 life sentences for murder; he hanged himself in his cell in 2004. It is estimated he may have murdered more than 230 people.

Robert Pickton Vancouver

Robert "Willy" Pickton – Vancouver, Canada. Nicknamed "the Butcher," this Canadian farmer and serial killer murdered 49 women and purportedly disposed of their bodies by feeding them to his pigs. Many of the victims were from Vancouver's crime-ridden Downtown Eastside. In 2007 he was charged with 49 counts of murder, convicted of six, and sentenced to life.

Clockwise from top left: Belle Gunness of Chicago. Responsible for around 40 deaths; Samuel Little, who murdered people all across the United States and is thought to be America's most prolific serial killer—mainly of poor black women; Dr. Harold Shipman, an English GP practicing in Hyde, Greater Manchester. With an estimated murder count of 230, he is one of Britain's worst serial killers; Vancouver farmer Robert "Willy" Pickton—"The Butcher," pictured here smiling as he begins to butcher one of his pigs. Most of his estimated 49 murder victims were dismembered and fed to his animals.

ANGELS OF DEATH
NURSES WHO KILL

Above: Nurse Kristen Gilbert, sentenced to four consecutive life sentences after being found guilty of four confirmed murders, though it's possible she killed over 350 veterans.

Referred to ironically as Angels of Mercy, nurses who kill patients are often found trying to revive their victims, motivated by the need to appear heroic to their peers. Even though nurses do not take an oath to "do no harm," as is required of doctors, the vast majority of nurses are caring and dependable medical professionals. Yet in the annals of serial crime there are quite a number of nurses who left a trail of bodies in their wake.

Kristen Gilbert Massachusetts

A New England nurse with a history of violent behavior, Gilbert killed four patients and attempted to murder another two at the Veterans Affairs Medical Center in Northampton, Massachusetts. Her method was to induce cardiac arrest in a patient by injecting large amounts of untraceable epinephrine, a heart stimulant, into their IV bags . . . and then attempting to resuscitate them herself. It is possible she killed more than 350 veterans, but was only tried for the four confirmed deaths. In 2001 she received four consecutive life terms.

Genene Jones San Antonio

A Texas native and licensed vocational nurse, Jones was the adopted daughter of a nightclub owner and his wife. Originally a beautician, she attended nursing school in the late 1970s. While working in the pediatric ICU at the Bexar County Hospital (now University Hospital of San Antonio), an unusual number of children died in her care. It was later revealed that she injected digoxin, heparin, and succinylcholine into her young patients to induce medical crises. She was eventually tried for the murder of two children, but the exact number of deaths may be closer to 60. The truth will never be known as the records of Jones's activities were misplaced and destroyed by the hospital, possibly to avoid additional litigation.

Niels Högel
Oldenberg, Germany

Born in the former West Germany, Hogel was the son of two nurses who followed in his parents footsteps and generally earned esteem from colleagues. But in 1999, while employed at the Oldenberg Clinic in the cardiac

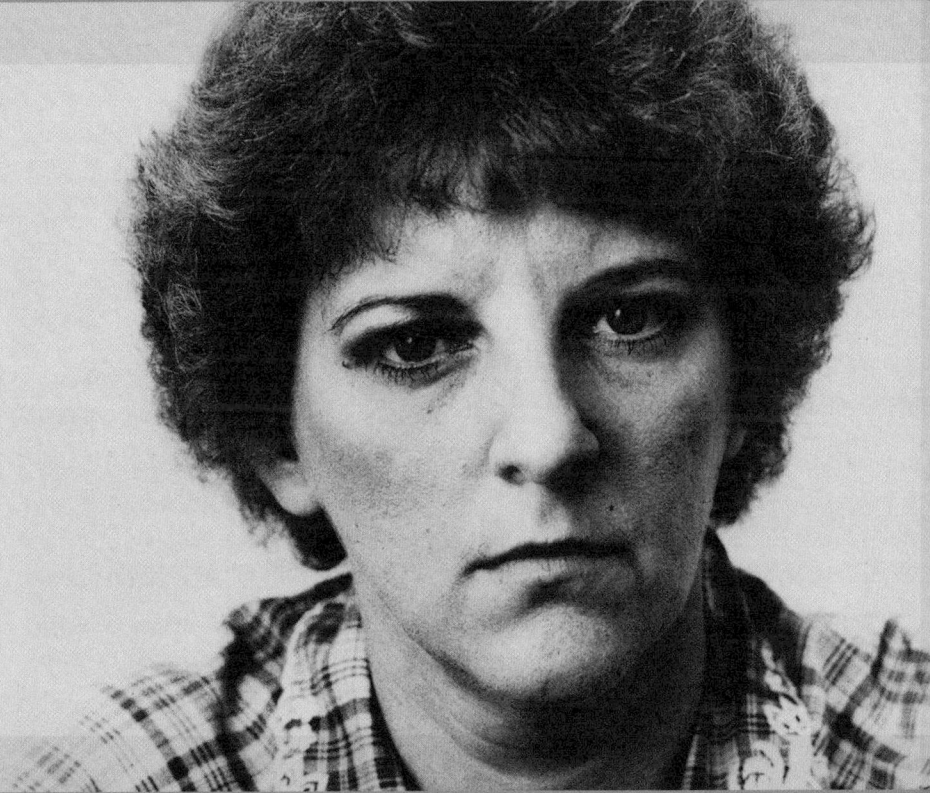

surgical ICU, a surprising number of patients died while in his care. A similar spike occurred at his next job at the Delmenhorst Clinic. When he was caught manipulating a patient's ajmaline (an anti-arrythmia medication) pump, Högel was arrested. After he received a life sentence for the murders of six patients in 2015, further investigations resulted in his conviction for a total of 85 deaths. By his own account, he murdered more than 300 patients. The prosecution claimed he acted out of boredom and the need to show off his resuscitation skills.

Beverly Allitt
Grantham, England

A British-licensed practical nurse from Lincolnshire, Allitt worked at the Grantham and Kestevan Hospital, where she killed four children, attempted to murder another three, and caused grievous bodily harm to six more.

Her methods ranged from fatal shots of insulin to injecting air bubbles, which can cause heart attack or stroke. She received 13 life sentences at her 2007 trial in Nottingham. She was believed to suffer from Munchausen by proxy syndrome, a mental disorder where people endanger or abuse those in their care to bring attention to themselves.

Aino Nykopp-Kosk Finland

This Finnish nurse killed five elderly patients using sedatives and opiates—and attempted to kill five more—while working at various hospitals, care homes, and private residences. Although she pleaded not guilty, and a mental health assessment classified her as psychotic with an antisocial personality disorder, in 2010 the court convicted her and issued a life sentence, with a minimum of 12 years served.

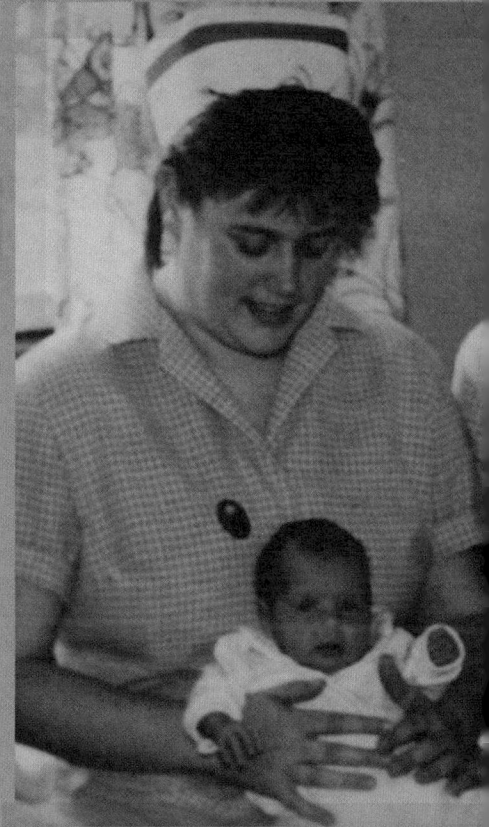

Above left: Nurse Genene Jones around the time she was beginning her killings; **Top:** Nurse Beverly Allitt, before her crimes were discovered; **Center:** Finnish nurse Aino Nykopp-Kosk during questioning; **Above:** Nurse Niels Hogel. He was convicted of a total of 85 deaths.

WEST COAST KILLERS

California is the third-largest state behind Alaska and Texas, but it is the most populous state, with more than 39 million residents as of 2020. Therefore, it is not statistically surprising that a number of high-profile serial killers have been found among its residents.

Top: Arthur Leigh Allen, who was always the prime suspect in the Zodiac Killings, though nothing was ever proved; **Above:** *San Francisco Chronicle* crime reporter Paul Avery, who covered the murders, was drawn deep into the case and at one point was even targeted by the Zodiac Killer.

The Zodiac Killer

The Zodiac was the self-anointed name of an unidentified serial killer who preyed on Northern California during the 1960s. He typically phoned in his crimes and used the newspapers to whip up a frenzy of publicity, insisting his letters be published or he would increase the frequency of his murders. Some letters included coded messages or cryptograms, one claiming that his victims would "become his slaves in the afterlife."

The Zodiac murdered five people between 1968 and 1969 in rural, urban, and suburban settings, using a knife or a gun. His targets were young couples, although two of the men survived the murder attempts. He also shot a cab driver and later included pieces of his bloody shirt in letters to police and journalists.

The Zodiac once claimed to have killed 37 people, and police did find links to some cold cases. Author Robert Graysmith's book *Zodiac* indicates his first victim, Darlene Ferrin, may have known her killer. This acquaintance, a child molester named Arthur Leigh Allen, was already the police's most promising suspect. But the evidence against him was circumstantial, and he was never prosecuted.

The Golden State Killer

Responsible for three crime sprees in California between 1974 and 1986, he committed 120 burglaries, 50 rapes, and 13 murders. Each spree generated a different press name: Visalia Ransacker in the San Joaquin Valley; East Area Rapist in the Sacramento region; and, as his crimes escalated to serial murder, the Night Stalker or Original Night Stalker in Santa Barbara, Ventura, and Orange Counties.

The investigation lasted decades, with some suspects cleared by DNA testing. (The case helped advance California's DNA database, which includes DNA from all suspected and convicted felons.) The killer, identified as a tall, athletic-looking, blond man, often taunted the police with obscene phone messages or written communications.

More than 40 years after his first crime, the FBI and local law-enforcement announced a renewed nationwide effort, with a $50,000 reward, to capture the Golden State Killer. On April 24, 2018, Sacramento County Sheriff's deputies arrested Joseph James DeAngelo, then 73 years old, after the killer's DNA—taken from a rape kit—matched DeAngelo family DNA accessed from a commercial DNA repository.

Zodiac Killer

1. **David Faraday and Betty Lou Jensen.** December 20, 1968. Lake Herman Road, Benicia
2. **Darlene Ferrin and Michael Mageau.** July 4, 1969. Blue Rock Springs Park, Vallejo
3. **Bryan Hartnell and Cecelia Shepard.** September 27, 1969 Lake Berryessa, Napa County
4. **Paul Stine.** October 11, 1969. Presidio Heights, San Francisco

Five murders, with two intended victims surviving

The Night Stalker

1. **Jennie Vincow.** June 28, 1984. Glassell Park, Los Angeles
2. **Dayle Yoshie Okazaki.** March 17, 1985. Rosemead
3. **Tsai-Lian "Veronica" Yu.** March 17, 1985. Monterey Park
4. **Vincent and Maxine Zazzara.** March 27, 1985. Area north of Whittier
5. **Bill Doi.** May 14, 1985. Monterey Park
6. **Mary Louise Cannon.** July 2, 1985. Arcadia
7. **Joyce Nelson.** July 7, 1985. Monterey Park
8. **Lela and Maxon Kneiding.** July 20, 1985. Glendale
9. **Chainarong Khovananth.** July 20, 1985. Sun Valley, Los Angeles
10. **Elyas Abowath.** August 8, 1985. Diamond Bar
11. **Peter Pan.** August 18, 1985. San Francisco

13 murders, including torture and rape, and at least 16 attempted murders

Golden State Killer

1. **Claude Snelling.** September 11, 1975. Visalia (Visalia Ransacker Case)
2. **Katie and Brian Maggiore.** February 2, 1978. Rancho Cordova, Visalia (East Area Rapist Case)
3. **Debra Manning and Robert Offerma.** December 30, 1979. Goleta (Original Night Stalker Case)
4. **Charlene and Lyman Smith.** March 13, 1980. Ventura (Original Night Stalker Case)
5. **Patrice and Keith Harrington.** August 19, 1980. Dana Point (Original Night Stalker Case)
6. **Manuela Witthuhn.** February 5, 1981. Irvine (Original Night Stalker Case)
7. **Cheri Domingo and Gregory Sanchez.** July 27, 1981. Goleta (Original Night Stalker Case)
8. **Janelle Cruz.** May 5, 1986. Irvine (Original Night Stalker Case)

Thirteen murders, plus robbery and rapes

Hillside Stranglers

1. **Yolanda Washington.** October 17, 1977. Her body dumped near the Ventura Freeway
2. **Judith Miller.** November 1, 1977. Her body dumped in Alta Terrace Drive in La Crescenta
3. **Lissa Kastin.** November 6, 1977. Her body left near the Chevy Chase Country Club, Glendale
4. **Dolores Cepeda and Sonja Johnson.** November 20, 1977. Their bodies dumped near Dodger Stadium
5. **Kristina Weckler.** Her body found on a hillside near Glendale on November 20, 1977.
6. **Evelyn Jane King.** On November 23 1977 her body found by the Los Feliz off-ramp of the Golden State Freeway
7. **Lauren Wagner.** November 29, 1977. Her body found in the hills around LA's Mount Washington
8. **Kimberly Martin.** December 14, 1977. Her body found in deserted lot near LA City Hall.
9. **Cindy Hudspeth.** February 16, 1978. Her body found in the trunk of her orange Datsun, some way down a cliff on the Angeles Crest Highway.

Ten murders, including torture and rape

WEST COAST SERIAL KILLERS: MURDER LOCATIONS DECEMBER 1968 TO MAY 1986

Top left: Joseph DeAngelo, The Golden State Killer, was the first criminal arrested by means of *genetic genealogy*, using the perpetrator's crime scene DNA to trace family connections from a DNA database; **Center and above:** Cousins Bianchi & Buono—the Hillside Stranglers. At the time, their joint trial was the most expensive in Californian legal history; **Top right:** A grim Hillside Stranglers murder scene awaits the coroner.

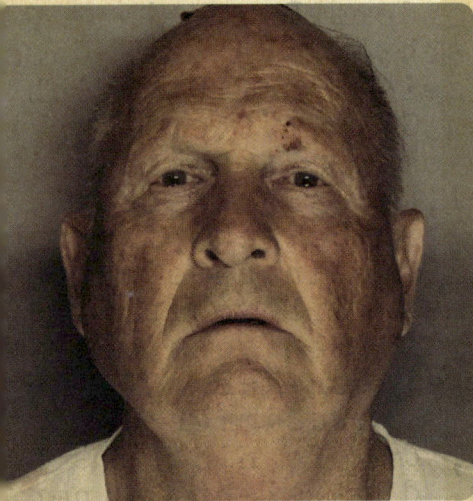

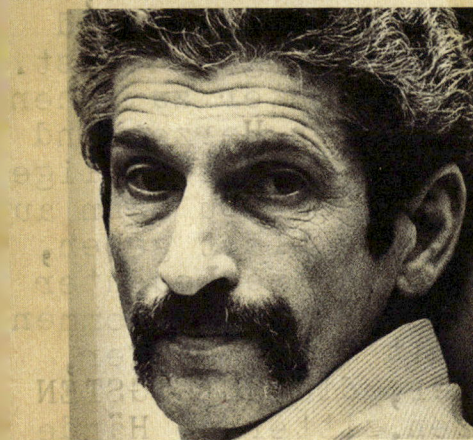

DeAngelo was born in New York state, but graduated from high school east of Sacramento. He enlisted in the Navy, saw action in Vietnam, then got a degree in criminal justice. From 1973 to 1976, he worked as a police officer in Exeter, close to Visalia. In 1976, he served with the Auburn Police, until his dismissal for shoplifting. After his arrest, he was charged with eight counts of first-degree murder, pled guilty to avoid the death penalty, and received 26 life sentences.

The Hillside Stranglers

The Hillside Stranglers haunted the Los Angeles region from October 1977 to February 1978. It is unusual for serial killers to have partners or accomplices. Yet this was the case with the Hillside Stranglers, so named because victims' bodies were found in the Los Angeles hills. When the police realized, based on the positions of the bodies, that two killers were working as a team, they kept that information from the public.

The first three murders were of sex workers, found naked and strangled in the scrub, but then the men abducted and killed five girls from middle-class neighborhoods. That was

when the media began to cover the murders and publicize the killer. After two more murders, in December and February, the killing stopped. Still the investigation continued, and finally, when Kenneth Bianchi was arrested in 1979 for the murder of two girls in Washington, he agreed to implicate his cousin for the Hillside murders in return for leniency. This led to the arrest of Angelo Buono, Jr.

Bianchi had left his hometown of Rochester, NY, to live in California with Buono. The two decided to become pimps and forced several girls to work for them. When the girls eventually ran away, they bought a "pimp" list of regular "johns" from a friend of another prostitute, Yolanda Washington. When they realized they'd been tricked, they killed Washington, and began their murder spree. The dual court case was the most expensive in California's legal system up to that time. Both men were convicted of rape, torture, kidnapping, and murder and received life sentences. Buono died of a heart attack in 2002.

The Night Stalker

The Night Stalker was responsible for a terrifying series of home invasions and murders in

KING COUNTY
WASHINGTON
BA   DATE
1 3 5 9 0 0 5 1 2 '82

"I've killed 20 people, man. I love all that blood...."

RICHARD RAMIREZ, THE NIGHT STALKER

the Greater Los Angeles area—and later the San Francisco Bay area—from June 1984 to August 1985. The killer, dubbed the Night Stalker, used a range of weapons: handguns, knives, a machete, a tire iron, and a claw hammer. When Texas native Richard Ramirez was finally apprehended after a 1985 manhunt, he told police a harrowing story from his youth, how his older cousin Miguel Ramirez, a Green Beret and Vietnam veteran, showed 12-year-old Richard Polaroid photos of atrocities he'd committed during the war, including raping women suspected of being

Vietcong collaborators and then beheading them. Richard also witnessed Miguel kill his wife during an argument. A year later Richard began to take LSD and became involved with Satanism and the occult. Ramirez may have been psychologically damaged, but he never expressed any remorse for the 13 deaths, 5 attempted murders, and 11 sexual assaults on his ledger. He served 24 years on death row before succumbing to lymphoma.

Above: Richard Ramirez, The Night Stalker, in 1985.

The Green River Killer

Just north of California lies the Pacific Northwest, where a serial killer targeted sex workers and underage runaways during the 1980s and 1990s. The bodies of his first five victims were found in the Green River in Washington, thus his press name. He typically strangled the women, hid them in forests, and sometimes returned to have sex with them. On November 30, 2001, truck painter Gary Ridgway was arrested after DNA profiling linked him to the murders of four separate women. Originally from Salt Lake City, Utah, Ridgway had been dominated by his mother as a child and confessed he was both sexually attracted to her and wanted to kill her. Ridgway arranged a plea bargain, revealing the locations of his victims in return for being spared execution. He is the second most prolific American serial killer after Samuel Little. The police attributed 49 murders to Ridgway, but he claimed a total of 71.

THE YORKSHIRE RIPPER

THE ONE THAT ALMOST GOT AWAY

Top: The 13 confirmed victims of the Yorkshire Ripper; **Center:** Peter Sutcliffe's mugshot, taken by the South Yorkshire Police Anti-Vice Squad after his arrest in Sheffield, January 1981. He was apprehended entirely by chance. A local woman happened to be in his car at the time; **Above:** The crime scene of Sutcliffe's tenth victim, Jo Whitaker, in Halifax, West Yorkshire.

The police are not infallible. Sometimes during a large investigation key factors get overlooked or there is a breakdown in communication. In the search for a brutal serial killer in the rugged landscape of Yorkshire, a series of outdated investigative procedures was likely the element that hamstrung law enforcement.

Peter Sutcliffe was born to a working-class Catholic family in the West Riding of Yorkshire. His father, an abusive alcoholic, reportedly smashed him over the head with a beer mug for sitting in his chair at Christmas. Sutcliffe developed a fixation on prostitutes and their pimps, often watching the women soliciting men on the streets of Leeds and Bradford. After leaving school, he had a series of blue-collar jobs but eventually trained as an HGV (heavy goods vehicle) driver and married teacher trainee Sonia Szurma in 1974. In 1977 the couple used her teacher's salary to buy a house in Heaton, in Bradford, where he lived until his arrest. For his job, Sutcliffe was required to travel extensively, criss-crossing the North of England.

By then he had already begun murdering women, initially targeting girls in residential neighborhoods, then switching to prostitutes because, he claimed, the voice of God told him to. Leeds was his main killing field, with six murders

and four attacks, including his first and last victims. Sutcliffe murdered at least 13 women and tried to kill 10 more. His weapons of choice were a hammer and a knife: he would stun the victim with a blow, then slash her torso. His first victim, Wilma McCann, mother of four children, died of repeated stabs to her throat, chest, and abdomen. Second victim Emily Jackson was stabbed 52 times. The press quickly dubbed the killer "the Yorkshire Ripper."

An extensive inquiry involving 150 officers of the West Yorkshire Police gained little traction. Yet the police interviewed Sutcliffe in relation to the murders on NINE separate occasions—including over a £5 note found on one of the bodies, issued from his bank, and again when a survivor's description of her attacker resembled Sutcliffe *and* the tire tracks at the scene matched the brand on his car. Still he was not detained. Four years after the first murder, the killings continued unabated. The police were sidetracked by a taped message from an imposter that sent them hunting for a man with a Sunderland accent.

An Endless Urge to Kill

In April 1980, Sutcliffe was arrested for driving drunk. While awaiting trial, he murdered two more women and attacked three. By that time,

> "The women I killed were filth. Bastard prostitutes who were littering up the streets." PETER SUTCLIFFE

he said, he "had the urge to kill any woman." When he was routinely stopped by the South Yorkshire Police anti-vice squad in Sheffield, in January 1981—with a prostitute as a passenger, no less—a quick radio check revealed his car had false number plates. He was arrested and transferred to Dewsbury Police Station in West Yorkshire. A strip search revealed an inverted V-neck sweater worn under his pants, exposing his genitals and padding his knees. The sexual implications were obvious. After sustained questioning, he finally admitted he was "the Ripper," and calmly supplied details of the attacks, calling his victims "filth." On trial for 13 counts of murder, he claimed diminished responsibility. The judge overruled a diagnosis of paranoid schizophrenia, and the jury sentenced him to 20 consecutive life sentences. He died in prison in 2020.

Afterward, the West Yorkshire Police were heavily criticized on several fronts, not least for institutional sexism. Key descriptions of Sutcliffe by female survivors of his attacks were not trusted by the officers in charge of the case, and some were even left in an intray for over a year. Essentially, the West Yorkshire Police had not properly equipped themselves for such a massive investigation—one of the biggest in British criminal history. Since the 19th century, information on crime suspects was written on index cards, but in a case this large there were difficulties in storing and accessing them. Case notes of thousands of pages were further complicated by false confessions. Post-Ripper, revolutionary new investigative systems were put in place for major crimes, and the first computerized alternative system—the Home Office Large Major Enquiry System (Holmes)—was instituted.

Above left: George Oldfield, the Assistant Chief Constable of West Yorkshire Police. Oldfield, along with his boss, Chief Constable Ron Gregory, and Acting Chief Constable Jim Hobson, were the three men in charge of the Ripper manhunt, and regular targets of the British tabloid press; **Top:** With each killing, dozens of constables would be assigned to fruitless searches of the surrounding crime scene; **Above:** In 1979 Detective Constables Andy Laptew (pictured) and Graham Greenwood interviewed Sutcliffe whilst following up multiple sightings of a Ford Corsair driven by a lone male. They detailed their suspicions and recommended Sutcliffe be investigated further. However, their concerns were dismissed by a senior officer and their report was filed away. In 2019, the *Guardian* described the hunt for the Ripper as "stunningly mishandled."

ANDREW CUNANAN
CELEBRITY ASSASSIN

Andrew Cunanan has the dubious honor of being both a spree killer (killing multiple people during one—possibly prolonged—incident) and a serial killer (killing multiple people in separate incidents).

Above: The FBI's mugshot of Andrew Cunannan. He was thought to suffer from antisocial personality disorder, which is marked by a lack of remorse and empathy. His various aliases included Andrew DeSilva, Lt. Cmdr. Andy Cummings, Drew Cunningham, and Curt Matthew Demaris; **Top right:** The entrance to Casa Casuarina, Versace's Miami Beach mansion, where on the morning of July 15, 1997, Cunanan shot the designer twice in the head.

Although he is known to much of the public as the murderer of Italian fashion designer Gianni Versace, Cunanan was responsible for the deaths of five men. His link, if any, with Versace is considered tenuous, but sometimes in the case of a sociopath, even a slight connection is enough to arouse feelings of anger or a desire for revenge.

Cunanan was born in National City, California, just outside San Diego, and was of Filipino- and Italian-American heritage. Enrolled in private school by his father, he was a bright, talkative child with a high IQ. As a teenager, he became a proficient liar and teller of tall tales . . . and was known to alter his appearance to make himself as attractive as possible.

He identified as gay and was soon arranging liaisons with wealthy older men. After Andrew's father fled to the Philippines to avoid arrest for embezzlement, he became openly gay; during a fight with his mother over his sexual orientation, he threw her into a wall and dislocated her shoulder. In 1989 he moved to the Castro, a culturally gay neighborhood in San Francisco. He began to live off a string of wealthy male patrons and started dealing drugs. His friends recalled he was increasingly under the influence of methamphetamine and painkillers as well as alcohol.

The Killings Begin . . .

Cunanan's first victim, in April 1997, was his friend and former roommate, Jeffrey Trail, who had recently distanced himself from Andrew. Cunanan flew to Minneapolis, argued with Trail, then lured him to the home of Cunanan's former lover, architect David Madson, and beat Trail to death with a hammer . . . in front of Madson. Andrew then rolled the body in a rug and hid it behind the couch. He likely kept Madson as a hostage for several days before shooting him with a gun he had stolen from Trail and dumping the body near a local lake.

On May 4, he drove to Chicago and attacked wealthy real estate developer Lee Miglin, binding him with duct tape, stabbing him more

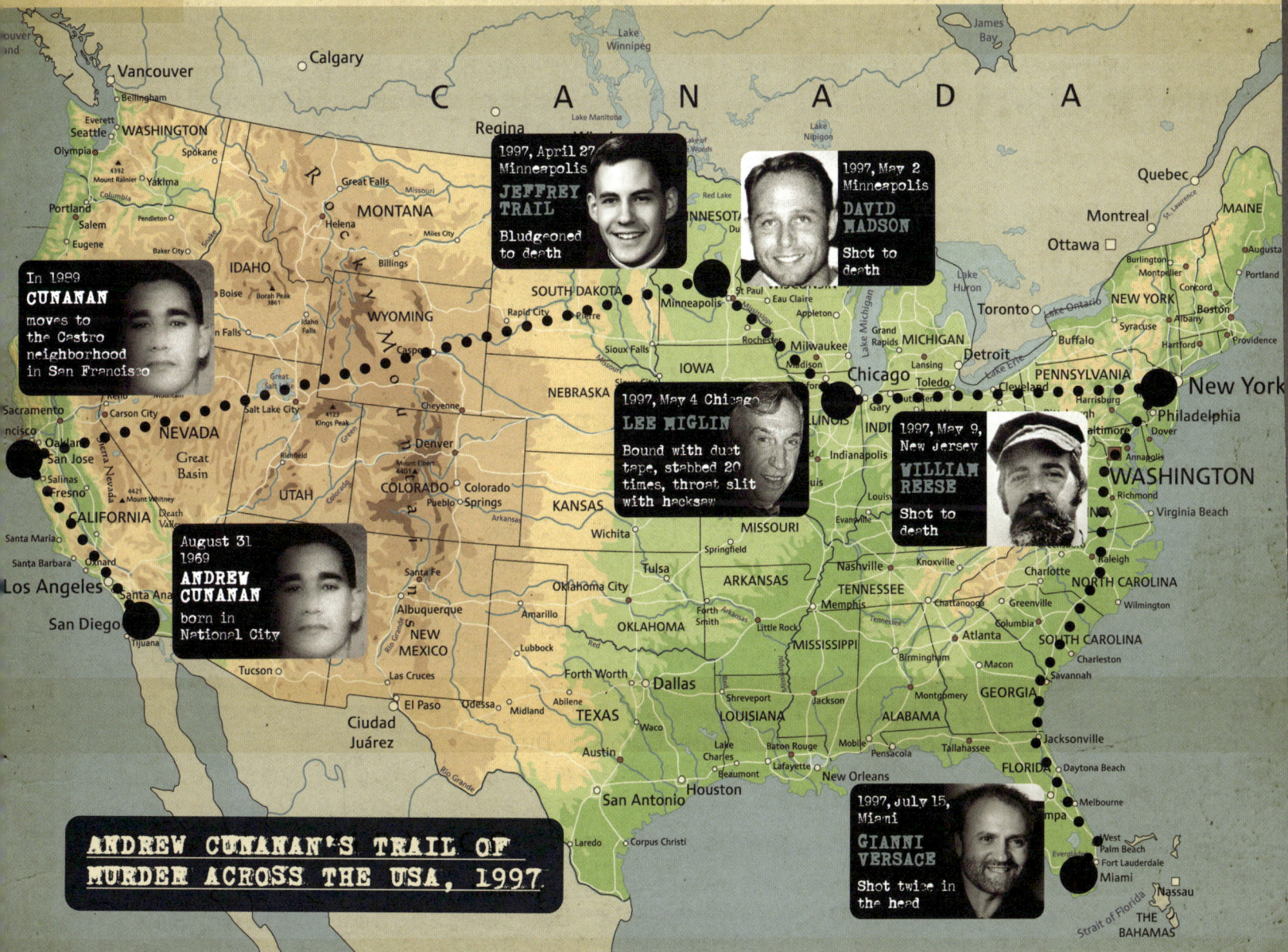

1997, April 27 Minneapolis
JEFFREY TRAIL
Bludgeoned to death

1997, May 2 Minneapolis
DAVID MADSON
Shot to death

In 1989 CUNANAN moves to the Castro neighborhood in San Francisco

1997, May 4 Chicago
LEE MIGLIN
Bound with duct tape, stabbed 20 times, throat slit with hacksaw

1997, May 9, New Jersey
WILLIAM REESE
Shot to death

August 31 1969
ANDREW CUNANAN born in National City

ANDREW CUNANAN'S TRAIL OF MURDER ACROSS THE USA, 1997

1997, July 15, Miami
GIANNI VERSACE
Shot twice in the head

than 20 times with a screwdriver, and slitting his throat with a hacksaw. The motive behind this brutal killing has never been explained. He ultimately stole Miglin's Lexus LS sedan and fled. In New Jersey, Cunanan cold-bloodedly shot cemetery worker William Reese in order to take Reese's Chevy pick-up truck. He then headed to Florida, apparently with the intention of killing Gianni Versace.

If, indeed, the two men had met—which Versace's family denies ever happened—it was probably some time in 1990, when the fashion designer was in San Francisco working on

costumes for Richard Strauss's opera *Capriccio*. In spite of being on the FBI's Ten Most Wanted list, Cunanan managed to hide out in Miami for two months. Then, on the morning of July 15, he accosted the designer on the front steps of his Miami Beach mansion, and shot him twice in the head with Trail's gun. Cunanan escaped, but on July 23 the police found his body on an unoccupied luxury houseboat. He had shot himself in the head. When Reese's truck was located, it contained Cunanan's clothing and clippings about his string of murders.

Above: The celebrity assassin's trail of murder across the continental United States in 1997.

The US may be home to the largest number of serial killers, but Latin America has given rise to some of the most barbarous and prolific examples in history. Some had "careers" that went on for years, and death tolls in the dozens or even the hundreds.

LATIN AMERICAN SERIAL KILLERS

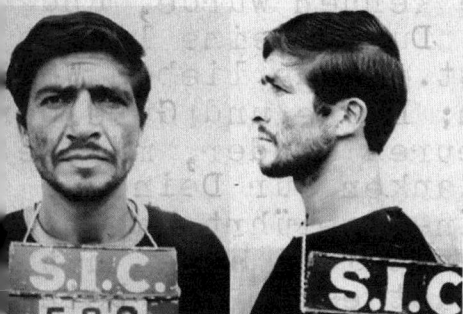

Many of these killers avoided capture by targeting indigenous women, the homeless, and outcast boys . . . victims whom few people would report missing and whose deaths the police spent little time investigating. There was also the lack of a deterrent—the legal systems here were not set up to respond to such heinous acts . . . so that even when a vicious multiple child murderer received the maximum sentence, it might only be for 14 years.

Pedro Lopez Monster of the Andes

Pedro Lopez, the Colombian-born "Monster of the Andes," is one of the most well known of the South American serial killers. Lopez was convicted of raping and killing 110 girls and women in Ecuador, but is suspected in the deaths of more than 300. After being tossed from his home for molesting his sister, he went into foster care, where he himself was assaulted and raped. As an adult he traveled across South America from Peru to Ecuador to Colombia, killing sometimes two or three victims a week. In 1978, Peruvian tribal elders almost put him to death for his crimes. After his capture by police in Ecuador he confessed to everything and served the maximum sentence of 16 years. After his release and deportation to Colombia, where he served four years in a psychiatric hospital, he re-entered private life and disappeared.

Pedro Ludeña The Apostle of Death

Pedro Pablo Nakada Ludeña of Lima, Peru, was known as the "Apostle of Death." The son of an alcoholic father and a mother with mental health issues, Nakada's sisters would dress him as a girl and then mock him. As an adult he paid a Japanese man to adopt him and changed his surname to Nakada in preparation for emigrating to Japan (a common way for criminals to flee persecution), but the plan fell through. He claimed to have killed 25 prostitutes "at God's command," using 9mm pistols with homemade silencers. He was arrested at his workplace after a shootout and convicted of 17 homicides. Meanwhile, apparently influenced by Pedro, his younger brother Jonathan went on a killing spree in Japan, stabbing 6 people.

Pedro Filho Killer Petey

Pedro Rodrigues Filho of Brazil, also known as "Pedrinho Matador" or "Killer Petey," was a vigilante who pursued and killed other criminals during the late 1960s. He'd received a skull-deforming head injury while in utero after his father kicked his pregnant mother during a fight, and claimed he first felt the urge to kill at age 13. To avoid arrest, he hid from the police in the tenements of Greater São Paulo, taking over for the drug dealers he'd eliminated, and then executing his father for killing his mother, cutting out his heart and biting into it—all before he turned 18. He murdered at least 71 people, including the 43 or so convicts he dispatched in prison.

Top: "The Monster of the Andes," Pedro Lopez;
Center: Pedro Ludena, "The Apostle of Death";
Above: Pedro Filho, "Killer Petey."

LATIN AMERICAN SERIAL KILLERS

MEXICO 1950s-60s
LAS POQUIANCHIS In the 1950s and 60s, four sisters responsible for the deaths of at least 91 victims

COLOMBIA, "THE BEAST" Raped, tortured, murdered and decapitated an estimated 189 boys in the 1990s. Despite this catalogue of depravity, he will be eligible for parole in 2023...

ECUADOR By 1978, **"THE MONSTER OF THE ANDES"** had killed a suspected 300 girls and women

COLOMBIA, DANIEL BARBOSA Raped, murdered and dismembered over 223 girls and women. In 1994 he was stabbed to death in prison by a fellow inmate

PERU, "THE APOSTLE OF DEATH" convicted of the murder of 25 sex workers

BRAZIL, TIAGO GOMEZ DA ROCHA Suspected of killing 39 people. Convicted and sentenced to 30 years in 2016

SAO PAULO, "KILLER PETEY" murdered at least 71 people, including the 43 fellow convicts he killed whilst in prison

ARGENTINA, "THE BLACK ANGEL" Convicted of robbery, rape, sexual abuse, kidnapping and the murder of 11 people in the 1970s and '80s

121

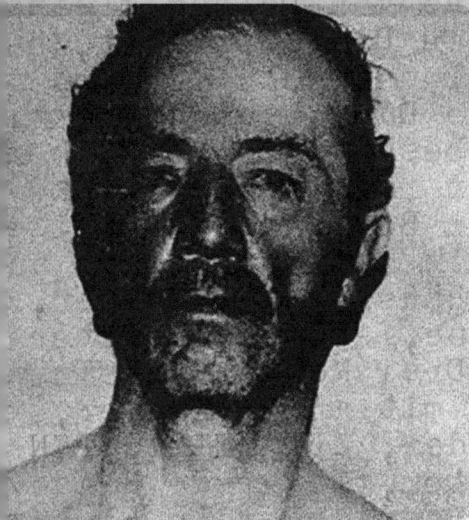

Top: Robledo Puch—The Black Angel of Buenos Aires; **Above:** It's believed that during the 1970s and '80s Daniel Camargo Barbosa raped, murdered, and dismembered over 223 young girls in Colombia and Equador;

Robledo Puch The Black Angel

Carlos Eduardo Robledo Puch is an Argentinian serial killer and thief known as the "Angel of Death" or the "Black Angel." He killed 11 people during the 1970s and 1980s and also faced charges of rape, sexual abuse, robbery, and kidnapping. During a hardware store robbery he accidentally shot his accomplice, while an earlier accomplice died in a mysterious car crash, which Puch fled. He was arrested and convicted in 1980, and is now the longest-serving prisoner in Argentina.

Daniel Camargo Barbosa

Daniel Barbosa of Colombia was the child of an overbearing, distant father and an abusive stepmother. He did well in school but was forced to leave in order to help his family financially. He married, then fell in love with another women, Esperanza, who was no longer a virgin. Barbosa agreed not to leave her if she could furnish him with virgins, whom he then drugged

and raped. Unfortunately, one of them reported him to the law, and he and Esperanze were incarcerated. After being released from prison, Barbosa raped and murdered a nine-year-old girl, assuring she would not report him. It is believed that he raped, murdered, and dismembered over 150 young girls in Colombia and Ecuador. When he escaped from his island prison, he killed 72 more females. In 1994 he was stabbed to death in prison by the nephew of a victim.

Tiago da Rocha

Tiago Henrique Gomes da Rocha of Brazil is a former security guard who possibly killed 39 people. He would pretend to be a mugger as he accosted his victims from a motorbike, shouting out "Robbery!" before shooting them dead. His main targets were homeless people, women, and sex workers. He claimed that sexual abuse by a neighbor during his childhood was what left him with homicidal urges. In 2016 he was sentenced to 30 years.

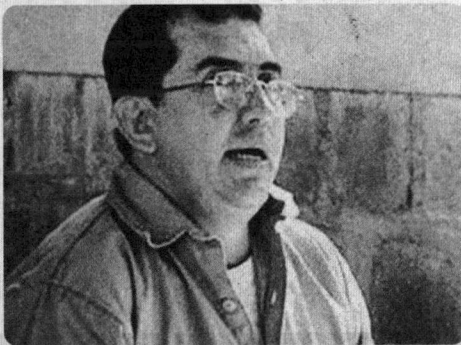

Luis Garaviti The Beast

Luis Alfredo Garavito, known as "the Beast," was born in Genova, Colombia. He grew up with an abusive father, who labeled him, among other slurs, an imbecile and bastard. His mother was likely a prostitute, and he was often forced by his father to watch his mother with clients, and then allow the clients to sexually abuse him. Perhaps it is not surprising that he murdered small animals and was attracted to young children—who could not harm him. He had relationships with women, but they were probably not consummated. Friends categorized him as kind but easy to anger. He soon began spiraling into mental illness, molesting children throughout the 1970s and 1980s. In 1992, he murdered his first victim, Juan Carlos, because the moon "compelled" him. After that he began rapidly targeting poor boys of six to 13 by luring them with offers of money, often wearing disguises to hide his identity. He would bind their hands, torture them, sexually abuse them, then decapitate them. Necrophilia was also involved. It is believed he raped and killed from 147 to 189 boys while he was active. A broken leg in 1995 left him with a limp that later helped police identify him after he was arrested in 1999—for an attempted rape. A DNA sample from his cell matched the sample from one of his earlier murders. The police had finally captured the Beast. He received a sentence of 1,853 years . . . but is eligible for parole in 2023.

Las Poquianchis

Carmen, María de Jesús, Luisa, and Delfina González, also known as *Las Poquianchis*, were four depraved Mexican sisters who owned brothels in Guanajuato and Jalisco during the 1950s and 1960s. They kept their prostitutes, often trafficked abductees, enslaved by debt and would abort their babies if they got pregnant. If the girls "lost their bloom," they were frequently murdered. The sisters killed at least 91 victims, maybe more. After a thorough police investigation, they were finally arrested, convicted, and sent to prison.

Left top: Tiago da Rocha, believed to have killed 39 people. He preyed on sex workers and the homeless of the city of Goiânia in Central-West Brazil; **Left above:** "The Beast", aka Luis Garaviti of Colombia. He raped and killed an estimated 189 young boys, frequently binding and torturing his victims before killing them. **Top right:** Maria and Delfina Gonzalez, two of the four Mexican sisters known as *Las Poquianchis*. The sisters pictured are generally believed to be the two main killers; **Above:** "The Angels," survivors of the depraved sisters' brothel regime

The British have a reputation for being an emotionally cool lot and rarely prone to violent or impetuous acts. Yet as was seen in earlier chapters, they regularly appear in the ranks of spousal and insurance-scam murderers, and are here significantly represented among serial killers.

BRITISH SERIAL KILLERS

Top: Possibly the most prolific serial killer in history—Amelia Dyer. It's estimated she murdered over 400 infants; **Above:** George Smith, the seven-times bigamist, was hanged for the murder of three of his wives.

Amelia Dyer The Ogress of Reading

Dyer killed hundreds of infants over a 30-year span of the Victorian era, becoming one of the most prolific murderers in history. She had trained as a nurse, and after being widowed in 1869, she began baby farming—adopting unwanted infants for money—to support herself. At first she legitimately took care of the babies along with her own children, but when several of them died while in her care, she was convicted of negligence and served six months at hard labor. After that, she made no pretense of care and began murdering the infants, most often strangling them with cloth edging tape. When the body of a baby in a package was found in the Thames, its wrapping led back to Dyer, and she was arrested. After a sensationalized trial in 1896, she was found guilty of the murder of Doris Marmon, a barmaid's infant daughter, and hanged. It is estimated "the Ogress of Reading" may have killed as many as 400 infants.

On a similar note, Amelia Sach and Annie Walters of London also operated a baby farm around 1900, taking in the offspring of unwed mothers for a fee. They reportedly murdered dozens of babies with a chemical compound containing morphine. Their execution at Holloway Jail was the last double-hanging of women in modern times.

George Smith The Brides in the Bath

George Joseph Smith was a serial killer and seven-time bigamist who perpetrated the sensationalized "Brides in the Bath" murders. In 1915, he was convicted and subsequently hanged for drowning three of his wives for their money or an insurance settlement. The case turned out to be significant in the history of forensic pathology and detection: similarities between connected crimes were used to prove deliberation, a technique that became invaluable in subsequent prosecutions.

John Haigh The Acid Bath Murderer

John George Haigh, known as the "Acid Bath Murderer" and the "Vampire of London," was an English serial killer active during the 1940s. Convicted of murdering six people, he claimed to have killed nine. His MO was either battering victims to death or shooting them. He disposed of their bodies using sulphuric acid and then forged their signatures in order to sell their possessions. Haigh was executed in 1949.

BRITISH SERIAL KILLERS

Lanarkshire, Scotland "The Beast of Birkinshaw" PETER MANUEL Killed at least seven people, 1956–58

Glasgow, Scotland "Bible John" An unknown killer who murdered at least three women, 1968–69

Practicing in Hyde, Greater Manchester, DR. HAROLD SHIPMAN has a murder count of 230 of his patients, 1977–98

Leeds, "The Yorkshire Ripper" PETER SUTCLIFFE Killed at least 13 women, 1975–80 (see p.116)

"The Beast of Manchester" TREVOR HARDY Killed three teenage girls, 1974–76

Manchester, "The Moors Murderers" IAN BRADY & MYRA HINDLEY Killed five children, 1963–65 (see p.126)

Harrogate, Baxendon, West Midlands & Shropshire, "The Black Panther" DONALD NEILSON Armed robbery, kidnapping, and murder of four people, 1971–75

Cricklewood & Muswell Hill, London DENNIS NILSEN Killed at least 15 people, 1978–83 (see p.104)

London, "The Acid Bath Murderer" JOHN HAIGH Killed nine people, 1944–49

Whitechapel, London JACK THE RIPPER Killed at least 5 women, 1888 (see p.86)

Reading, Berkshire AMELIA DYER Killed over 400 infants, 1870–96

Southend-on-Sea "The Gay Slayer" COLIN IRELAND Killed five gay men in 1993

London, Blackpool, Weymouth "The Brides in the Bath" GEORGE SMITH Killed three of his seven wives, 1912–14

125
FRANCE

BRITISH SERIAL KILLERS:
THE MOORS

The Moors Murders was a series of five child killings that happened between July 1963 and October 1965 in the Manchester area.

As the horrific tale unfolded, 1960s Britain was shocked and stunned, and even today, in Britain, the "Moors Murderers" is a cipher for absolute depravity and evil. The bodies of the murdered children were buried up on the Pennine Hills near Saddleworth. At least four of the victims were also sexually assaulted. These crimes were finally traced to a young couple—Ian Brady and Myra Hindley.

Ian Brady was born in Glasgow, the son of an unmarried waitress. He had run-ins with the law from an early age and was sent to several "borstals," custodial institutions for youthful offenders. After trying to

straighten out his life, he was hired to work at Millwards, a wholesale chemical distribution firm. Still, he found himself drawn to dark subjects, like Hitler's *Mein Kampf* and books on Nazi atrocities.

Myra Hindley was born outside Manchester and grew up poor, with a physically abusive father who expected her to do battle out in the world. After a series of low-level jobs, she became a typist at Millwards, where she met and was attracted to Brady. He soon had her reading books on Nazi torture and trying to create the perfect Aryan look—blond hair and dark red lipstick.

Inevitably, the two talked about committing the perfect murder—deciding to emulate Leopold and Loeb by killing a child. Consequently, Pauline Reade, a 16-year-old schoolmate of Myra's sister, was lured into a borrowed van and taken up to Saddleworth Moor; Brady sexually assaulted her, slit her throat, and buried her there. The next four victims were knifed or strangled. Hindley's brother-in-law, David Smith, who had witnessed the final murder, informed on the couple. They were each sentenced to life imprisonment . . . and both died while incarcerated.

MURDERS

"We do whatever we enjoy doing. Whether it happens to be judged good or evil is for others to decide..." IAN BRADY

Pauline Reade   John Kilbride   Keith Bennett   Lesley Ann Downey   Eddie Evans

Top, left to right: Ian Brady, Myra Hindley; **Inset pictures above:** The five children murdered. Brady and Hindley's first victim was Pauline Reade, 16-year-old. Victim two was 12-year-old John McBride. Victim three was Keith Bennett, also 12-year-old; Victim four was 10-year-old Lesley Ann Downey. Brady and Hindley's final victim was 17-year-old Eddie Evans, killed in their house by an axe blow to

his head, and witnessed by Myra Hindley's brother-in-law, David Smith. Smith promptly telephoned the police. His statement led to the discovery of Eddie Evans's body at the house. Of the four victims buried on Saddleworth Moor, Keith Bennett's remains have yet to be found;

Main Image: Volunteers scour Saddleworth Moor in 1965.

These European serial killers are some of the most prolific and cringeworthy in history. The crimes range from Mafia casualties shot during a mob war to the cold-blooded slaying of entire families in their homes.

EUROPEAN SERIAL KILLERS

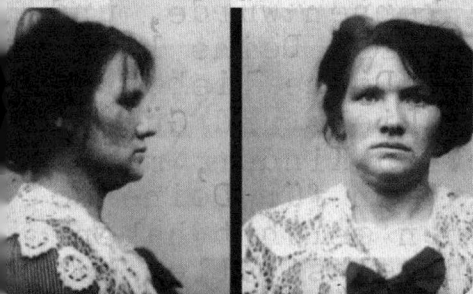

Top: Dagmar Overbye, "The Angelmaker";
Center: Vera Renczi, "The Black Widow";
Above: Andrei Chikatilo, "The Butcher of Rostov," killer of 53 women and children.

Dagmar Overbye Denmark

Known as "The Angelmaker," Dagmar Overbye was a Danish child caretaker who was paid to look after the babies of unwed mothers. Between 1913 and 1920 she killed between nine and 25 babies by strangulation, burning, or drowning. One of her victims was her own child. At her trial she received a death sentence, was reprieved, but died in prison at the age of 42. Her highly publicized case helped change Danish legislation regarding childcare.

"The Black Widow" Romania

Vera Renczi, a Romanian serial killer nicknamed "the Black Widow," was convicted of murdering 35 men between 1920 and 1930 using arsenic poisoning. Although Renczi was one of the world's most prolific female serial killers, there is little information about her and her crimes; some criminologists even believe she is a figure of Romanian folklore rather than an actual person.

"The Bluebeard of Kharkiv"

Ivan Maleshoff, known as "the Bluebeard of Kharkiv," was a Ukrainian electrical engineer who possibly dispatched a woman a week during his most active period in the early 1930s. Labeled a "lust killer," he used a dagger on his victims and left notes at the scene taunting local police. He was arrested while stalking a fresh victim and stood trial for his known 20 murders. After his conviction, Maleshoff then admitted to killing another 30 women in the nearby capital city of Kyiv. In 1935 he was executed by firing squad.

"The Butcher of Rostov"

Andrei Chikatilo, a Ukrainian who preyed on women and children from 1978 to 1990, was called "The Butcher of Rostov," "The Red Ripper" and "The Rostov Ripper." A child of poverty who did not taste bread until age 12, he was mentally scarred by the Nazi occupation during World War II. While working as a teacher, he began sexually assaulting female students, which led to his dismissal. He eventually found work as a factory supply clerk. His first murder victim, a 9-year-old girl he intended only to rape, was killed while struggling to get free. Chikatilo realized how aroused he became while taking a life. He was eventually arrested and convicted of murdering 53 women and children. Earlier, another man had mistakenly been executed for the first murder. Chikatilo himself was executed by gunshot in 1994.

Giuseppe Greco Sicily

Greco was an Italian hitman and high-ranking member of the Sicilian mafia. During the Second

Mafia War, which ran from 1981 to 1983, he carried out dozens of murders with his favorite gun, an AK-47. Convicted in absentia of killing 58 people, he probably took the lives of between 80 and 300 victims. In classic mob fashion, he was "rubbed out" in his home in 1985.

Serhiy Tkach Ukraine

A former police criminal investigator, Serhiy Tkach was a Soviet and Ukrainian serial killer who began his attacks on young girls in 1984. His MO was to suffocate his victims and afterward perform sexual acts on them. He often left bodies near newly tarred railway lines to throw off police sniffer dogs. While attending the funeral of one of his victims, he was recognized by her friends and apprehended. Convicted of 37 murders, he claimed to have killed a total of 100 girls. Although sentenced to life, he fathered a child while in prison via conjugal visits from a girlfriend he later married. He died of heart failure in 2018.

"The Terminator" Ukraine

Anatoly Onoprienko, a Soviet Ukrainian serial/spree killer, was known as "the Beast of Ukraine," "the Terminator," and "Citizen O." The second son of a decorated World War II soldier, he nevertheless ended up in an orphanage after his mother died and his grandparents gave him up, while his elder brother remained at home with their father. He started killing in 1989, murdering a family of 10 when someone interrupted him during a burglary. After that, his modus operandi became the stuff of nightmares. He would target a secluded home, kill the father or adult male first, then the mother, followed by the children. His weapons included a sawed-off shotgun, a hammer, and an axe. He often torched the house afterward and dispatched any witnesses. When Onoprienko was finally arrested seven years after his first murder, he confessed to killing 52 people. The police found a number of weapons in his home along with items belonging to the victims. His death sentence was commuted to life imprisonment; he died from heart failure in 2013.

"The Werewolf" Siberia

Mikhail Popkov, a former Russian policeman and serial killer known as "the Werewolf," confessed to an astonishing 83 murders. Raised in Siberia, Popkov became a policeman in that remote region. He began murdering in 1992, perhaps in retaliation for a cheating wife, targeting prostitutes or inebriated women that he classified as immoral. He lured victims by offering them rides while still dressed in his police uniform. Using knives, axes, baseball bats, and screwdrivers, he mutilated the bodies so grotesquely that he earned another name: "the Angarsk Maniac." After avoiding detection for two decades, he was finally caught when the 4x4 tire tracks found near numerous crime scenes were identified as those from a police vehicle. Popkov's DNA was then matched to crime scene evidence. Convicted of 22 murders in 2015, he confessed to an additional 61. Needless to say, he was sentenced to life.

"The Chessboard Killer" Moscow

Alexander Pichushkin struck between 1992 and 2006 in southwest Moscow's Bitsa Park. A sociable child, he suffered a distressing personality shift after he fell backward off a swing and the seat struck him in the forehead, possibly damaging his frontal cortex. To stimulate him mentally, his grandfather taught him to play chess, at which he excelled, often challenging the players at nearby Bitsa Park. After the grandfather's death, Pichushkin began to consume large quantities of vodka and started videotaping himself terrorizing children. In 1992 he graduated to murder, his first victim a classmate invited along on a "killing mission." When Pichushkin realized his friend thought it was all a joke, he killed him instead. Pichushkin vowed to murder 64 people, the number of squares on a chessboard and ended up dispatching between 48 and 60, killing many with hammer blows, then leaving a vodka bottle in the gaping wound. He chose older homeless men, young men, women, and children. Captured after a metro ticket found in a female victim's pocket led to security footage of her and Pichushkin on the subway platform, he was sentenced to life at the Arctic penal colony "Polar Owl."

Top: Mikhail Popkov—"The Werewolf," murdered an estimated 83 women, mainly female sex workers;
Above: Alexander Pichushkin, the Moscow "Chessboard Killer."

FEELINGS OF INADEQUACY

According to Russian lawyer Yuri Antonyan, "Sexual serial murders have common characteristics that are always associated with the intimate life of the perpetrator, his psycho traumatic sexual experiences, his feelings of sexual inadequacy . . . which allows one to call such murders sexual." He points out that these killers had serious sexual failings: Chikatilo (the butcher) was impotent; Golovkin (the child killer) and Ershov (the axe murderer) were virgins, and Dzhumagaliev (the cannibal) was disgusted by intercourse. So many serial killers were sexually inferior or felt they were.

ICELAND
Vatnajokull
2119 ▲
REYKJAVIK ★ Hvannadalshnukur

SWE

Trondheimsfjorden

Trondheim
1796 ▲
Alesund

NORWAY

Sundsvall

Faroe Islands
(Denmark)

Suduroy

2469
Galdhopiggen

Shetland Islands
(UK)

Bergen

OSLO ★

STOCKHOLM

Orkney Islands

Boknafjorden

Drammen

Norrkoping

EUROPEAN SERIAL KILLERS

Isle of Lewis

Wick

Stavanger

Kristiansand

NORTH

Denmark, "The Angelmaker"
DAGMAR OVERBYE
Killed between 9 and 25
infants, 1913-20

Hebrides

SCOTLAND Aberdeen

SEA

DENMARK

Ola

British

Perth

COPENHAGEN ★ ● Malmo

BAL

Isles

Glasgow ● Edinburgh

KA
(RL

Rockall

ULSTER

Gdans

ORTH

IRELAND

Belfast ●

UNITED

Frisian Is.

Newcastle

Hamburg

KINGDOM

Liverpool ● ● Manchester

● Amsterdam

NETHERLANDS

BERLIN ★

POLA

DUBLIN ●

Birmingham ●

● Rotterdam

Dusseldorf

● Leipzig

Cork ●

WALES

ENGLAND

BRUSSELS ● ● Antwerp

GERMANY

PRAGUE

Cardiff ●

● LONDON

BELGIUM

Frankfurt

CZECH.REP.

CELTIC SEA

Plymouth ●

Southampton

Lille ●

LUX.

Brest ●

Le Havre

PARIS ★

Stuttgart

VIENNA ●

Strasbourg

Munich ●

AUSTRIA

HU

English Channel

Seine

Rennes ●

FRANCE

BERNE ● LIECHT.

SLOVENIA

B

Nantes ●

Geneva ●

SWITZ.

Milan ●

LJUBLJANA ●

ZAGR

ATLANTIC

Lyon ●

4810
Mt Blanc

Venice ●

CROATIA

BOSN

Bay of
Biscay

Bordeaux ●

Massif
Central

Turin ●

Florence ●

SARAEVO

MONTE

OCEAN

Toulouse ●

Montpellier ●

Nice ●

M.C.

S.M.

ITALY

PODO

Bilbao ●

Pyrenees
3404 ▲
Aneto AND.

Marseille ●

Corsica

VAT. ★ ROME

Bari ●

Vigo ●

Valladolid ●

Gulf of
Liona

Naples ●

Porto ●

Douro

Zaragoza ●

Barcelona ●

In the 2nd Mafia War, Sicilian hitman
GUISEPPE GRECO Murdered
an estimated 300 men, from 1981-83

Coimbra ●

Ebro

MADRID ★

Palermo ●

Messina ●

Tage

Valencia ●

Balearic Is.

MEDITERRANEAN SEA

3323
Etna ▲

Sicily

PORTUGAL

SPAIN

Ibiza

LISBON ★

Sierra Morena

ALGIERS

TUNIS ★

VALLETTA ▼

Seville ●

Cordoba ●
3482 ▲ Mulhacen

Chlef ●

Annaba ●

MALTA

Gibraltar (U.K.)

Oran ●

Constantine ●

TUNISIA

Strait of Gibraltar

Ceuta (Spain)

2236 ▲

Sfax ●

Tangiers ●

Melilla(Spain)

Tlemcen ●

Gabes ●

RABAT ★

Fes ●

ALGERIA

MED

Casablanca ●

MOROCCO

FINLAND

RUSSIAN FEDERATION

Siberia, "The Werewolf"
MIKHAIL POPKOV
Murdered 83 people from 1992-2012

Oulu

Lake Oulu

Lake Vyg

Arkhangel'sk

Pori

Vaasa

Petrozavodsk

Syktyvkar

Lakes Region

Lake Onega

Turku

Tampere

HELSINKI

Lake Ladoga

Lake Beloye

Sukhona

Kudymkar

Gulf of Finland

St Petersburg

Vologda

Viatka

Kama Reservoir

TALLINN

Novgorod

Rybinsk Reservoir

Nijni Reservoir

Perm'

ESTONIA

Lake Peipus

Iaroslavl

Kostroma

Yoshkar-Ola

Izhevsk

RIGA

Pskov

Ivanovo

Nizhniy

Yekaterinburg

LATVIA

Tver

Moscow, "The Chessboard Killer"
ALEXANDER PICHUSHKIN
Killed up to 60 people 1992-2006

Kazan'

LITHUANIA

MOSCOW

Ryazan'

Simbirsk

Ufa

Chelyabinsk

RAD

VILNIUS

Smolensk

Kaluga

Tula

Saransk

Tol'yatti

KALININGRAD (FED.)

MINSK

Penza

Samara Reservoir

Ural Mountains

WARSAW

BELARUS

Bryansk

Orel

Saratov Reservoir

Samara

Orenburg

Ukraine, SERHIY TKACH
Convicted of 37 murders, he claimed over 100, dating back to 1984

Ukraine, "The Bluebeard of Kharkiv"
IVAN MALESHOFF Murdered 50 people in the early 1930s

Ural'sk

Volga

Ord

Krakow

KIEV

Kharkiv

Voronezh

Aktyubinsk

Lviv

KAZAKHSTAN

AKIA

Dnipropetrovsk

Do

Ukraine, "The Butcher of Rostov"
ANDREI CHIKATILO Murdered 53 women & children from 1978-90

Caspian Depression

Atyrau

Romania, "The Black Widow"
VERA RENCZI Murdered 35 men between 1920-30

Carpathians

UDAPEST

UKRAINE

Odesa

Rostov-na-Donu

Aral Sea

RY

ROMANIA

Ukraine, "The Terminator"
ANATOLY ONOPRIENKO
Murdered 52 people 1989-96

Elista

Astrakhan'

BELGRADE

BUCHAREST

Sevastopol

Stavropol'

UZBEKISTAN

SERBIA

Danube

Maykop

5642

Groznyy

Makhachkala

Nukus

KOSOVO

SOFIA

BULGARIA

BLACK SEA

Elbrus

Caucasus

CASPIAN

Urgench

SKOPJE

2925

Musala

Sinop

GEORGIA

TBILISI

SEA

Garabogaz

F.Y.R.O.M.

Istanbul

Bosporus

AZERBAIJAN

TURKMENISTAN

IA

2911

Salonica

ANKARA

TURKEY

Bursa

YEREVAN

ARMENIA

BAKU

Turkmenbashi

Turkmenabat

Olympus

Izmir

Anatolia (Asia Minor)

5137

Mt Ararat

Kara - Kum

Mary

ATHENS

Konya

Kayseri

4810

ASHGABAT

Mashhad

onnesus

GREECE

Adana

Gaziantep

Lake Urmia

Tabriz

Gorgan

AEGEAN SEA

Antalya

Mersin

Tigris

Mt. Demavend

2542

NICOSIA

Aleppo

Al Mawsil

Kirkuk

TEHRAN

5671

Salt Desert

Crete

CYPRUS

3088

SYRIA

IRAQ

Qom

NEAN SEA

LEBANON

BEIRUT

BAGHDAD

Kermanshah

IRAN

DAMASCUS

AFGH.

Many countries in Asia suffer from overpopulation, where larger cities teem with people living in poverty. This overcrowding and economic strain often generates a criminal class, men and women who acquire a "dog-eat-dog" mentality to survive. Here, human life may have little value, except to the ones who prey on the weak and vulnerable.

ASIAN SERIAL KILLERS

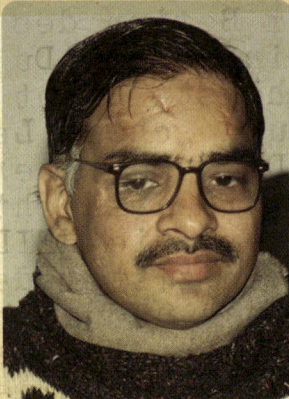

Charles Sobhraj "The Serpent"

Charles Sobhraj, a French serial killer of Sindhi and Vietnamese heritage, was known as "the Serpent" and the "Bikini Killer." Described as attractive but remorseless, he murdered at least 20 people in Southeast Asia. First operating as a thief and scam artist, he soon gained a following of other criminals. He also partnered with his wife Chantal robbing tourists on the popular "hippie trail" that ran from Turkey to Nepal and with his half-brother Andre, who eventually served 18 years for his crimes.

Meanwhile, Charles stayed steps ahead of the police, using 10 fake passports to cross borders with members of his "clan." In 1975 he committed his first murder: Teresa Knowlton was found drowned, wearing a floral bikini, on the Gulf of Thailand. It is assumed she had been enlisted to join his crew and threatened to betray him to the police.

Sobhraj often poisoned his victims, as well as new associates, nursing them back to health to gain their loyalty. His downfall came in 1976, when he tried to poison some graduate students he was guiding through New Delhi—in preparation for robbing them—and they overpowered him and called the police. His 20-year sentence would at least keep him from being extradited to Thailand—and facing

certain execution. When it looked like he might be released early, he held a party and drugged all the guards, then walked out the prison doors.

The escape added 10 years to his sentence, at which time the Thai charges would have expired. By 2003 he was free and gambling in Nepal when he was arrested for the 1975 murder of two tourists. This time he received a life sentence; he currently remains incarcerated and in poor health.

Javel Iqbal Lahore, Pakistan

A Pakistani known as "Kukri," Javel Iqbal killed 100 runaway boys ranging in age from six to 16. After sexually abusing them, strangling and dismembering them, he dissolved their bodies with acid. He was arrested in 1999, thanks to a confessional letter he sent to a newspaper. In his defense, he claimed his earlier arrest for sodomy so shamed his mother that she died of a heart attack, and so he desired to inflict that pain on the mothers of 100 boys.

He was set to be executed in the manner in which he killed his victims, described by the judge who stated, "You will be strangled to death in front of the parents whose children you killed. Your body will then be cut into 100 pieces and put in acid, the same way you killed the children." He committed suicide, however, before the sentence could be carried out.

Top: A still from the BBC drama production, *The Serpent*, with Tahar Rahim as Charles Sobhraj, and Jenna Coleman as his acolyte Marie-Andrée Leclerc; **Above:** Javel Iqbal after his arrest in Lahore.

Ahmad Suradji Indonesia

A native of Medan, Indonesia, Ahmad Suradji was a shaman who often consulted with female clients. He was convicted of strangling at least 42 women and girls in 1988. As a defense, he expressed his belief that a series of ritual slayings would give him magical powers. He died in front of a firing squad in 2008.

Yang Xinhai "Monster Killer"

A Chinese itinerate laborer known as the "Monster Killer," Yang Xinhai was active from 1999 to 2003. He would enter his victims' homes during the night and use a mixture of weapons—axes, meat cleavers, hammers, and shovels—to maul and kill those he found. When he acted nervous during a normal police inspection of entertainment venues, he was apprehended. He confessed to 67 murders and 23 rapes, making him the most prolific serial killer since the establishment of the People's Republic. In 2004, he was executed by firing squad.

Yoo Young-chul "Raincoat Killer"

This South Korean career criminal was a serial killer and possible cannibal. Between 2003 and 2004, he slayed 21 people, mostly prostitutes and wealthy old men, often using a large, homemade hammer. He also confessed to eating the livers of some victims, but there is no proof. During his trial, Yoo repeatedly attacked attendees, including judges, and even attempted suicide. He was sentenced to death and is currently awaiting execution in Seoul.

Lê Thanh Van Ho Chi Min City

Lê Thanh Van, a Vietnamese woman from Ho Chi Min City, used her pretty face, sweet manner, and familiarity with medicine to befriend wealthy people . . . before poisoning them with water or food laced with cyanide. By forging new wills, she appropriated at least US $20,000 from her victims. She also poisoned her father- and mother-in-law and her foster mother, and enlisted her boyfriend to help murder a motorbike taxi driver. In total, she killed 13 people. After being tried and convicted in 2004, she received a death sentence.

Top: The real Serpent, Charles Sobhraj, after his arrest in New Delhi in 1976. He subsequently drugged his guards and walked out to freedom; **Right, top to bottom:** Yoo Young-chul, "The Raincoat Killer" of South Korea. He murdered 21 people using a homemade hammer, and reputedly ate some of their livers. As of October 2021 he is awaiting execution; Indonesian killer Ahmad Suradji was convicted of murdering at least 48 women and girls in 1988. He died by firing squad; Lê Thanh Van, who killed and embezzled fortunes from her 13 victims; Yang Xinhai, "The Monster Killer." The most prolific serial killer in The People's Republic of China, he was executed by firing squad.

Africa during the nineteenth and twentieth centuries was a continent of political strife, with European interests vying to establish domain over both its geography and its rich resources. Most killings that took place were a result of European oppression, anti-colonial sentiments, or hate-fueled genocides. Yet serial killers have cropped up in Africa, though some are not well documented.

AFRICAN SERIAL KILLERS

Above: The marketplace in Marrakesh, circa 1906, where "The Marrakesh Arch-Killer" was walled up; **Pictures opposite, from top:** On the carriage roofs of trains such as this, running between Cairo and Alexandria, Ramadan Abdel Rahim Mansour (next picture down) and his accomplices raped, tortured and murdered their 32 young male victims; Norman Simons, "the Station Strangler," currently serving 35 years; Moses Sitole, who killed at least 38 women before 1995.

"The Express Train"

Ramadan Abdel Rahim Mansour, an Egyptian street gang leader known as al-Tourbini— "the Express Train"—and "the Butcher of Garbia," was active from 1999 to 2006. He and other gang members would ride the trains between Cairo and Alexandria and lure homeless children onto the carriage roofs, mostly boys aged 10 to 14 years old. They then stripped, raped, and tortured them. The dead or dying victims were thrown off the moving trains. Sometimes Mansour tossed the bodies into the Nile or buried the boys alive. After he was captured by police, he claimed a female jinn (genie) had possessed him and commanded him to commit the 32 murders. Mansour and an accomplice, Farag Mahmoud, were executed by hanging in 2010.

"The Marrakesh Arch-Killer"

Hadj Mohammed Mesfewi, was a shoemaker in Morocco at the turn of the 20th century. Known as "the Marrakesh Arch-Killer," he drugged, mutilated, murdered and beheaded his female clients, with a possible 36 victims buried under or next to his shop. In 1906 he stood trial and was found guilty and a sentence of death by crucifixion was decreed. However, this was considered cruel and inhumane, so he was executed in a particularly vengeful manner—by immurement—walling up.

"The Station Strangler"

Norman Afzal Simons of South Africa, called the "Station Strangler," was a primary school teacher who raped and killed 22 young boys from 1986 to 1994. He blamed his behavior on a childhood sexual assault by his older stepbrother and said he often heard his brother's voice telling him to kill. In 1995 he was convicted for the death of one of his victims and is currently serving a 35-year sentence.

"The South African Ted Bundy"

Moses Sitole, known as the "South African Ted Bundy," preyed on unemployed women. He would pose as a businessman and lure his victims with the prospects of a job, before leading them to an isolated spot, where he raped, tortured, and murdered them. He killed at least 38 people before his arrest in 1995, after a police skirmish where he was shot. Ultimately, he was sentenced to 2410 years imprisonment.

Cairo-Alexandria railway,
"The Express Train"
RAMADAN MANSOUR
Killed at least 32 young
boys between 1999 and 2006

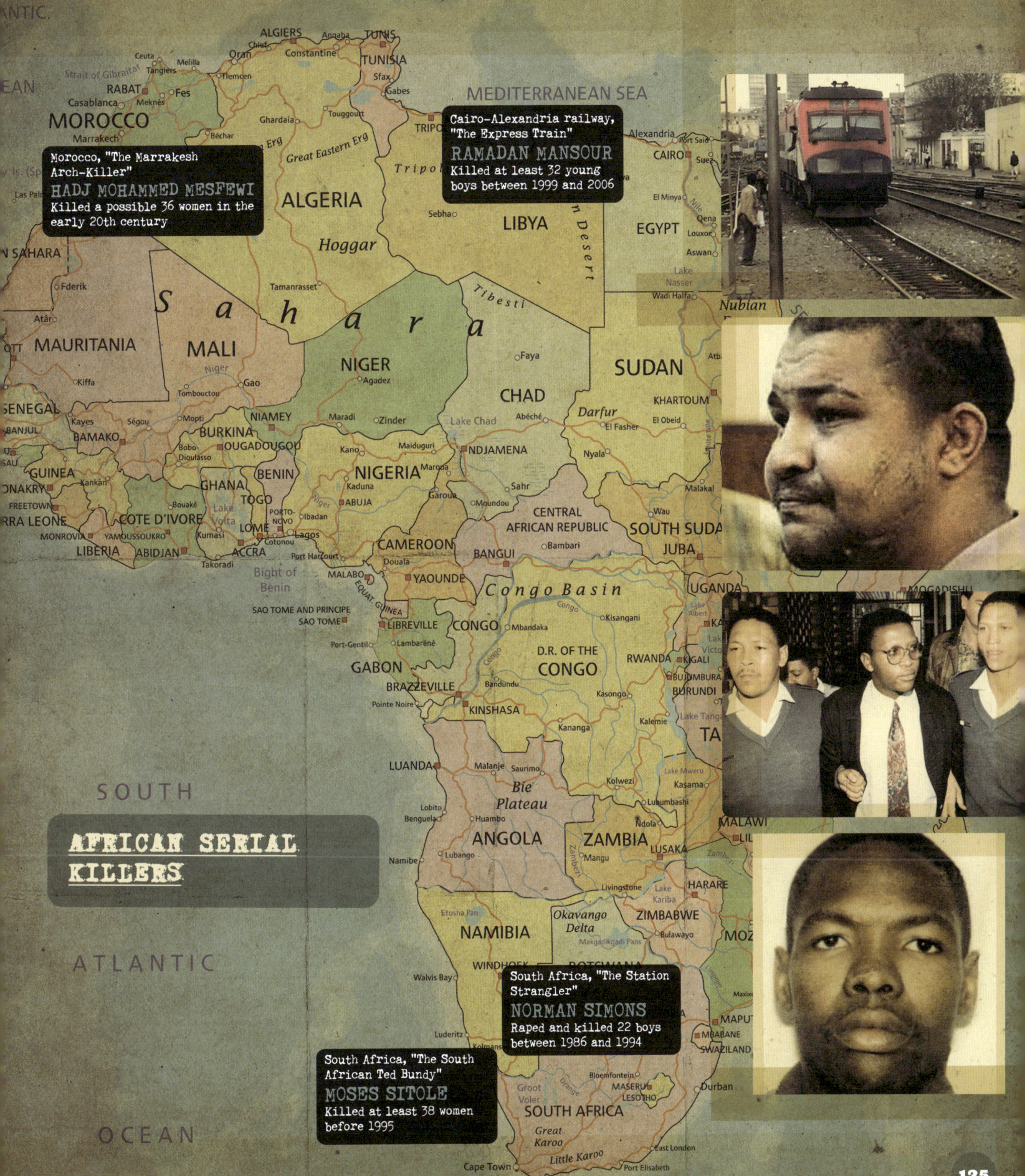

Morocco, "The Marrakesh
Arch-Killer"
HADJ MOHAMMED MESFEWI
Killed a possible 36 women in the
early 20th century

AFRICAN SERIAL KILLERS

South Africa, "The Station
Strangler"
NORMAN SIMONS
Raped and killed 22 boys
between 1986 and 1994

South Africa, "The South
African Ted Bundy"
MOSES SITOLE
Killed at least 38 women
before 1995

> **"Truly, whoever we are and wherever we reside, we exist upon the whim of murderers."**
>
> ALAN MOORE, BRITISH COMICS AUTHOR

7 Chapter Seven

Rampage Killers

Also known as mass murderers or spree killers, rampage killers are classified as different from serial killers because their crimes are committed during one, often impulsive, event, not stretched out over weeks or months . . . plus they often take place in a public space. Serial killers and mass murderers can display the same characteristics of manipulation and lack of empathy, but spree murders frequently end with the death of the perpetrator. Serial killers live to strike again.

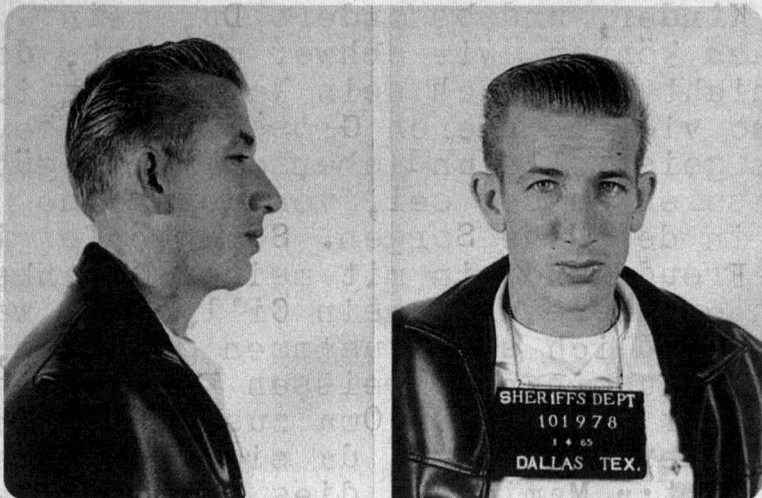

America was still fairly naive in 1966 when it came to horrific crimes . . . the darkness of Manson and Bundy, Dahmer and Gacy had not yet stirred up the media and invaded the family living room. So when Americans heard the news report that a stranger had entered a student nurses' residence in Chicago and killed eight young women, they could not quite believe it. . .

RICHARD SPECK
BORN TO RAISE HELL

Top: Richard Speck's mugshot taken by the Sheriff's Dept., in Dallas, Texas, January 4, 1965, 18 months before the Townhouse Invasion in Chicago; **Center:** Student nurses at South Chicago Community Hospital, July 1966. Four of the group were murdered days later by Speck: Mary Ann Jordan (left), Suzanne Farris (third left), Nina Jo Schmale (fourth left), and Pamela Wilkening (right); **Above:** Corazon Amurao, who survived Speck's attack;

Criminals killed people while committing crimes, mobsters killed other mobsters, or sometimes unlucky police officers, but human beings just didn't go out and murder other humans for no reason at all. The very notion opened the doors of the imagination to unthinkable possibilities. Were any of us safe when we might have "enemies" we knew nothing about?

Richard Benjamin Speck was born in Illinois, the seventh of eight children of a religious family. After his father died, his mother remarried and the family relocated to Dallas, Texas. Speck and his siblings suffered abuse at the hands of their alcoholic stepfather. He was also mocked in school and had a dread of public speaking.

As a teen Speck turned to petty crime and was labeled a juvenile delinquent. When he got his 16-year-old girlfriend pregnant, he married her, but theft and check fraud landed him in prison in 1963. He was back inside, arrested for assault, four weeks after his release. After having "Born to Raise Hell" tattooed on his arm, he relocated to Monmouth, his hometown in Illinois. In April 1966, two Monmouth women

were attacked, the second one—a local barmaid—beaten to death. He was questioned by police, then quickly left for Chicago.

The Townhouse Invasion

His brother-in-law found him work on a lake ore freighter and, not surprisingly, female bodies started turning up wherever his ship berthed. Once back in Chicago, Speck began visiting the National Maritime Union looking for another ship. Nearby was a townhouse that served as a group residence for student nurses. Speck obviously noticed them. On the night of July 13, he knocked on the door and when Corazon Amurao answered, he forced his way inside with a gun. He rounded up all the girls, told them to empty their purses, then tied them up.

Then began a night of horror, as he brutalized each one as the others looked on. Nurses who had been out when he broke in were also brutalized as they arrived home. Eight student nurses between the ages of 18 and 24 were bound, beaten, stabbed, and strangled in what appeared to be a frenzy of bloodlust. At least one was raped. Yet Amurao had somehow

managed to hide under one of the beds, cowering there until Speck left, after gathering up the money they pooled. She waited hours before gaining the courage to seek help.

During her police interview, Amurao recalled the killer's "Born to Raise Hell" tattoo, which helped law enforcement narrow their search. Still, it took a week for the townhouse fingerprints to be processed and identified as Speck's. Seeing his picture on the front page of every newspaper, Speck knew the noose was tightening. He attempted suicide in his hotel room, but was taken to Cook County Hospital, where the tattoo again betrayed him. During his trial he maintained he could not recall the night of the murders, but Amurao, in spite of her trauma, was able to recall almost every detail. The jury took less than an hour to find him guilty on all eight counts. The judge sentenced him to death, but it was later commuted to to 50 to 100 years. He died of a heart attack in 1991 while still in prison, and possibly undergoing female hormone treatments.

Above: The eight student nurses Speck brutally killed on July 13, 1966. Top row, left to right: Pamela Wilkening, Valentina Pasion, Pat Matusek, and Gloria Davy. Bottom row: Suzanne Farris, Nina Jo Schmale, Merlita Gargullo, and Mary Ann Jordan. **Below:** Speck, convicted killer of the student nurses, is surrounded by newsmen as he leaves Peoria County Court House on June 5, 1967, after receiving the death sentence.

Sniper attacks involve a single marksman in a hidden, elevated location where the shooter can hit multiple human targets. The sniper, who needs to fire with accuracy and at long range, typically uses a special rifle with a high-powered telescopic sight.

SNIPER ATTACKS
DEATH FROM ABOVE

"This massive, muscular youth seemed to be oozing with hostility..." MAURICE DEAN HEATLY, CHARLES WHITMAN'S PSYCHIATRIST

Top: Charles Whitman, the ex-Marine who killed his mother and wife, then shot dead 14 people and wounded 31 from the the top of the university tower before Austin policeman finally reached the observation deck and shot him to death. **(top right background)**: **Above:** Whitman family portrait. He was brought up in a strict family, with, most probably, an abusive father.

Charles Whitman Austin, Texas

Charles Joseph Whitman, the "Texas Tower Sniper," was a former Marine from Lake Worth, Florida. He attended the University of Texas at Austin for mechanical engineering through a military education program and there he met wife, Kathleen. Due to struggles with bad grades and a drinking problem, he eventually lost his scholarship in 1963. In 1966 he sought professional counseling for mental health problems (possibly caused by his abusive father), including the urge to shoot people from a tower. On the morning of August 1, he stabbed his mother and then his wife, "to save them from future humiliation." He purchased an M1 carbine at a hardware store and a 12-gauge semi-automatic shotgun at Sears. He then packed his footlocker with the M1, a hunting rifle, a pump rifle, two pistols, a revolver, the new shotgun, and 700 rounds of ammunition.

Near noon, he entered the Main Building at the university and rode the elevator to the top, 27 stories above the campus. He killed three people inside the building, then barricaded himself on the 28th-floor observation deck. From there he randomly shot 42 students and passersby, killing 11 and wounding 31. Among the dead was the unborn baby boy of first outdoor victim, Claire Wilson. Many people on the ground mistook the shots for noise from a nearby construction site; others near the tower risked their lives to help the injured to safety. Two Austin policemen, Sergeant Ramiro Martinez and Patrolman Houston McCoy, finally made their way to the observation deck, where Whitman was shot and killed.

Stephen Paddock Las Vegas

Stephen Paddock holds the dubious record for the most people killed in a single sniper attack. The 64-year-old native of Mesquite

KEY STATS

There were 2,128 mass shootings in the US between 2013 and 2019, or roughly one per day.

CHARACTERISTICS OF RAMPAGE KILLERS

According to a 2000 New York Times study of 100 "rampage" mass murders, where 425 people were killed and 510 injured, many killers displayed the qualities below.

- Serious mental health issues
- Not usually motivated by exposure to videos, movies, or television
- Not using alcohol or other drugs at the time of the attacks
- Unemployed
- Not usually Satanists or racists
- White males; a few Asians or African Americans
- Have college degrees or some years of college
- Have military experience
- Give pre-attack warning signals
- Carry semiautomatic weapons obtained legally
- Do not attempt escape
- Half commit suicide or are killed by others
- Most have a death wish

Nevada, was a real estate agent and high-stakes gambler who was often comped luxurious suites in Las Vegas. On October 1, 2017, he stationed himself in a suite on the 32nd floor of the Mandalay Bay Hotel. His target was the 22,000 attendees at the Route 91 Harvest Music Festival on the famous Las Vegas Strip.

His arsenal, which a bellman helped him bring to the room, consisted of 14 AR-15 rifles (some with "bump" stocks that use the weapon's recoil to fire bullets in rapid succession), eight AR-10 rifles, a bolt-action rifle, and a revolver. Between 10:05 and 10:15 p.m., he killed 60 people and injured 411, firing more than 1,000 rounds over a distance of roughly 490 yards. The ensuing panic brought the number of injured to 867. An hour after the attack, the police broke into Paddock's room and found him dead from a self-inflicted gunshot wound. His motives for the senseless killing were never made clear.

Top: Stephen Paddock, who at the time of writing, holds the dubious record for the most people killed in a single sniper attack—sixty dead, with 411 wounded or injured; **Above:** The Mandalay Bay Hotel in Las Vegas, from the roof of which Paddock shot his random victims.

141

TRIALS OF THE CENTURY

> ## "I never thought I was normal, never tried to be normal..."
> CHARLES MANSON

MANSON MURDERS
THE FAMILY THAT SLAYS TOGETHER...

Above: Charles Manson, who died in prison in 2017; **Top left:** Manson after his arrest, complete with the self-inflicted "X" scraped into his forehead; **Top right:** Three members of the Manson "Family," from left: Pat Krenwinkel, Susan Atkins, and Leslie Van Houten.

If there were a 20th century version of the bogey man, who stalked the dreams of adults and children alike, Charles Manson would make a very good candidate. A charismatic manipulator with aspirations of becoming a rock star, in the late 1960s Manson created his own "cult of personality" in Southern California, based at the Spahn Ranch, a former movie ranch. There, in the role of philosophical guru, he attracted other drifters and outsiders, including a number of young women who became his sexual servants.

In July 1969, Manson killed Bernard Crowe, a drug dealer who had threatened the Family. Manson's group also targeted Gary Hinman, a music teacher they believed was wealthy. When Hinman refused to join the Family and turn over his money, Manson ordered Bobby Beausoleil to stab him.

On the night of August 9, 1969, Manson upped the ante. He sent a group—Tex Watson, Susan Atkins, Patricia Krenwinkel, and Linda Kasabian—to 10050 Cielo Drive in Benedict Canyon with orders to kill. It had been the rental home of music producer Terry Melcher, the son of Doris Day.

Melcher had met Manson through Beach Boy Dennis Wilson, and had considered making a documentary about him. When both Wilson and Melcher cut ties with Manson, they angered him greatly. But Melcher had moved, and his landlord had rented out the property to Polish director Roman Polanski and his pregnant wife, actress Sharon Tate. Manson must have known this, as he entered the property in March of 1969 and

> **"You know, a long time ago being crazy meant something. Nowadays everybody's crazy..."** CHARLES MANSON

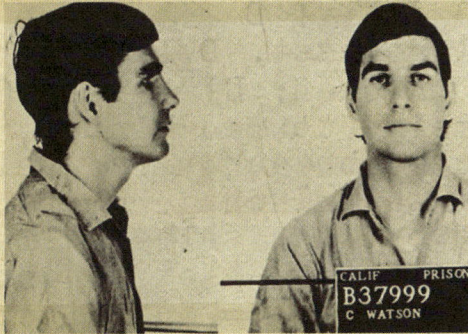

KEY STATS

The Manson trial was the longest murder trial in America up to that time. The jury ended up sequestered for 225 days. The trial transcript was 31,716 pages.

Oh, we take care of George.

actually encountered Tate briefly. She mentioned "that creepy-looking guy" to the landlord.

Whatever his motives, Manson sent his followers to the house, where they broke in and haphazardly butchered five people: Sharon Tate, Jay Sebring, Abigail Folger, Wojciech Frykowski, and Steven Parent. Folger and Frykowski fought back and nearly escaped: Sharon Tate's unborn child died of asphyxiation.

A Second Night

Manson, angry that the murders had been so chaotic, ordered another killing the following night. The four members from the Tate murder, plus Manson, Leslie Van Houten, and Steve "Clem" Grogan, arrived at the home of supermarket executive Leno LaBianca and his wife Rosemary. There, Manson tied up the couple, then left with Atkins, Grogan, and Kasabian; meanwhile, Watson and the two girls entered

the house and Watson brutally dispatched both LaBiancas with a steel bayonet. He carved "war" into Leno's abdomen, and Krenwinkel wrote "Death to pigs," and "Healter Skelter" (sic) on the kitchen wall with his blood. Manson believed the Beatles song "Helter Skelter" used secret code to predict a major American race war.

The L.A. Police took months to track down the killers. After a lot of false starts and missed clues, they finally connected the two August murders, and Manson and his followers were indicted. During the nine-month trial, the sardonic Manson turned the proceedings into a grim circus, appearing at one point with an X carved into his forehead. Along with Van Houten, Atkins, and Krenwinkel, he received the death penalty, which was later commuted to life in prison. Tex Watson was tried separately and his death sentence was also commuted.

Top left: Sharon Tate poses on a flight with Jay Sebring; **Top right:** Sharon Tate with director husband Roman Polanski; **Center left:** Charles "Tex" Watson mugshot; **Center:** Leno and Rosemary LaBianca, the second night victims. Although Tex Watson killed both, Leslie Van Houten stabbed Rosemary LaBianca a further 14 times; **Above:** Two stills from scenes at the Spahn Ranch in Tarantino's re-imagining of the Sharon Tate murders, *Once Upon a Time in Hollywood.*

CRIME GOES

Left, top to bottom: A studio portrait of Edward G. Robinson; Virginia Mayo and James Cagney in *White Heat* (1949); Jeffrey Lynn, James Cagney and Humphrey Bogart revisited a tumultuous decade in US history in Raoul Walsh's *The Roaring Twenties* of 1939; The actor George Raft crossed the line between artifice and reality, becoming close to mobster Bugsy Siegel; **Top, center:** Anthony Hopkins in his role as Dr. Hannibal Lecter in *The Silence of the Lambs* of 1991.

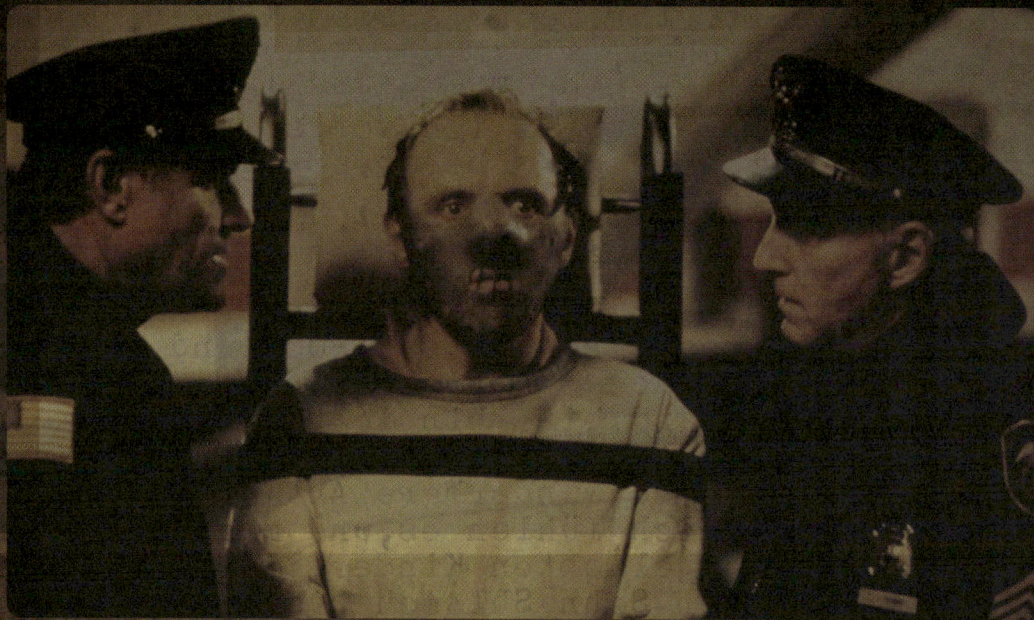

Crime makes a natural subject for motion pictures—offering vivid characters on both sides of the law along with action, tension, ingenious plots, and the battle between right and wrong, with an outcome where right usually prevails.

During the 1930s and 1940s, films featured memorable criminal portrayals, like Edward G. Robinson as *Little Caesar*, James Cagney in *The Public Enemy* and *White Heat*, Humphrey Bogart in *The Petrified Forest*, and Barbara Stanwyck and Ida Lupino portraying husband murderers in *Double Indemnity* and *They Drive By Night*. The late 1940s and 1950s introduced the antihero, with Burt Lancaster as a robber awaiting his fate in *The Killers*, and Marlon Brando as a motorcycle gang leader in *The Wild One*. Swearing revenge against former jewel thief Victor Mature, Richard Widmark was a chilling Tommy Udo in *Kiss of Death*. In fact, during that era a new film genre arose, *cine noir*, or *film noir*, which focused on the criminal class and the dark side of human nature.

By the 1960s and 1970s, viewers were introduced to more charismatic crooks like Warren Beatty and style icon Faye Dunaway as *Bonnie and Clyde* and Paul Newman and Robert Redford as *Butch Cassidy and the Sundance Kid*. The two again costarred as a pair of con men in *The Sting*, which won Best Picture at the Academy Awards, proving that cinema crime, at least, does pay.

The 1980s and 1990s focused on the psychopath, the sociopath, and the cannibal. Movies offered uber villains like Darth Vader in the *Star Wars* franchise or Hannibal Lecter in Thomas Harris's triptych, *Red Dragon*, *The Silence of the Lambs*, and *Hannibal*. Quentin Tarantino helped reinvigorate the crime genre by combining retro sensibilities with nonlinear storylines in *Reservoir Dogs* and *Pulp Fiction*. Martin Scorsese, director of 1973's *Mean Streets*, continued his fascination with men outside the law by delivering classics like *Taxi Driver*, *Goodfellas*, *Casino*, *Gangs of New York*, *The Departed*, and *The Irishman*. Film's greatest mafia saga, Francis Ford Coppola's *Godfather* trilogy, gave rise to a wildly popular TV show, *The Sopranos*, again beckoning the public to follow a deeply entrenched crime family. British director Guy Ritchie also enlivened the gangster genre with romps like *Lock, Stock, and Two Smoking Barrels* and *Snatch*.

TO THE MOVIES

Films or TV biopics about real criminals have always found an audience: Burt Lancaster in *The Birdman of Alcatraz*; Tony Curtis in *The Boston Strangler* (see p92), Steve Railsback as Charles Manson in *Helter Skelter* (see p142), Richard Attenborough as John Christie in *10 Rillington Place* (see p90), Cuba Gooding Jr. in *The People v. O.J. Simpson* (see p82), and Charlize Theron earning Oscar gold as Aileen Wuornos in *Monster* (see p106).

Do Movies Promote Crime?

Religious groups and parents' organizations frequently complain that movies and TV lend glamour and even prestige to outlaws, mobsters, and murderers. Yet watching crime dramas can be cathartic and offer a release from daily stress. Psychologist Chivonna Childs says watching true crime stories does not indicate a tendency toward criminal behavior. "It's curiosity," she writes, explaining that our inquisitive human natures crave a glimpse into the mind of a criminal or killer, wanting to understand their capacity for cruelty. Research also indicates that crime stories may disproportionately appeal to women, who, says Dr. Childs, want to be prepared in case they are ever in that situation.

Top left: Marlon Brando as Don Vito Corleone in *The Godfather* (1972); **Top right, from left:** Steven Van Zandt as Silvio Dante, James Gandolfini as Tony Soprano, and Tony Sirico as Paul "Paulie Walnuts" Gualtieri in a scene from Season 6 of *The Sopranos* (2006); **Above center, from left:** Ray Liotta as Henry Hill, Robert De Niro as Jimmy Conway, Paul Sorvino as Paul Cicero, and Joe Pesci as Tommy DeVito in Martin Scorsese's *Goodfellas* (1990); **Above:** Faye Dunaway as Bonnie Parker and Warren Beatty as Clyde Barrow in *Bonnie and Clyde* (1967); **Above right:** The inimitable Barbara Stanwyck and Fred MacMurray in *Double Indemnity* of 1944. The film was directed by Billy Wilder, and Raymond Chandler wrote the screenplay.

Latin America has been home to some of the world's most disturbing spree killings, including family massacres and revenge murders . . . and one involving demonic possession in a haunted home.

RAMPAGE KILLERS OF LATIN AMERICA

Top right: A newspaper illustration of Pedro Rosa da Conceicao, who killed three and wounded 13 others in 1904; **Top left:** Campo Elias Delgado, the former US serviceman who killed 29 and wounded 12 in 1986; **Above:** Genildo Ferreira de Franca, who killed himself after dispatching 14 people in and around Santo Antonio do Potengi in 1997; **Opposite left:** Claudia Mijangos, "The hyena of Queretaro", who stabbed her three children to death; **Opposite right:** The bloody Mijangos crime scene.

Pedro Rosa da Conceição

Pedro Rosa da Conceição was an early Brazilian mass murderer ... and possible serial killer. On April 22, 1904, the railway worker rode a train to Rio das Pedras, a region of Rio de Janeiro, and with a bayonet killed three people and wounded 13 others. The next day he was arrested hiding among some trees. In 1911, while in prison, he killed his cellmate Joachim Alves Jr. and an unnamed guard, who tried to restrain him. It was also rumored Rosa had murdered a family of 12 in Rio das Pedras.

Campo Elias Delgado

Campo Elias Delgado Morales was a Colombian spree killer who had been a US serviceman from 1975 to 1978. During his childhood in Chinácota in northeast Colombia, he witnessed his father's suicide and blamed his mother for the death and for his growing sense of estrangement. He eventually began teaching English to support himself. On December 3, 1986, after withdrawing all his money, nearly COP$50,000, from the Banco de Bogota, he argued with the cashier for shorting him 43 cents.

Soon after, he purchased a .32 caliber Smith & Wesson revolver and 500 rounds of ammunition. On December 4, he fatally stabbed a woman who employed him as a tutor for her daughter, then killed the girl. Next he returned to the apartment he shared with his mother and killed her with a single blow. He set her body on fire, then ran through the apartment building shouting "Fire!" and shooting anyone who came to their door. He went into an Italian restaurant and ordered a meal and drinks. Once he was done, he opened fire on the diners, hitting 32 people, 20 of them fatally. Delgado was either taken down

UNITED STATES OF AMERICA

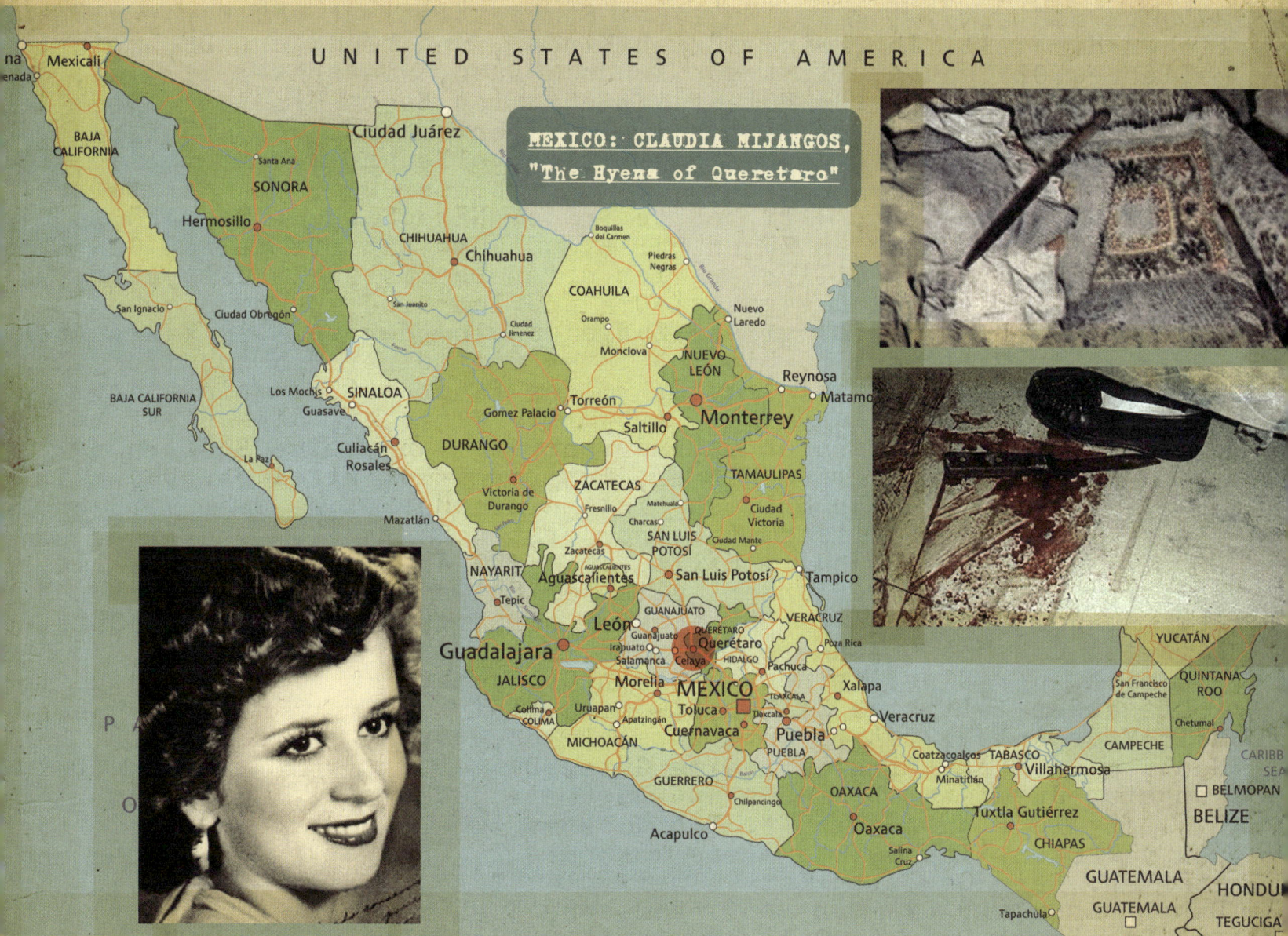

MEXICO: CLAUDIA MIJANGOS,
"The Hyena of Queretaro"

by a police officer or shot himself in the temple. He killed a total of 29 people and wounded 12.

Genildo Ferreira de França

Genildo Ferreira de França murdered 14 people in and around Santo Antônio do Potengi, Rio Grande do Norte in Brazil. He had served in the 7th Battalion of Combat Engineers and was judged an expert marksman. Married twice, he had three children and ran a grocery store. But seeing his son hit and killed by a taxi cab altered him. His second wife left him and began hinting to others that he was a homosexual. On May 21, 1997, he shot his ex-wife's lover, a taxi driver; then shot his father-in-law and a family friend; shot another three men who had spread rumors about him; and finally murdered his wife. The next day he killed a police sergeant; his mother-in-law; his ex-wife and her mother; a neighbor; a truck driver; and a messenger. When Ferreira was cornered by police, he committed suicide by shooting himself in the chest.

Claudia Mijangos "La hiena de Querétaro" (The Hyena of Querétaro)

Claudia Mijangos Azrac of Mazatlan, Mexico, a beauty queen in her youth, was married and had three children. Sadly, she developed serious mental health issues around age 33, hallucinating visions of angels and demons. Her estranged husband fought with her over her obsession with a priest who taught at the local school and she threatened him. That night, Claudia awoke with loud voices in her head. From the kitchen she took three knives and went upstairs to where her son and two daughters slept and stabbed each of them to death, despite their pleas for mercy. Claudia received a jail sentence of 30 years. The house where the murders took place was said to be haunted, and some years after the tragedy it featured in a TV documentary about the supernatural, on Mexican television.

147

European rampage killers are almost exclusively males who use firearms to commit their attacks, which are often termed "massacres."

RAMPAGE KILLERS OF EUROPE

Above: Ernst August Wagner. The teacher who murdered his family and a further nine people when he went on a killing spree in the German village of Mühlhausen an der Enz.

Ernst Wagner Germany

A German teacher with an irritable, nervous nature, Ernst August Wagner had become increasingly paranoid that those around him knew of his drunken sodomy of a farm animal. On September 4, 1913, he finally cracked. He killed his wife and four children in Degerloch, then drove to Mühlhausen an der Enz, where he set a number of fires and shot 20 people, nine fatally. The incensed villagers beat him unconscious. At his trial, he was found not guilty on grounds of insanity and spent the rest of his life in an asylum in Winnenthal, where he wrote plays.

Peter Grachev Russia

Peter Grachev, a Russian peasant farmer in Ivankovo, felt simmering anger over a Decree on Land enactment that caused him to lose a desirable piece of land to a neighbor. Vowing vengeance, on July, 26, 1925, he set his neighbors' homes on fire while they were in the fields. As they rushed back to the village, he ambushed them from cover along the road. He killed 17 residents and shot at the firemen trying to save the blazing homes as well as killing 12 horses. He fled, but was captured by state militia. It is believed he killed his family and household

staff and burned down his own house before perpetrating the Ivankoko massacre.

Christian Dornier France

The son of a French farmer, Christian Dornier had troubled relationships with those around him, which 12 months in the military in 1981 did nothing to ease. His father promised him oversight of the family farm, but after a short stay at agricultural school he had a mental collapse. Any interest in farming was gone and his behavior grew increasingly erratic. In July 1989, while his family dined, he waited in the kitchen with a 12-gauge shotgun. He shot a visiting cattle inseminator by mistake, then murdered his sister and mother and wounded his father. After that he drove through the village of Luxiol, shooting randomly at people, including several children. He killed fourteen and wounded eight in a 15-minute rampage. After a diagnosis of schizophrenia, he was sent to a psychiatric hospital.

Michael Ryan England

Michael Robert Ryan was the English farm laborer behind the Hungerford massacre that took place on August 19, 1987. Ryan used a handgun and two semi-automatic rifles to kill

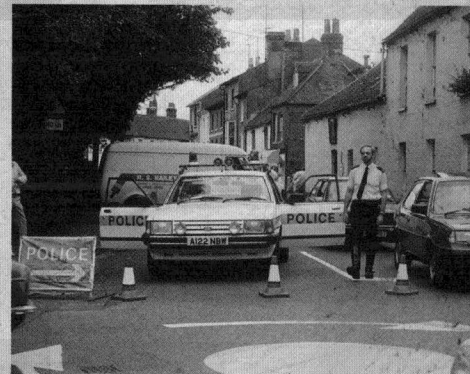

16 people, including his own mother and an unarmed policeman. Fifteen other victims were wounded. One of those killed, Susan Godfrey, was picnicking with her two young children and managed to place them in her car before the armed Ryan ordered her into the forest. There he shot her 13 times in the back. Because Ryan killed himself, no motive for the attack was ever discovered. The Home Secretary order a report on the incident, and in 1988 the Firearms Act was passed, which bans the ownership of semi-automatic center-fire rifles and restricts shotguns that hold more than three cartridges. The Ryan shooting remains one of the deadliest firearms incidents in British history.

Friedrich Leibacher Switzerland

Friedrich Leibacher was a businessman and convicted felon in the Swiss city of Zug. Leibacher felt his convictions for fraud, public obscenity, and obscene acts with children were unwarranted, and he decided he was being unfairly persecuted by the government. So on September 27, 2001, he struck back. Armed with a Swiss army assault rifle, a SIG Sauer pistol, a pump-action shotgun and a revolver, and disguised as a policeman in a homemade police vest, he entered the Zug canton's parliament building unimpeded. Once inside, he managed to shoot to death 14 people and wound 18, in what was called the Zug massacre, before killing himself.

Above, main image: Michael Ryan, the English farm labourer who shot dead 16 people, including his mother, before killing himself; **Above top right pictures:** The British authorities tour the old English market town of Hungerford in the immediate aftermath of the shootings; **Right, center and bottom:** Christian Dornier, the son of a farmer who shot dead most of his family and then drove through the French village of Luxiol, killing 14 and wounding eight.

Africa has given rise to numerous rampage killers from the 1950s onward, of whom a significant number were police officers or military personnel. Like Africa, Asia has had some notable mass murderers, a number of them beginning their assault by attacking family members or loved ones.

RAMPAGE KILLERS OF AFRICA & ASIA

Top: William Unek, responsible for two spree killings in the Belgian Congo, and then British Tanganyika, a total of 57 dead, including his own wife; **Above:** Carel Delport of Ladysmith, who shot nine people dead—including his father—and wounded a further 11.

William Unek Belgian Congo

William Unek, a police constable, engaged in two separate spree killings. In 1954 he killed 21 people with an axe in the Belgian Congo. After fleeing, he ended up in British Tanganyika Territory. In 1957 he experienced a social misunderstanding with his boss that resulted in another massacre: armed with a stolen police rifle and an axe he killed 36 people, including his own wife, whose hut he set on fire. Nine days later, he was hunted down and shot.

Carel Johannes Delport Ladysmith, South Africa

Carel Johannes Delport was a mentally unbalanced farmer from South Africa, who, in 1992 killed his father over the sale of three calves. He then shot the housemaid and the two black men who had bought the calves and in the streets of Ladysmith shot another five strangers and wounded 11. The many black victims he killed stirred up racial tension after his arrest.

Richard Komakech Kampala, Uganda

Richard Komakech of Uganda was a private in the military police and the perpetrator of the Kampala wedding massacre in 1994. Komakech, a wedding guest, grew angry when Irene Ati repeatedly refused his offer to dance. He caused a scene and was asked to leave. The drunken soldier returned to the party with his semi-automatic rifle, shot Ati, then killed another 25 guests. He tried to shoot himself in the head, but was only superficially wounded. The police tried to prevent the other guests from killing him, but Ati's father broke through and smashed Komakech's skull.

Alfred Ogwang Uganda

Alfred Ogwang of Uganda was a police officer responsible for a mass killing at the Kamwenge Trading Centre. While attending a disco dance at the Centre in 1994, he got into an argument in the canteen. He returned to his barracks and brought an SMG rifle back to the bar, where he shot four men, shouting, "I will finish you all!" Firing onto the dance floor, he killed another nine people and wounded 14. Sentenced to hang, his term was commuted to life in 2010.

Raman Raghav Mumbai, India

Raman Raghav not only raped and killed his own sister in the late 1960s, he went on a rampage in Mumbai, India, bludgeoning 41 people to death in their huts as they slept. After being examined by doctors, he was declared "certifiably not sane." In 1995 he died of renal failure in prison.

Woo Bum-Kon South Korea

Woo Bum-Kon, a South Korean policeman, killed 55 people and wounded 35 during a spree killing in 1982. After a physical assault on his girlfriend, he gathered weapons at a reservist armory, then claimed victims in a post office, a marketplace, and in a number of villages.

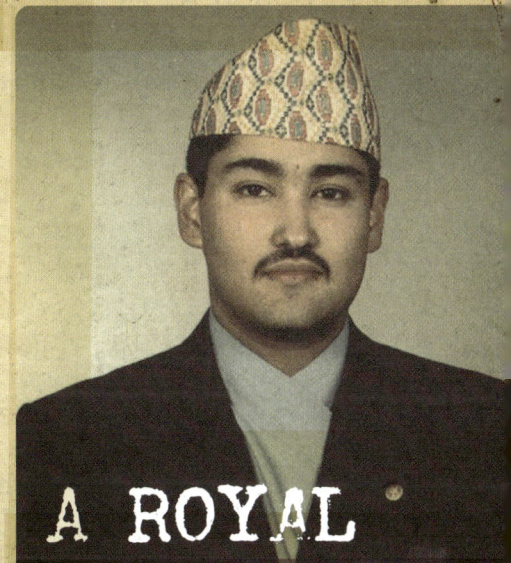

A ROYAL MASSACRE

Like a jaw-dropping plot development from a TV mini-series, in 2001 Nepalese Crown Prince Dipendra shot and killed nine members of his family during a royal family gathering at Narayanhity Palace. The deceased included King Birenda and Queen Aishwarya. Dipendra fell into a coma after attempting suicide and died three days later—after being declared king. His uncle Prince Gyanendra succeeded him.

Jin Ruchao China

Jin Ruchao, the perpetrator of the Shijiazhuang, China, bombings in 2001, was targeting buildings where his ex-wife, ex-mother-in-law, and a lover lived. A total of 108 people were killed and 38 wounded by the ammonium nitrate bombs that exploded near four apartment buildings. Just prior to the attack, he had stabbed his girlfriend to death. At his trial, Jin received the death penalty.

Top: The Belgian Congo Force Publique. William Unek was a member of this police force; **Above, left to right:** The trial of the Shijiazhuang bomber, Jin Ruchao, in 2001; **Right:** The rubble from the apartments after the ammonium nitrate bombs exploded, killing 108 and maiming 38. Jin Ruchao received the death penalty for his crimes.

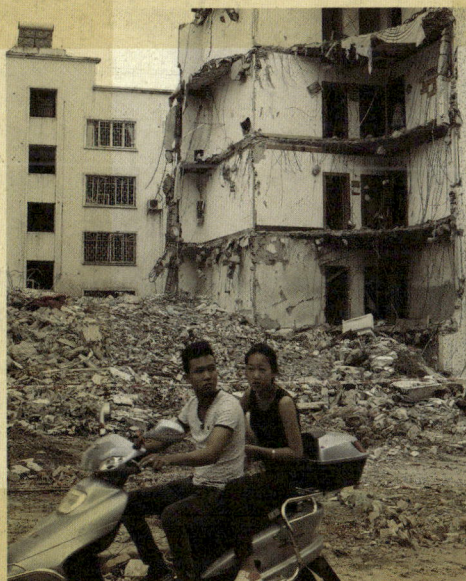

151

"My consuming lust was to experience their bodies. I viewed them as objects, as strangers."

JEFFREY DAHMER

8 Chapter Eight

Cannibals in Our Midst

Advanced cultures consider cannibalism the ultimate taboo; more heinous than killing a human, is killing and consuming them. "Of the estimated 2,000 active serial killers in the United States, between five and 10 are probably cannibals as well," claims Dr. Eric Hickey, professor of forensic psychology at Walden University. Yet the planet's fossil record shows human tooth marks on human bones, indicating some early cultures adopted the practice either out of necessity or as part of a ritual.

"He had lost his only friend and one true love. And he was absolutely alone in the world..." BIOGRAPHER HAROLD SCHECHTER ON THE DEATH OF GEIN'S MOTHER

ED GEIN
THE PLAINFIELD GHOUL

Above: Ed Gein. There's a general consensus that Gein was not a typical cannibal. But because he had a fetishistic attraction to women's bodies and cannibalized their skin to make a female "suit," he is included in this chapter.

Born in LaCrosse, Wisconsin, Edward Theodore Gein grew up in a repressive household with a mousy, alcoholic father and a controlling, religiously puritanical mother who spouted warnings about sin and carnal lust. In 1915, the family moved to a farm outside Plainfield.

After their father died, Ed and his older brother Henry took on many jobs around the town. Ed contributed by working as a handyman and, shockingly, as a babysitter. One day when the brothers were burning brush, the fire surged out of control. Afterward Henry was found dead but unburnt, his demise attributed to asphyxiation. Looking back, some criminologists believe it was Gein's first kill.

Gein, who was obsessed with his mother, never dated and rarely left the farm.
When she died in 1945, he came unglued. He kept her rooms pristine while the rest of the neglected farmhouse deteriorated. Meanwhile, he developed an unhealthy interest in anatomy books and pulp magazines featuring cannibals and Nazi atrocities. As time passed, locals began disappearing, among them Mary Hogan, who ran a tavern that Gein frequently visited. Three

years later, when Bernice Worden went missing from her Plainfield hardware store, police found a trail of blood that led out the back door. Her son, Frank, a deputy sheriff, suspected Gein and tracked him to a grocery store, where he was apprehended.

A Gruesome Discovery

When the police drove to Gein's farm to search the grounds, they were sickened by what greeted them. Among the horrors were Bernice Worden's headless, gutted body hanging from the ceiling of a shed; human organs stored in jars, human skin used as fabric to make clothing, lampshades, and chair seats, skulls used as soup bowls . . . and Bernice's head in a burlap sack. Gein confessed to killing Worden and also Hogan three years earlier. He told them of robbing graves while in a "daze," taking the recently buried bodies of women who resembled his mother and tanning their skin. He'd planned to make a "woman suit," so he could literally crawl into the skin of his figurative mother.

Gein was arraigned on one count of murder in November 1957, but pleaded not guilty. Having been diagnosed with schizophrenia, he was judged

INSPIRING HORROR

The most brutal and bizarre crimes in America

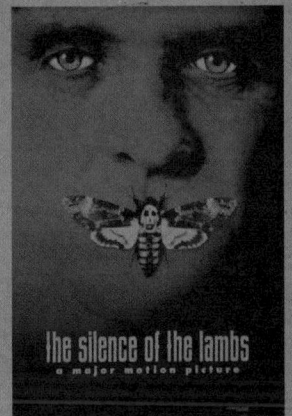

unfit to stand trial and was placed in a hospital for the criminally insane. Fast forward to November 1968, when doctors declared Gein now mentally fit to confer with lawyers and help with his own defense. The trial lasted one week: Gein claimed he'd accidentally shot Worden in her store while looking at a rifle. Judge Gollmar, presiding without a jury, found him guilty.

After a second trial to establish his mental fitness, Gollmar found him not guilty by reason of insanity. His house and effects were to be sold at auction, but the house burned down before it took place. Arson was suspected, but investigating it was not a high priority for Fire Chief Frank Worden, son of Bernice, Gein's final victim. Gein spent the rest of his life in a mental hospital and died of lung cancer in 1984.

Top: The Gein house, November 1957, after his arrest; **Center:** The house is boarded up after Gein had been placed in a hospital for the criminally insane; **Above:** As with the murderer Christie's house at Rillington Place in London (see p90), the Gein house also attracted ghoulish sightseers.

Ed Gein's gruesome deeds formed the model for many popular slasher novels and movies. His career as a killer, necrophile, and grave robber gave rise to such characters as Norman Bates in *Psycho*, Buffalo Bill (Jame Gumb) in *The Silence of the Lambs*, and Leatherface in *The Texas Chainsaw Massacre* film franchise.

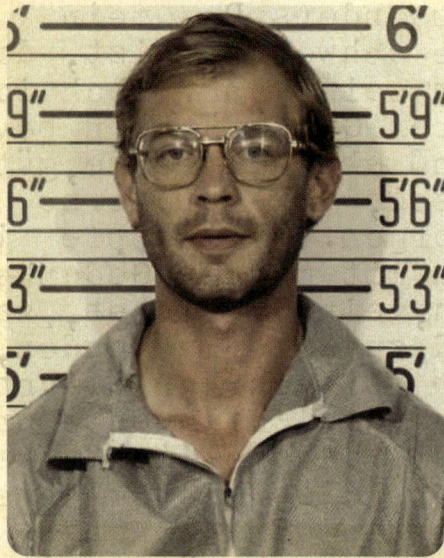

Jeffrey Dahmer—serial murderer, necrophile, and cannibal—became one of the late 20th century's most detestable criminals after killing and dismembering 17 young male victims.

JEFFREY DAHMER
THE MILWAUKEE MONSTER

TRIALS OF THE CENTURY

Top: Dahmer mugshot; **Above:** 14-year-old victim Konerak Sinthasomphone, who thought he had escaped Dahmer's clutches, only to be handed back to him by police;

Dahmer was born in 1960 in Milwaukee, Wisconsin. He was reportedly a normal, happy child, but at the age of four required surgery for a double hernia. Afterward, he grew increasingly withdrawn and by high school was a tense, detached loner.

Dahmer claimed he was 14 when his thoughts first turned to murder and necrophilia, and his parents' bitter divorce possibly spurred him to act on his dark fantasies. In June 1978 Dahmer brought hitchhiker Steven Hicks to the family home, got him drunk, and strangled him with a barbell. The dismembered body was buried behind the house, but Dahmer eventually crushed the bones and scattered them in a ravine.

After a short stint in college—and by now a heavy drinker—he joined the army. He was posted to Germany, but was discharged due to drink. (Authorities later tried, unsuccessfully, to tie his presence in Germany to several unsolved murders.) His time back home included a stay in Ohio, a move back to Wisconsin, and several arrests for indecent exposure. He began killing in earnest in 1987 with second victim Steven Tuomi. Dahmer said they drank together at a hotel, then he woke up next to the man's corpse with no memory of what had occurred. He dismembered the body in his grandmother's basement.

Dahmer soon developed a system, picking up young African-American men at gay bars, bus stops, and malls ... luring them with offers of sex or money. He would serve them drugged alcohol and then strangle them. After engaging in sexual acts with their corpses, he would dismember their bodies and dispose of the parts. He often kept skulls or genitals as mementos and took photos of the process so that he could relive it afterward.

He had a close call in September 1989, when an encounter with a 13-year-old Laotian boy resulted in charges of sexual exploitation and second-degree sexual

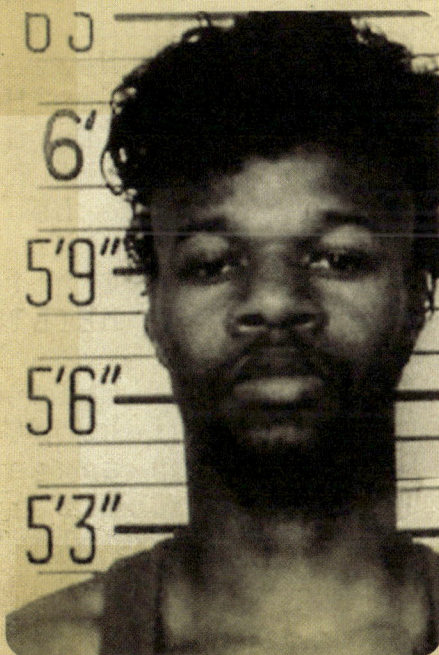

assault. In court he claimed that the boy had appeared older, promised he'd repent, and received a one-year sentence with "day" release. He went on to murder another 13 men, refining his process by adding torture to his killing rituals, using chemical to dispose of the bodies, and often consuming the flesh of victims.

On the night of May 27, 1991, police were called to investigate an Asian boy running naked in the street. When they arrived, Dahmer reassured them the youth was his 19-year-old lover. The Laotian boy was actually the 14-year-old brother of Dahmer's earlier molestation victim. When the police left, Dahmer killed the boy. A simple police check of his home would have found the body of his 12th victim, Tony Hughes. Dahmer was finally apprehended when a disoriented black man wearing dangling handcuffs led

police to the "weird dude" who had drugged him. While in Dahmer's apartment, they found Polaroids of dismembered bodies. A further search disclosed a head in the refrigerator and three more in the freezer, plus a host of sickening souvenirs.

The jury at Dahmer's trial determined he was sane, found him guilty of all charges, and recommended 16 life sentences. He "found religion" in prison, but in 1994 was beaten to death, along with another inmate, by convicted murderer Christopher Scarver. Ironically, Dahmer, who killed his first victim with a barbell, was himself dispatched with a weight room iron bar.

Top: Dahmer is led into court; **Left:** Convict Christopher Scarver, who murdered Dahmer in prison.

No matter how genteel the culture or how civilized the society, cannibals manage to infiltrate almost every setting—be it rural, suburban, or urban.

ENGLISH AND EUROPEAN CANNIBALS

Leonarda Cianciulli
Reggio Emilia province, Italy

Leonarda Cianciulli, of Italy's Reggio Emilia province, was known as the "Soapmaker of Correggio." A troubled child who attempted suicide twice, as a married mother she was highly protective of her own children. When her eldest son announced his intention to join the army just before World War II, she decided to ensure his safety with human sacrifices.

To this end, she murdered and dismembered three of her female neighbors between 1939 and 1940. She made soap and teacakes from their remains . . . serving the cakes to her other neighbors and giving the soap away to friends. She was convicted of murder in 1946 and died in prison in 1970.

Joachim Kroll Ruhr Region
of Germany

Joachim Kroll, was a German serial child killer, necrophiliac, and cannibal, who operated in the Ruhr region from 1955 until 1976. He began killing after the death of his mother and claimed 14 victims—staying active partly due to other killers in the region distracting the police.

Known for surprising victims and strangling them quickly, he would strip the body, have intercourse with it, then slice off pieces of flesh

to be eaten later. He was finally arrested for the murder of four-year-old Marion Ketter; someone in Kroll's building complained about a blocked waste pipe, and Kroll told him it was "guts." The police found the girl's dismembered body in his flat, her small hand simmering on his stove. Kroll somehow believed he would receive an operation to cure him and be set free.

Nikolai Dzhumagaliev Kazakh
Soviet Socialist Republic

Nikolai Espolovich Dzhumagaliev, a fireman in Kazakh SSR, was also known as Metal Fang and Kolya the Maneater. A practicing cannibal, he acquired a taste for human flesh in 1979 after his first kill, a young peasant woman walking alone on a rural path. He slit her throat, drank her blood, then brought her butchered body parts home in a backpack, where it took him a month to consume them. The police found the woman's mutilated body, but had no leads.

He killed five more times before accidentally shooting another firefighter while drunk, after which he was arrested. While in a psychiatric hospital he was diagnosed with schizophrenia. Upon his release, he killed three more people. Then, during a house party with some friends, he decided to kill and dismember one of his guests. He lured him into another room, but

Top: Leonarda Cianciulli, "The Soapmaker of Correggio"; **Center and Above:** Joachim Kroll. The police found four-year-old Marion Ketter's severed hand simmering on his stove.

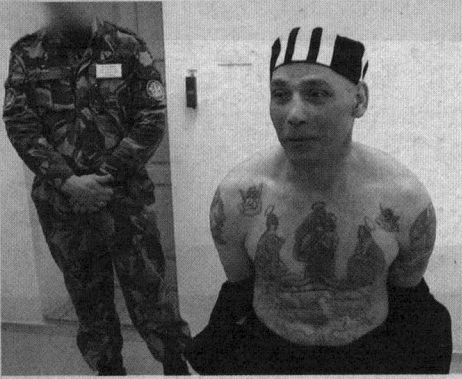

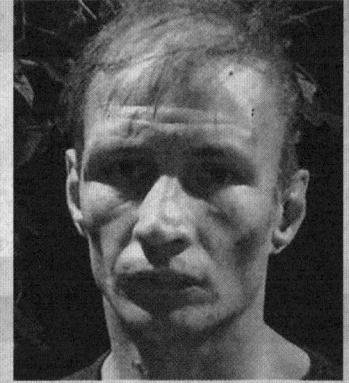

when the remaining guests came looking for him and saw what Nikolai had done they fled in terror and called the police. The police found him naked and covered in blood. He was able to escape to the nearby hills with just a hatchet, but was found and arrested the next day. (At the same time as Dzhumagaliev's crimes, another murderer named Alexander Skrynnik was killing and dismembering women in Chisinau, Moldavia, making those residents fear that Dzhumagaliev had escaped and reached Moldavia. Skrynnik was eventually caught and executed.)

Meanwhile, Dzhumagaliev was declared insane, and spent eight years in a treatment center . . . before he escaped in 1989. He was rumored to have murdered people in Moscow, but was again apprehended after several years on the run, and is now housed in a specialized psychiatric clinic fenced with barbed wire.

Vladimir Nikolayev
Novocheboksarsk, Russia

Vladimir Nikolayev, a resident of Novocheboksarsk, a city in Eastern Russia, was known as the Ogre. He had a history of robbery before he killed a drinking buddy during a fist fight. He carried his "unconscious" friend to his apartment, realized he was dead, and so dismembered him in the bathtub, where he first had the idea to eat him. He roasted part of his thigh and found it palatable.

He continued to find victims to butcher, distributing some of the meat to friends and even selling a kilo in a market, labeled as kangaroo meat. He used the money to buy alcohol. But when some people grew suspicious of what Vladimir claimed was antelope meat,

they had it analyzed. Once it was shown to contain human blood, Nikolayev was arrested. In his flat, police found human remains and a very bloodstained bathtub.

Peter Bryan North London

Peter Bryan, who grew up in London, was the youngest of seven children born to parents from Barbados. He quit school at 14, worked at a clothing stall, then taught cooking at a soup kitchen. In 1987, the police were called to his East London rooming house, after he had attempted to throw another resident out his sixth-floor window. The police did not charge Bryan, however.

In 1994, he admitted to killing a young shop assistant, Nisha Sheth, with a hammer. This resulted in his being sent to Rampton Secure Hospital, a psychiatric facility. The staff felt he was making progress in behavior and maturity. Eventually he was released into the care of a psychiatrist and social worker. He began living in the Riverside Hostel in North London and was free to come and go.

In 2004, he was transferred back to a psych ward after an alleged indecent assault on a 16-year-old girl. Just hours after he was discharged, he killed his friend Brian Cherry: police found the body dismembered and a frying pan on the stove containing tissue from Cherry's brain. Remanded to Broadmoor Hospital, Bryan killed a patient, Richard Loudwell, saying he would have "eaten Loudwell's flesh" if not interrupted by staff. After entering a plea of manslaughter on the grounds of diminished responsibility, he was sentenced to life in Broadmoor without parole.

Dmitri and Natalia Baksheev
Southern Russia

Dmitri and Natalia Baksheev were an antisocial married couple who lived in Krasnodar in southern Russia. Natalia worked for a time as a nurse, but was fired for alcoholism. Dmitri had a criminal history that had been extinguished by 2017, and he worked as a handyman.

One day Dmitri lost his cell phone, which was picked up by road workers who gave it to the police. On it they found photos of Dmitri holding human remains, including one shot of him with a human hand in his mouth. Both he and Natalia were questioned, but they claimed the body was found in the bushes. They later confessed to killing a local woman, Elena Vakhrusheva. Natalia said she and Elena quarreled during a drinking session, a jealous Natalia ordering Dmitri to kill her rival, but then participated in stabbing her multiple times. In their small flat, police found fragments of a body in saline, and food and frozen meat of unknown origin. More remains were found in the basement and surrounding area. The frozen meat turned out to be of human origin, taken from one person.

After both Baksheevs received prison sentences, wild stories about them began to circulate: they had been hunting victims for nearly ten years; they had tortured, murdered, and eaten 30 people, then canned the food they could not consume. An investigation found only the single murder for which they had been incarcerated.

Top left: Vladimir Nikolayev; **Center:** Peter Bryan; **Right:** Dmitri Baksheev

ENGLISH AND EUROPEAN CANNIBALS

In North London
PETER BRYAN Murdered, dismembered and ate the brain of his friend Brian Cherry, 2004

In Ruhr Region, Germany
JOACHIM KROLL Killed and ate 14 people, including a 4-year-old girl, between 1955–76

In Reggio Emilia province, Italy,
LEONARDA CIANCIULLI Murdered and dismembered three of her neighbors and made soap and teacakes from the remains, 1939–40

FINLAND

R U S S I A N F E D E R A T I O N

Oulu

Lake Oulu

Lake Vyg

Arkhangel'sk

Petrozavodsk

Pori

Vaasa

Lakes Region

Lake Onega

Syktyvkar

Turku

Tampere

HELSINKI

Gulf of Finland

St Petersburg

Vologda

Viatka

Perm'

Novgorod

Rybinsk Reservoir

Severnaya Dvina

Sukhona

1990s, Novocheboksarsk, Eastern Russia
VLADIMIR NIKOLAYEV Killed and ate numerous people, even selling their dismembered carcasses as kangaroo and antelope meat

TALLINN

ESTONIA

Lake Peipus

Iaroslavl

Kostroma

Nijni Reservoir

Yoshkar-Ola

Izhevsk

Yekaterinburg

Pskov

RIGA

LATVIA

Ivanovo

Nizhniy Novgorod

Kazan'

Kama

LITHUANIA

Tver

Vladimir

Cheboksary

Simbirsk

Ufa

Chelyabinsk

VILNIUS

MOSCOW

Ryazan'

Samara Reservoir

Smolensk

Kaluga

Tula

Saransk

U r a l M o u n t a i n

MINSK

Penza

Tol'yatti

BELARUS

Bryansk

Orel

Saratov Reservoir

Samara

Orenburg

WARSAW

Gomel

Pripet

Koursk

Saratov

Volga

Ural'sk

Oral

Lipetsk

Tambov

In Chisinau, Moldavia
LEONARD SKRYNNIK Murdered and dismembered women around the same time as Dzhumagaliev, "Metal Fang" (far right box)

Belgorod

Voronezh

Aktyubinsk

Lviv

KAZAKHSTAN

Carpathians Mts.

AKIA

In Krasnodar, Southern Russia
DMITRI & NATALIA BAKSHEEV Wild stories of 30 people killed and eaten, over 10 years—even canning the meat, but imprisoned for just one murder in 2019. Dmitrri died in prison in 2020.

DAPEST

MOLDOVA

UKRAINE

Depression

Atyrau

Aral

RY

CHISINAU

Odesa

akhan'

NIKOLAI DZHUMAGALIEV In Kazak Soviet Socialist Republic, "Metal Fang" killed 10, eating nine of them, 1979-1990s

ROMANIA

Sea of Azov

Krimea

BELGRADE

BUCHAREST

Danube

Sevastopol

Krasnodar

Stavropol'

UZBEKISTAN

SERBIA

BLACK SEA

Maykop

5642 Elbrus

Groznyy

Makhachkala

Nukus

KOSOVO

SOFIA

BULGARIA

C a u c a s u s

CASPIAN

Urgench

SKOPJE

2925 Musala

Sinop

GEORGIA

TBILISI

TURKMENISTAN

F.Y.R.O.M.

Bosporus

Istanbul

ANKARA

TURKEY

YEREVAN

AZERBAIJAN

ARMENIA

5137

BAKU

Kara - Kum

Turkmenbashi

Turkmenabat

NA

2911 Olympus

Salonica

Bursa

Anatolia (Asia Minor)

Mt Ararat

4810

SEA

ASHGABAT

Izmir

Kayseri

Lake Van

Lake Urmia

Mary

ATHENS

onnesus

GREECE

Konya

Gaziantep

Tigris

Tabriz

Gorgan

Mashhad

Adana

Euphrates

Mt. Demavend

Salt

AEGEAN SEA

Antalya

Mersin

Aleppo

Al Mawsil

Kirkuk

TEHRAN

5671

Desert

Rhodes

NICOSIA

3088

SYRIA

Qom

Herat

2542

Crete

CYPRUS

LEBANON

BEIRUT

IRAQ

Kermanshah

IRAN

AFGH.

ANEAN SEA

DAMASCUS

BAGHDAD

These killer-cannibals strayed beyond aberrant behavior into the realm of the truly bizarre...

DISHONORABLE MENTIONS

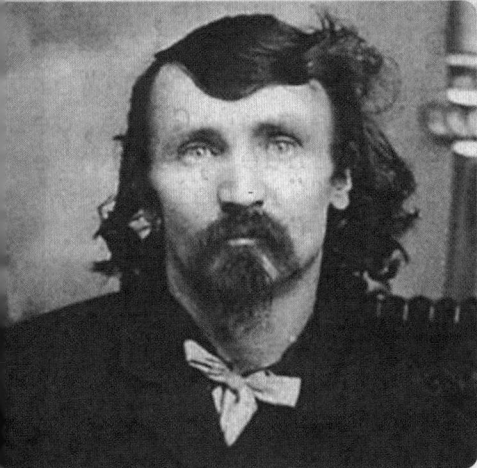

Boone Helm The Old West

Boone Helm, might have been just another colorful mountain man and gunfighter from America's Old West ... except for his habit of killing and eating the people he met. Born to a respectable Kentucky family that moved to Missouri while he was a child, the adult Helm liked showing off and thumbing his nose at the law, once riding his horse into a courthouse to challenge a judge.

After failing as a husband, he headed to California in search of gold. When a cousin who had promised to accompany him changed his mind, Helm killed him and set out alone. He was arrested and placed in a mental asylum, but soon escaped and headed West again. En route he killed several more men, even admitting to strangers that he was "often obliged" to feed on those he'd slain. In California he killed a rancher who had aided him, continued to rob and murder in Oregon, and in 1864 was finally captured in Montana and hanged. "Let 'er rip," he instructed the hangman before jumping off the box he stood on to his death.

Albert Fish The Brooklyn Vampire

Albert Fish was known as the Gray Man, the Werewolf of Wysteria, the Brooklyn Vampire, the Moon Maniac, and the Boogey Man. A serial child killer, sexual fetishist, and cannibal, he once bragged he had "children in every state" and was responsible for a possible 100 deaths.

Born in Washington, DC, Fish spent years in a brutal orphanage after the death of his father, the place he said he learned to enjoy pain. He moved to New York in 1890, where he began raping boys. His mother arranged a marriage for him, and he and wife Anna Hoffman had six children, but she eventually left him.

In 1919, after a stint in Sing Sing for grand larceny, he began a sadomasochistic affair with Thomas Keddon, 19. Ten days later he took Keddon to an old farm house, tortured him, cut off half his penis, and left him with a $10 bill. He'd also begun embedding needles into his own groin and abdomen; at least 29 showed up on x-rays after his arrest.

The child killing began around 1919, with the stabbing of a mentally disabled boy. (Fish targeted children who were mentally handicapped or black, believing no one would care if they went missing.) He called his tools the "implements of Hell"—a meat cleaver, butcher knife, and hand saw. In 1934 he sent a letter to the mother of victim Grace Budd claiming to be an "acquaintance" of the man who killed and ate her. An emblem on the envelope allowed police to trace it back to Fish's rooming house, where he was arrested. At his trial for the murder of Budd, the jurors concurred privately that he was insane, but found him guilty anyway and sentenced him to death. He went to the electric chair in Sing Sing.

Top: Boone Helm, mountain man, gunfighter, murderer. The Kentucky cannibal; **Above:** A frail Albert Fish, the Brooklyn Vampire, is helped into court in 1936.

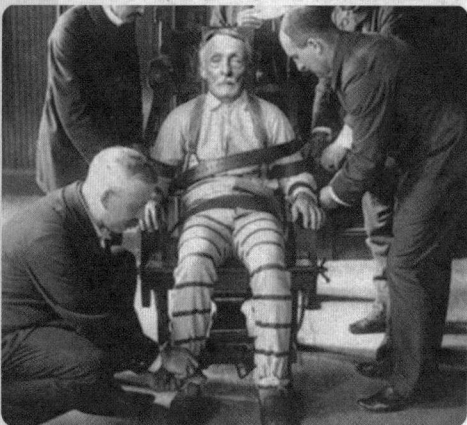

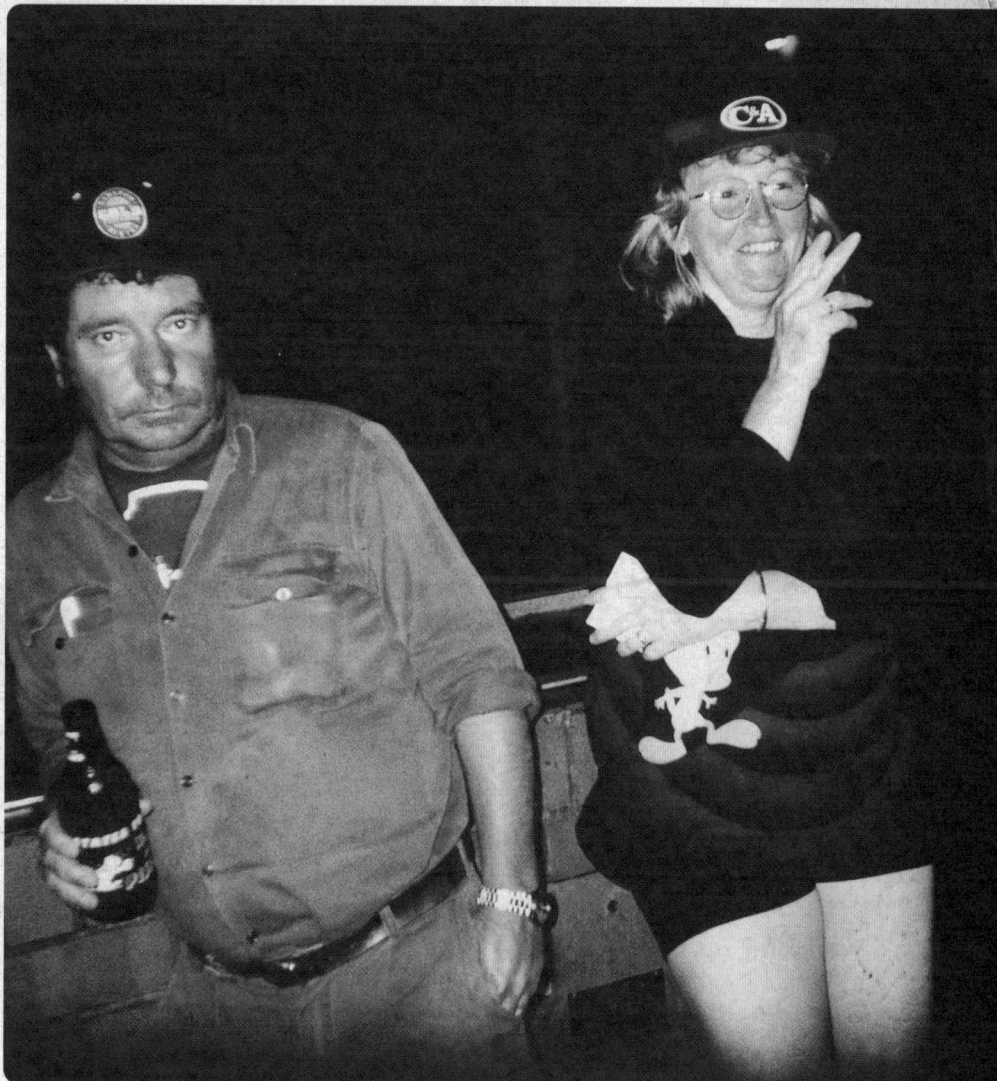

Katherine Knight Australia

Katherine Knight was an Australian from New South Wales. Her married mother lived with her lover, Knight's father. He ended up raping her mother repeatedly, often ten times a day, and her mother told her details of their sexual relationship. Knight grew into a loner and a bully who assaulted at least one boy at school.

In 1974 she married hard-drinking David Kellet, her co-worker at an abattoir—a place she'd called her dream job. Knight tried to kill him on their wedding night for falling asleep before satisfying her sexually. Even while heavily pregnant, she hit him on the head with a frying pan for coming home late. She was in and out of mental wards, most notably after placing her baby on the train tracks.

After Kellet left her, she had a series of affairs with local men. She eventually moved in with popular miner John Price, who lived with two of his children. But her temper grew so foul he had to take out a restraining order. She managed to seduce him one night, then stabbed him 37 times. Afterward she skinned him, decapitated him, and cooked a full meal for his children using his body parts. When the police entered the home they found the table set and place cards for each child. A third meal had been thrown into the back yard, as if Knight had tried to eat it and could not. She was sentenced to life in prison without parole.

Top left: Albert Fish, a study in the absurdity of existence, and **Center left:** Fish is prepared for death via the electric chair; **Top:** Katherine Knight with the unfortunate John Price; **Above:** The young Katherine Knight.

Top: Issei Sagawa is led out of the Police Judiciaire in Paris after his arrest in 1981;
Above: Sagawa, the Kobe Cannibal, interviewed some years later in Japan, a free man.

Issei Sagawa The Kobe Cannibal

Issei Sagawa, known as the Kobe Cannibal, was born prematurely to wealthy parents and suffered poor health as a child. His earliest cannibalistic desire occurred in first grade, when he saw a naked male thigh. While at university, he followed a young woman home, broke in while she slept, and planned to slice off a bit of her buttocks. She awoke, though, and struggled with him.

This "attempted" rape" was covered up by his father. In 1981, while attending graduate school in Paris, he invited a fellow student to his flat, shot her in the neck, had sex with her corpse, and carved up her body in order to eat her. He took photos of her at each stage of consumption. His attempt to dump her remains in a nearby lake resulted in his arrest. He was eventually found insane and was placed in a mental institution.

After his story was published, he gained a certain celebrity, and the French decided to deport him back to Japan, where he was immediately committed to Matsuzawa Hospital in Tokyo. There, his psychologists all pronounced him sane. Because the French charges had been dropped and their court documents were not released to Japanese courts, Sagawa was legally a free man—and has continued as such since 1986.

Tsutomu Miyazaki The Rat Man

Tsutomu Miyazaki, the "Otaku Murderer" or "the Rat Man," was born in Tokyo, also to a wealthy family. Sadly, he had a rare birth defect that caused his hand joints to become fused. As

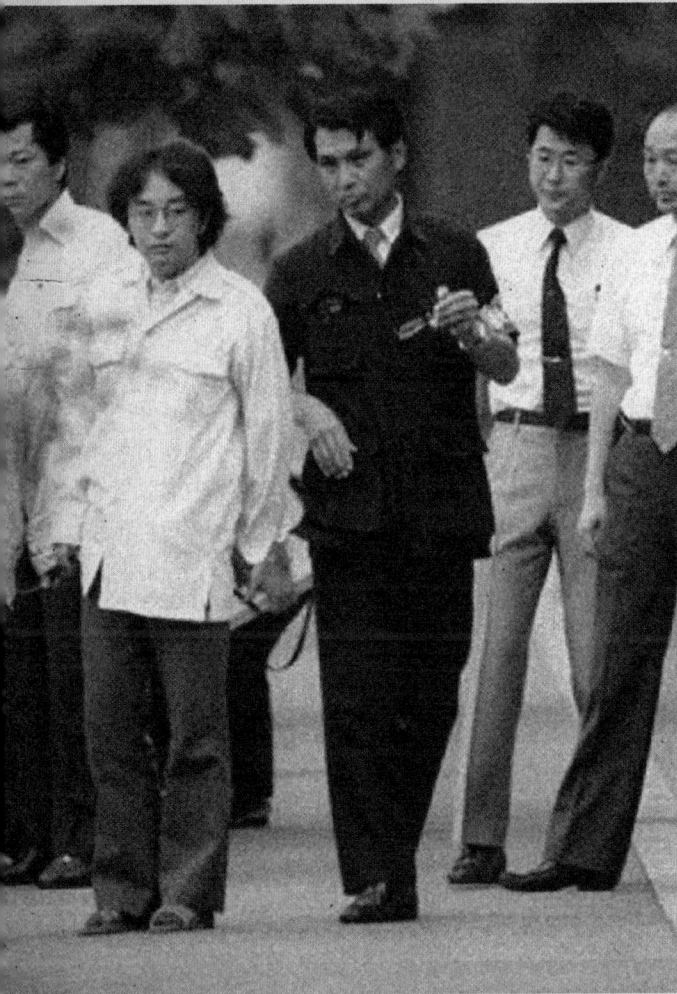

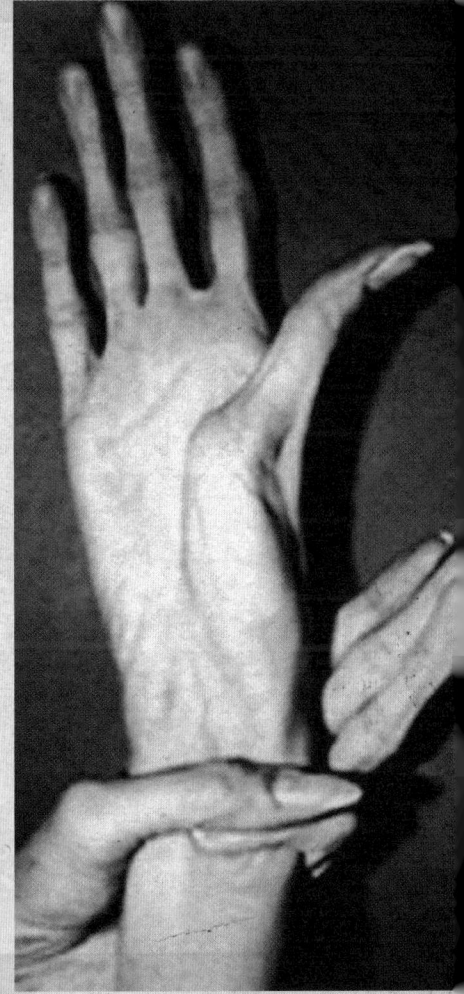

a child he felt alone and misunderstood, in part due to his deformed hands. When his beloved grandfather died, he consumed some of his ashes to "retain something from him." He started peeping on his older sister and even attacked his mother once.

From August 1988 to June 1989 he terrorized the parents of Tokyo with four murders that targeted little girls and included necrophilia and cannibalism. He preserved body parts as trophies and sent "mementos" such as clothing or teeth to the parents with taunting notes. His luck ran out while he was in a park taking photos of one of two young sisters, whom he had asked to remove her clothing, and their father came along and attacked him. He managed to escape, but when he returned later to fetch his car, the police were waiting.

During his 1990 trial, Miyazaki blamed the murders on the "Rat Man," an alter ego who ordered him to kill. After a grueling seven-year trial, he was finally determined to be sane enough to face punishment and so was hanged in 2008. Miyazaki was called the Otaku Murderer because the press mistakenly believed he'd been influenced to kill by pornographic anime and manga rather than traditional pornography and horror videos; *otaku* are people obsessed with anime and manga.

Above left and center: "The Rat Man" takes a stroll whilst in custody in Tokyo; **Above right:** Miyazaki's deformed, "Nosferatu-like hands"; **Right:** Miyazaki's mugshot. As an adult, Miyazaki became a photography technician, possibly to feed his voyeuristic tendencies.

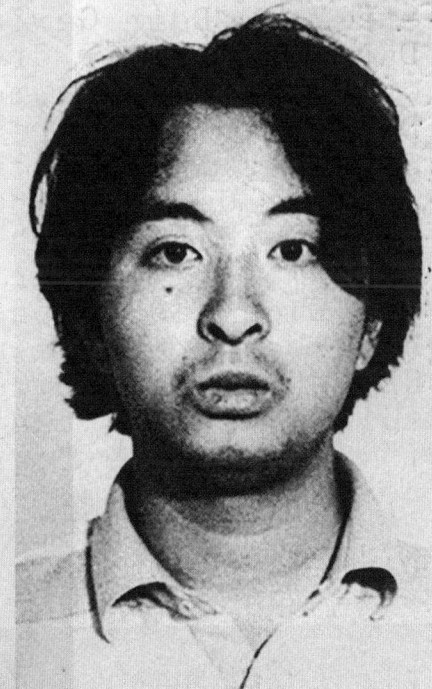

165

"I am alive, but I'm not living, I remember thinking as I walked. I am the living dead. I am nothing but a shell."

ELIZABETH SMART

9 Chapter Nine

KIDNAPPERS

Carrying people off against their will goes back to Biblical times, with the kidnapping of Jacob's daughter Dinah in the Book of Genesis. Today a kidnapping is generally performed to obtain a substantial ransom, money that will enrich the kidnappers themselves or, in certain regions of the world, help fund insurrectionists or terrorists. Sadly, far too many kidnappings have resulted in the death of the victim.

Certain infamous crimes linger in the imagination and continue to chill the heart. This is especially true when the criminals are promising young men who unleashed some base part of their natures.

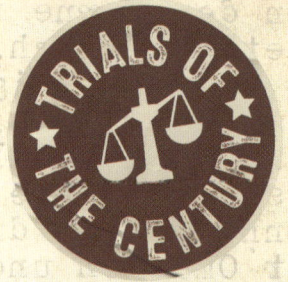

TRIALS OF THE CENTURY

LEOPOLD AND LOEB
THRILL KILLERS

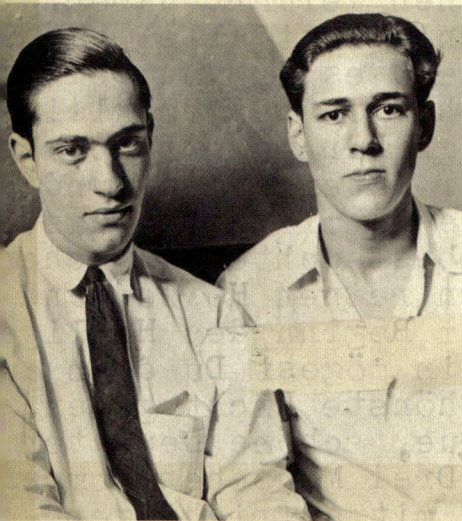

Above: Nathan Leopold Jr., left, and Richard Loeb in 1924.

In 1924, Nathan Leopold Jr. and Richard Loeb were two wealthy students of German-Jewish heritage attending the University of Chicago. Close friends, both lived in the affluent Kenwood section of Chicago's South Side. Inspired by their study of Nietzsche and desiring to prove their intellectual superiority, they decided to commit the "perfect crime."

They spent months planning a murder, which they intended to look like a kidnapping by sending ransom notes, and even buying a chisel to use as the murder weapon. After some consideration, they chose a victim—14-year-old Bobby Franks, the son of a wealthy watch manufacturer. Franks was a second cousin to Loeb and had played tennis at his house.

On May 21, the two college boys rented a car and drove around until they found Bobby walking home from school. He refused an offered ride, but when Loeb mentioned discussing tennis rackets, Bobby climbed into the front seat. It was never clear who was driving and who was in the back seat, but one the of two abductors stuck the boy in the head with the chisel, and then dragged him into the back seat and gagged him until he died. As planned, they drove 25 miles to Wolf Lake in Hammond, Indiana, then stripped the body, poured hydrochloric acid on his face and genitals—to hide his circumcision—and rolled him into a ravine. Leopold said later he wondered if he would feel different after the murder. He recalled feeling nothing.

The word quickly spread that Bobby was missing. Loeb stayed quiet, while Leopold freely told the press and police his theories on the abduction. Ransom notes arrived at the Franks's home, but before the payment could be made Bobby's body was discovered. The police also found a pair of glasses near the boy with custom hinges—which were traced to a pair that Leopold had ordered. The two friends were arrested and at first would say nothing, except to proclaim their innocence. But then Loeb cracked and confessed, implicating Leopold as the one who actually killed Bobby.

The court case became a media circus, and was quickly labeled the "trial of the century." It ran for 32 days in spite of the defendants' guilty pleas. Famous defense attorney Clarence Darrow was

hired by Loeb's family to lead the defense team. Darrow's summation alone lasted 12 hours, but the pair were found guilty and sentenced to "life plus a 99 years." Loeb's father died a month later of heart failure.

Loeb died in 1936 after being attacked by a fellow inmate with a straight razor, possibly after Loeb propositioned him. Leopold became a model prisoner and made significant improvements to the conditions at Stateville Penitentiary, including reorganizing the library, teaching students, and volunteering in the hospital. He even volunteered to be infected with malaria in order to test new treatments. Leopold was paroled in 1958 and accepted a medical

tech position in Puerto Rico, where he married a widowed florist. After receiving a masters degree, he taught at university, did research for the departments of health and urban renewal, as well as on leprosy, and became an island naturalist. He died in 1971 of a heart attack.

Top left: Richard Loeb, left, and Nathan Leopold during the media circus that their trial became; **Top right:** Their young victim, Bobby Franks; **Above, left:** The spectacles found close to Bobby Franks's body, which were traced back to Nathan Leopold; **Above:** The two charged suspects leave the court to the usual flurry of newsmen; **Inset:** James Stewart (center), Farley Granger (left), and John Dall, in Hitchcock's *Rope* of 1948.

A CLOSER LOOK:

A 1929 British play by Patrick Hamilton called *Rope* was based on the case. In 1948 Alfred Hitchcock created a film version of *Rope*, which starred Farley Granger and James Stewart. In 1959, the film *Compulsion* was also based on the crime.

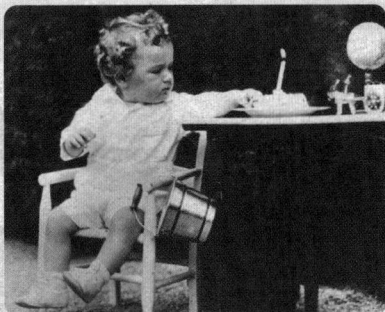

"THE CRIME OF THE CENTURY"
THE LINDBERGH ABDUCTION

Above: Colonel Charles Lindbergh. In 1927 he became the first aviator to fly solo across the Atlantic Ocean, becoming a huge celebrity in the process; **Top:** 20-month-old Charles Lindbergh Jr., the unfortunate little boy at the center of the whole saga.

When tall, blond Charles Lindbergh climbed into his single-engine monoplane, The Spirit of St. Louis, and became the first aviator to fly solo across the Atlantic Ocean in 1927, he gained instant celebrity. The public could not get enough of his boyish good looks and gladly celebrated his marriage to Anne Morrow, daughter of a US diplomat. His life was like something out of a storybook, with fame both popularizing and insulating him. When the Lindberghs' first child was born, the news was carried on all the wire services.

The family's country home, Highfields, was located in rural East Amwell, New Jersey. There, 20-month-old Charles Jr. had a nanny and household staff, as well as his parents to care for him. But something went terribly wrong on the night of March, 1, 1932. An intruder placed a ladder against the side of the house, climbed into the boy's bedroom, and abducted him. When nanny Betty Gow found the baby missing and a ransom note was discovered on the window sill, the police were immediately brought in. Lindbergh himself headed the investigation—a legal oddity to be sure.

The news media went into a frenzy once they learned of the abduction. The ransom of $50,000, mostly in documented gold certificates, was paid in a cemetery by a go-between, John Condon, who briefly glimpsed and spoke with the kidnapper. But Charles was never returned. The toddler's remains were found near the Lindbergh property, the baby killed by a blow to the head. Because a ladder, broken where two sections joined, had been found near the house it was proposed that the kidnapper had fallen and dropped the baby. Initial suspicion fell on staff members, specifically on nervous British servant Violet Sharp, who gave conflicting alibis for the night of the crime. She committed suicide by cyanide on June 10, but was belatedly vindicated when her alibi was confirmed.

The FBI stepped in once murder was involved, but it took a year before there was a break in the case. A gas station attendant phoned in the license plate number of a car whose driver had given him a $10 gold certificate. The plate led to a German immigrant, Bruno Hauptmann, a carpenter from the Bronx. Another $13,000 in ransom gold certificates were found

DAILY NEWS FINAL

BRUNO GUILTY — MUST DIE

SCENE IN COURT AS HAUPTMANN (ARROW) HEARS DOOM

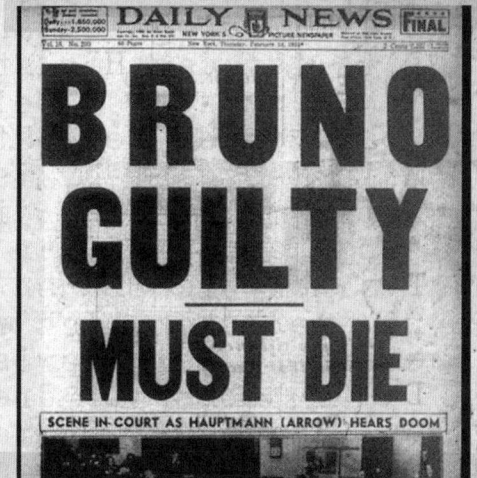

in his garage. He claimed he was holding the money for a friend who had since died. On October 8, 1934, Hauptmann was indicted for the murder. And even though the evidence was circumstantial, the German's fate was pretty much foregone. After a five-week trial, Bruno was found guilty and sentenced to death. Protesting his innocence to the end, on April 3, 1936 Hauptmann went to the electric chair.

Crime historians have unraveled this case and knit it back up a dozen times or more. There are no new answers. Either Hauptmann was guilty—with or without inside accomplices— or America's hero had become part of a gross miscarriage of justice regarding the defendant.

In some circles "Lindy" himself is considered suspect. He was known to have a skewed sense of humor, and only weeks before had hidden the baby for hours as a prank, to the distress of everyone, and perhaps had tried to repeat the "joke" and fatally dropped him from the ladder. Shortly after the trial, the Lindberghs departed for England, remaining in Europe for four years.

Top left: The jury in the Hauptmann trial at Wilmington, NJ; **Top center:** Lindbergh, on the stand; **Center:** The courtroom was packed to the rafters each day with newsmen; **Top right:** Bruno Hauptmann; **Center right:** The *NY Daily News* after the verdict; **Right:** Hauptmann in the electric chair at Trenton.

It is natural that kidnappers would go after people with enough money to pay a substantial ransom. Targets have also included political figures, like the prime minister of Finland, Karlo Juho Ståhlberg, and his wife, Ester. In the 1970s, the abductions of these two youthful scions of wealth made international headlines.

CELEBRITY ABDUCTEES

★ TRIALS OF ★ THE CENTURY

"For any victim of a violent crime, when you actually get to go in . . . and see their faces and know that they can't hurt you any more, there is no feeling like that. It really frees you from a lot of demons...." **PATTY HEARST**

Above: The 16-year-old John Paul Getty III in 1973.

John Paul Getty III

Born Eugene Paul Getty II, Paul was the grandson of American oil tycoon J. Paul Getty, one of the world's richest men. He was raised in Rome with his father, who looked after Getty oil interests there, and his stepmother. After his father's return to Britain, Paul stayed on in Rome, living an artsy, bohemian lifestyle. On July 10, 1973, the 16-year-old was kidnapped by the 'Ndrangheta, a Mafia crime syndicate, and held for $17 million ransom. (Ironically, he had earlier thought about getting himself kidnapped on purpose because he was in financial distress, but changed his mind, when he and his girlfriend found work as models.) He was transported to a cave in Calabria, while his abductors waited for the ransom. Unfortunately, his grandfather refused to pay it, saying it would encourage criminals to kidnap his 13 other grandchildren. His captors sent another demand, which was delayed by a postal strike. In frustration they killed Paul's pet bird and then cut off his ear, sending it to a daily newspaper. The grandfather finally agreed to pay $2.2million. Paul was found at a petrol station in Potenza, but when he called his grandfather to thank him, the old man refused to get on the phone. Nine men were eventually arrested, but only two were convicted of the crime.

Patty Hearst

Another child of wealth and privilege, Patricia Campbell Hearst was the granddaughter of famous newspaper magnate William Randolph Hearst. In 1974 she was kidnapped from her Berkeley apartment by the urban guerrillas of the Symbionese Liberation Army and held for 19 months. As ransom they wanted two jailed SLA members to be set free, and then for all needy Californians to be fed. Surprisingly Patty, now "Tania," appeared with the SLA in surveillance footage of a bank robbery wearing a dark beret, fatigues, and brandishing an M1 carbine. She was finally captured in the home of a fellow SLA member, but claimed she had been indoctrinated and threatened with rape if she did not cooperate. Found guilty of robbery, her sentence was commuted by President Jimmy Carter, and she was pardoned by Bill Clinton. She married police officer Bernard Shaw, who'd been part of her security detail while she was awaiting trial.

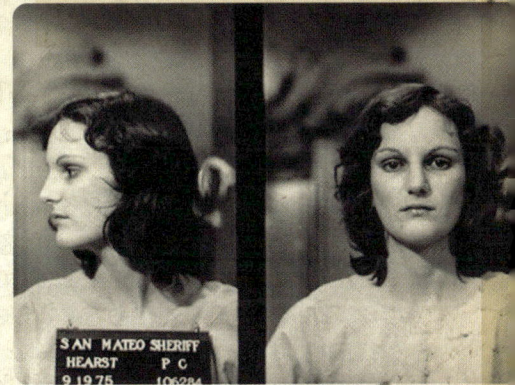

TYPES OF KIDNAPPINGS

In addition to the familiar abduction-and-ransom kidnappings, criminologists have identified a number of other types.

Bride kidnapping involves abducting a young woman against the will of her parents in order to marry her, even if she is willing to wed. It is a tradition in some nomadic tribes.

Express kidnapping, typically found in Latin America, involves taking a family member captive and demanding a ransom the family can easily afford.

Tiger kidnapping allows robbers to gain cooperation from an "inside" person at a bank or business by kidnapping and threatening harm to a family member. (See Hostage Heists on p194.)

Cult kidnapping is when families or friends attempt to physically free a loved one from the bonds of a cult or extreme religion. It is usually followed by a deprogramming process.

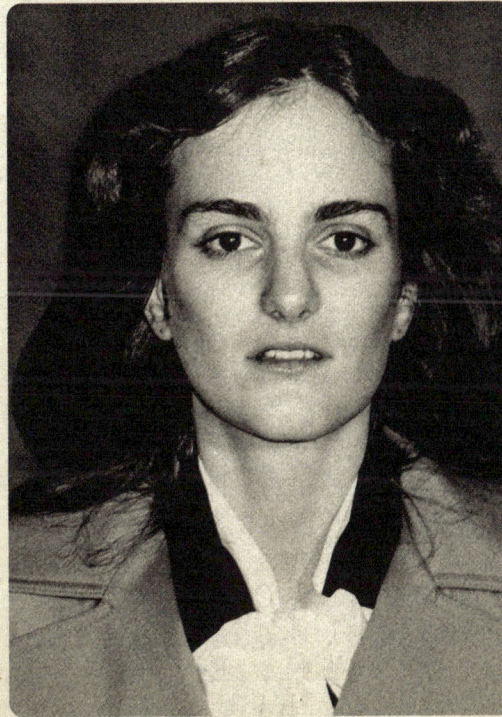

Top left: John Paul Getty III, released to the waiting world's press, minus his right ear; **Far left:** Patty Hearst—"Tania"— taking part in a bank robbery with members of the SLA; **Left:** Hearst during her trial; **Top right:** Patty Hearst's mug shot after her arrest for robbery.

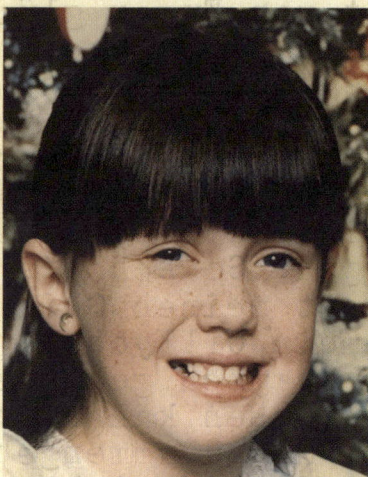

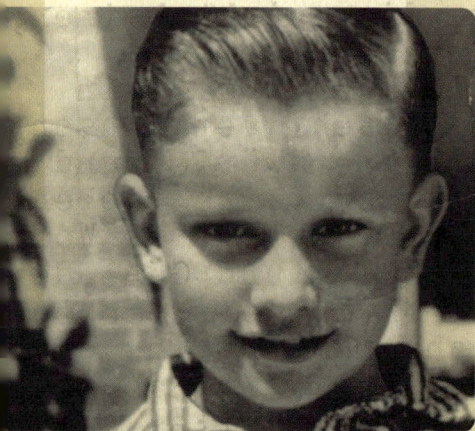

Sometimes in the aftermath of a terrible crime a law is improved, or a better system instituted—a beneficial outcome arising from a tragic circumstance.

KIDNAPPINGS THAT CREATED CHANGE

Top: A detail from a family portrait of Amber Hagerman. In 1996 she was kidnapped from a local store parking lot in Arlington, Texas, as she was cycling...and murdered; **Center:** Eight-year-old Graeme Thorne, also kidnapped and murdered; **Above:** A memento of young Graeme: **Opposite main image:** Twenty years on, the grandparents of Amber still grieve; **Opposite center:** In Bondi, Sydney, Bazil Thorne endures a press conference after his son's body is found; **Opposite bottom:** Amber's mom remembers her lost daughter; **Inset:** The 4 Square Store in Bondi from where Graeme Thorne was abducted in 1960.

Amber Hagerman Arlington, Texas

In 1996, nine-year-old Amber Hagerman of Arlington, Texas, was kidnapped while riding her pink bike in a grocery store parking lot. A neighbor witnessed the abduction and immediately called the police. Her parents and neighbors began searching for her. Unfortunately, four days after the kidnapping, a dog walker found her body in a creek bed with lacerations to the neck. Within days, her parents established People Against Sex Offenders (P.A.S.O.), hoping to force the Texas legislature to pass stricter laws to protect children. Meanwhile, the person who took Amber and killed her was never identified.

The "AMBER" Alert

The AMBER alert, an early-warning system begun in 1996, is issued as soon as law enforcement determines that a child has been taken and is at immediate risk. AMBER stands for America's Missing: Broadcast Emergency Response and it is meant to honor Amber Hagerman. It mobilizes the community at large to assist in the search. The alerts include the name and description of the child, description of the suspected abductor, and make, color, and license plate number of the car. They are broadcast on the radio, TV, LED road signs, and cell phones and other data-enabled devices. As of January 2021, these alerts have allowed the rescue and safe return of 1,029 children.

Graeme Thorne Sydney, Australia

In 1960, Bazil Thorne of Bondi, Australia, entered a special lottery to help fund the Sydney Opera House and won the top prize of A£100,000 (more than A£3 million today). No one in the media thought twice about publicizing lottery winners, and so the story of the Thorne family—Bazil, wife Freda, and their three children—made the front page of the Sydney newspapers. On July 7, the day the prize would be paid, Graeme Thorne, 8, went out to wait for his usual school ride, but when the family friend got there, he was missing. The Thornes immediately notified the police. An hour later a man with a foreign accent called the Thorne house: "I have your boy. I want £25,000 before 5 o'clock this afternoon . . . [or] I'll feed the boy to the sharks." The police began searching the neighborhood and an appeal was made on television by the police and Bazil.

The Tragic News

The following day Graeme's bookbag was found in Seaforth, a Sydney suburb. Then, nearly six weeks after his abduction, Graeme's body was found on some vacant land in Seaforth; he was wrapped in a tartan blanket, tied up with string, and gagged. Forensic clues—the woven blanket, human and dog hair, pink mortar, and tree debris, led police to the Seaforth home of Hungarian immigrant Stephen Bradley, who was by then on a ship bound for London. Two Sydney policemen apprehended him when the ship docked in Ceylon. Bradley confessed to the crime and told police the boy had suffocated in the trunk of his car. He died in prison in 1968.

After Thorne's death, which "marked an end of innocence in Australian life," lottery procedures changed; winners had the option of remaining anonymous. The case was also pivotal in the development of Australian forensic science and the updating of the country's kidnapping laws.

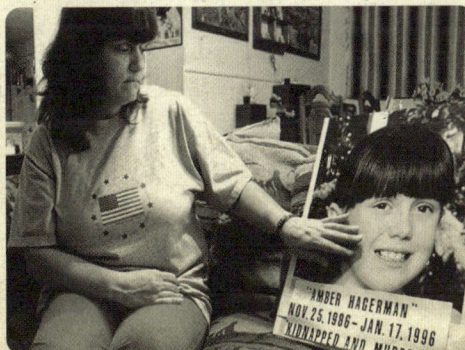

KIDNAPPING CONSEQUENCES

In Australia kidnapping is considered a criminal offense punishable by 14 to 20 years in prison. In Canada kidnapping without homicide may be punishable with a maximum possible penalty of life. In England, the kidnapping of a child is prosecuted based on whether the child gave consent or was too young to understand the risk.

A specific type of child molester kidnaps children, typically girls, with the intention of keeping them prisoner and grooming them as sexual partners. These deviants are often outsiders or loners, but sometimes they have wives and families who know nothing about the captives, even if the girls are hidden in the same house.

Captives in the Basement

Top: Elisabeth Fritzl of Amstetten, Austria—held captive for years by her own father, and raped repeatedly by him for over nine years, giving birth to seven children. Her mother was oblivious to everything. **Above:** Suzanne Sevakis—abducted, along with her sisters and brother by their stepfather

Elisabeth Fritzl Amstetten, Austria

Elisabeth Fritzl was held captive in the basement by her own father—who told his wife she'd joined a cult—and raped by him from 1984 to 1993. She gave birth to seven children, three of whom were brought upstairs as "foundlings." After the eldest captive girl fell ill, Fritzl took her to the hospital, but his story sounded suspicious. When Elisabeth was allowed out to visit the hospital, the alerted police rescued her. Fritzl was sentenced to life in prison.

Suzanne Marie Sevakis Georgia and Oklahoma

Suzanne Marie Sevakis and her two sisters and brother were abducted by their stepfather, Franklin Delano Floyd, in 1975. The girls were left at a shelter, but the boy disappeared. Floyd raised Suzanne, now Sharon, as his daughter, sexually abused her, and, after she had a child named Michael (by another man) he married her. Now an exotic dancer known as Tonya Hughes, she told coworkers if she left him Floyd would kill her and the boy, Michael Anthony Hughes. Floyd was a suspect in her death in a 1990 hit-and-run accident, and in 1994 he abducted Michael from school. Floyd was arrested for the kidnapping and sentenced to 52 years. In 2014, while on death row for the murder of another woman, Floyd admitted that he killed Hughes. Suzanne's missing brother came forward in 2019, his identity confirmed by DNA.

Jaycee Lee Dugard Meyers, California

In 1991, Jaycee Lee Dugard, 11, was abducted in Meyers, California, by Phillip Garrido, who stun gunned her and, with wife Nancy's help, thrust her into their car. Held captive for 18 years, Dugard was repeatedly raped by Garrido and bore him two children while in her teens. When Garrido brought those two teenage girls to a meeting at UC Berkeley, an events manager became suspicious and notified the authorities. Garrido was arrested and Dugard was freed, although her

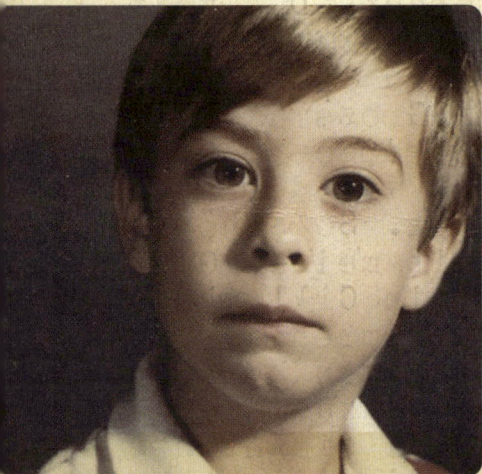

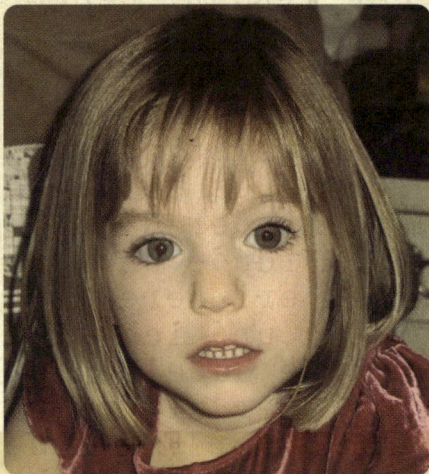

Child kidnappings often attract press coverage, but these two cases caused a furor. One case started with a boy's death, and featured an unconvincing confession, and the other was doggedly pursued, but never resolved.

MEDIA STORMS

Top left: Adam Walsh: kidnapped and murdered in July 1981; **Top right:** Madeleine McCann, kidnapped in May 2007. No trace of her has ever been found; **Above:** Adam's distraught parents, Reve and John Walsh; **Right:** The Walshes meet President Reagan in the aftermath of Adam's kidnap and murder.

Adam Walsh Hollywood, Florida

On July 27, 1981, Adam Walsh, age 6, was shopping with his mother Reve at the mall in Hollywood, Florida. She left him playing an Atari game with some kids while she shopped. When she returned, he and the kids had vanished. A store manager told her a scuffle had broken out, and all the kids had been ejected from the store. A frantic Reve had Adam paged to no avail, then contacted the police. She later conjectured he had been forced outside an unfamiliar exit and wandered off. On August 10, Adam's severed head was found floating in a drainage canal near Vero Beach. The rest of his body was never recovered. The coroner reported that he had died of asphyxiation.

A drifter, Ottis Toole, was questioned. He confessed that he had picked the boy up outside the Sears exit. He then drove the panicking child to a service road, strangled him, and decapitated him with a machete. Toole then recanted his story, and the police never charged him. Just before he died in prison, incarcerated for other crimes, Toole again confessed. But because he and confidant (and fellow serial killer) Henry Lee Lucas lied about their involvement in some 200 homicides, police discounted the story. The case was closed in 2008, with Toole named as the killer.

Aftermath

In 1984, the U.S. Congress passed the Missing Children's Assistance Act, in part due to the advocacy of John and Reve Walsh and parents of other missing children. In 1988, John Walsh became the creator and host of the popular TV reality show, *America's Most Wanted*. By the late 1990s, many malls and large stores had adopted a "Code Adam," locking down all exits if a child went missing.

CHILD MISSING

It's just
another headline.
Until it happens to your child.

Adam

Based on
the true story

The kidnapping case that shocked America...
and the courageous family that fought to survive it.

Starring
DANIEL J. TRAVANTI   JOBETH WILLIAMS
("HILL STREET BLUES")   ("POLTERGEIST")

3,40
4

BE THERE FOR THE
WORLD PREMIERE MOVIE!   **9PM**

*Show your support Monday: please drive with your headlights on
to symbolically light the way for America's missing children.*

Madeleine McCann Praia da Luz, Portugal

Few abductions generated worldwide press coverage like the disappearance of three-years-old Madeleine McCann, snatched from her bed in the Portuguese resort town of Praia da Luz on May 3, 2007. Her physician parents, Kate and Gerry McCann of Leicester, England, were on holiday with friends. They had left Madeleine and their twin toddlers alone in their Ocean Club apartment, while they dined at the resort's tapas restaurant, 180 feet away. During one of the frequent parental checks, Kate discovered Madeleine was missing and the locked shutters were broken open.

The rest of the story played out like a grim soap opera. Several sightings of men carrying a child came to naught. The lax police never alerted marine and border police and did no house-to-house searches, so a crack team from Leicester police was enlisted. Gerry McCann decided to "market" Madeleine to keep her in the public eye. Inevitably suspicion fell on the McCanns and even their friends. The tabloids subjected them to baseless allegations, and they

received damages from Express Newspapers. In 2008 the case was closed, then reopened in 2013. Madeleine remains missing.

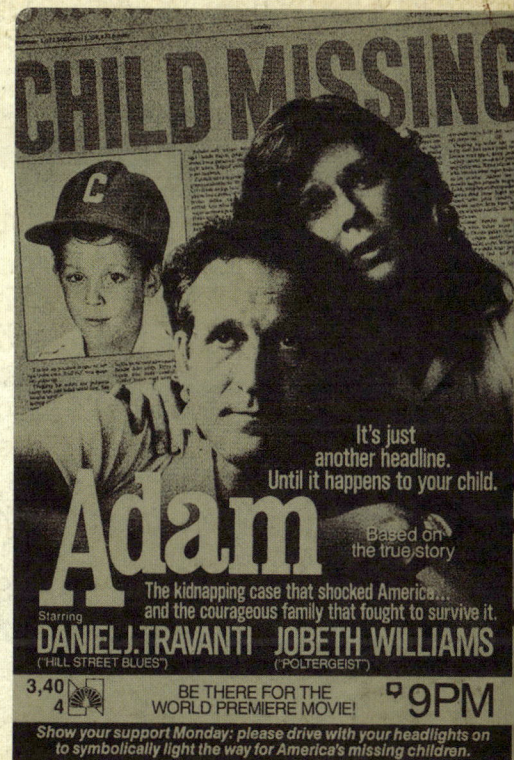

KEY STATS

After the TV film Adam was broadcast in 1983, 1984, and 1985, photos of missing children were shown to the millions of viewers. As a result, 13 of the 55 children were found and reunited with their loved ones.

A CLOSER LOOK

Adam's parents believed the Hollywood police botched their response to Adam's kidnapping. The police lost the bloodstained carpet from Toole's car, the bloody machete, and then the car itself.

Left: Maddie McCann, innocently enjoying the beach at the Portuguese resort of Praia da Luz, hours before she disappeared. **Top left:** Kate and Gerry McCann, Maddie's parents, prepare to commemorate what would have been Madeleine's 18th birthday; **Inset top right:** Press ad for *Adam*, the TV movie, which stimulated a nationwide effort to trace missing children.

"**Bank robbing is more of a sure thing than farming...**" ALLAN DARE PEARCE, AUTHOR

10 Chapter Ten

'THE BIG HEIST'

This is the theft that career criminals' dreams are made of—the fabulous score, the record-breaking boost, the ultimate payday— the one that enables a permanent retirement. Few ever achieve this elusive goal, and those who do did not operate alone. Major robberies require multiple accomplices and months, maybe years, of planning. But if everything goes like clockwork, the rewards can far outweigh the risks. At least until the police close in.

THE GREAT TRAIN ROBBERY

BRIDEGO RAILWAY BRIDGE, BUCKINGHAMSHIRE, ENGLAND
AUGUST 8, 1963

This train hijacking was among most famous thefts of the 20th century, in part due to its daring execution and also the way some of the robbers managed to stay ahead of the police. At least for a time. The robbery, which took place on the morning of August 8, 1963, focused on a Royal Mail train traveling from Glasgow to London on the West Coast Main Line.

The gang of 16, led by mastermind Bruce Reynolds, included Charlie Wilson, Buster Edwards, Gordon Goody, Roy James, John Daly, Jimmy White, Ronnie Biggs, Tommy Wisbey, Jim Hussey, Bob Welch, and Roger Cordrey, a signals expert, as well as three men known as 1, 2 and 3— Harry Smith, Danny Pembroke, and an unnamed retired train driver.

The thieves tampered with the signals to stop the train, then the men quickly boarded her. With information furnished by an insider called "the Ulsterman," they made directly for the second carriage behind the engine, the HVP, high-value package coach. Large quantities of money were carried here, usually in the range of £300,000, but because the previous weekend was a Bank Holiday weekend, the total take was between £2.5 and £3 million—valued today at well over $50 million.

With Reynolds disguised as a British Army officer, the robbers subdued the guards and removed all but eight of the 128 sacks from the HVP carriage, transferring them to their waiting army surplus truck by forming a human chain.

Roger Cordrey,
(signals expert)

Ronnie Biggs

Charlie Wilson

A CLOSER LOOK

A relatively minor member of the gang, Ronnie Biggs nevertheless achieved massive notoriety and even celebrity in Britain, when he escaped from Wandsworth Prison and fled to Paris, then Australia, with his share of the loot. By the late 1970s he was in Brazil and a regular in the British tabloids, passing his opinions on most subjects, and was famously visited by The Sex Pistols in 1978. After Johnny Rotten left the band, the remaining Pistols performed in *The Great Rock 'n' Roll Swindle* film with Biggs singing lead vocals on several tracks.

Bruce Reynold's son, Nick, was a member of the band Alabama 3, whose song "Woke Up This Morning" was the opening theme for the *The Sopranos* TV series.

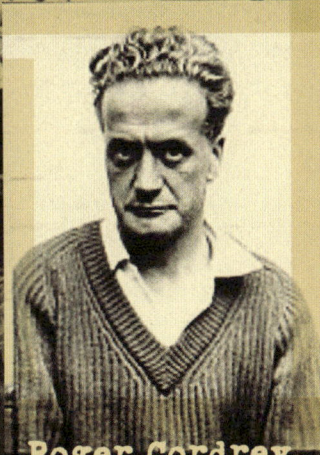

Although they used no firearms, the engineer, Jack Mills, was beaten over the head with a cosh.

The gang members then headed out along minor roadways in two military Land Rovers, each bearing the same license plate number, and drove back to their hideout, the run-down Leatherslade Farm. Fearing the police had gotten wind of their location, they dispersed in different cars and paid a local to burn the place down—which he failed to do. Following a tip-off from a herdsman, the police found Leatherslade Farm, but it furnished few clues except for the transport truck and the two Land Rovers.

At first the investigation did not go well for Scotland Yard, but then a convict offered to inform on the gang in return for a reduced sentence ... and he provided 18 names. This was

great news for Tommy Butler, the new head of the Met's robbery unit, the Flying Squad, and his six-man team. However, his predecessor, Earnest Millen, unwisely decided to publish photos of the thieves ... and most of them went to ground.

Eventually arrests were made, Roger Cordrey, the electronics expert, being the first. The majority of the other robbers and several assistants were all arrested. Meanwhile, Bruce Reynolds, still a free man, was "living it large" with his family in Mexico, where he was visited by Charlie Wilson—on the run after a prison escape—and Buster Edwards, who in 1966 turned himself in. Reynolds eventually moved back to England, where he was arrested in 1968. He served 10 years of a 25-year sentence.

Opposite, top left: The British Rail Class 40 Diesel Electric which hauled the train; **Opposite, top right:** Mastermind Bruce Reynolds; **Opposite left:** A rare aerial shot of the time, of the Great Train Robbers' hideout, Leatherslade Farm, near Aylesbury Vale, east of Oxford. It is some 56 miles north west of London; **This page, main image:** The now famous Bridego Bridge, with the loco reversed a little up the track from where the robbers left it. The steep bank to the left of the bridge is where the gang formed a human chain to pass the sacks of money out of the HVP and down into the waiting truck. The HVP carriage was kept by the police for evidence for seven years and then burned at a scrapyard in Norfolk in the presence of police and post office officials to thwart souvenir hunters. Another of the carriages is preserved at the Nene Valley Railway.

Members of organized crime are not the only ones who find it worthwhile to avail themselves of all the ready money, gold, and gems found in banks; a number of terrorist organizations have also helped fund their covert activities with stolen loot.

POLITICALLY MOTIVATED ROBBERIES
TERRORISTS AND MILITANTS

WANTED — Rita Darlene Brown and John William Sherman are being sought by Portland Federal Bureau of Investigation agents on charges of bank robbery. The pair, shown wearing wigs in FBI photos, are thought to be members of an organization that bombed two banks in suburban Seattle.

Above: FBI Wanted poster for Rita Brown and John Sherman of The George Jackson Brigade

The George Jackson Brigade
Seattle

Founded in the mid-1970s and lasting until around 1977, this revolutionary group was based in Seattle, Washington. It was named after George Jackson, a dissident prisoner and Black Panther member, who had been shot and killed during an alleged escape attempt at San Quentin Prison in 1971. The group combined members of the women's liberation movement, homosexuals, and Black prisoners and included both communists and anarchists. It advocated the use of force to overthrow the government of the United States and so engaged in a number of bombings and other attacks on governmental and business sites, as well as bank robberies over the years. After the death or imprisonment of most members, the group fell apart.

The British Bank of the Middle East Beirut

Sometimes robbers don't rely on well-thought-out plans to break into a bank. Sometimes they just use brute force to thrust their way inside. On January 20, 1976, a terrorist gang took advantage of the chaos occurring in war-torn Lebanon and robbed the British Bank of the Middle East in Beirut . . . by blasting a hole in a wall that the bank shared with the adjoining Catholic church. Supposedly several skilled Corsican locksmiths enabled the group to open the bank's vault and make off with from $20 million to $50 million in gold bars, mixed Lebanese and foreign currency, stocks, and jewels.

At first, international law enforcement remained uncertain about who was behind the robbery. It is currently attributed to Yasser Arafat's Palestine Liberation Organization, but earlier suspects included the Russian mob, Mossad (Israel's intelligence service), and the Irish Republican Army. Author Damien Lewis insisted he had evidence it was British SAS (Special Air Service) troopers, who were in search of documents of value to MI6—details of terrorist financial holdings. Somehow "in the confusion" the unit emptied the vault of its riches before heading back to base in Cyprus.

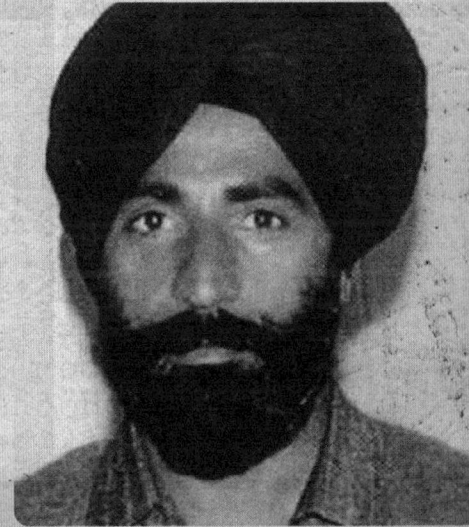

The Punjab National Bank
Ludhiana, India

The largest bank robbery in Indian history took place in February 1987, when militant Sikh leader Labh Singh (Sukhdev Singh Sukha), a former police officer, allegedly arranged a heist at the Millar Ganj branch of the bank in Ludhiana. Witness reports stated that 12 to 15 Sikhs dressed as policemen entered the bank carrying machine guns and rifles. It was described as a "neat operation" where no one was injured.

The thieves got away with 58 million rupees, or roughly US$4.5 million; a large portion of the money belonged to the Reserve Bank of India, the country's central bank. This doubtless allowed the Sikh terrorists to purchase sophisticated weapons.

Aryan Republican Army "Midwest Bank Bandits"

Members of the white nationalist Aryan Republican Army (ARA) were responsible for a series of 22 bank robberies in the Midwest from 1994 to 1996. To slow down any law enforcement who might pursue them, they often left behind fake explosive devices that appeared to need de-fusing. The group, which was fronted by Peter Kevin Langan, had connections to Neo-Nazism and allegedly conspired with convicted terrorist Timothy McVeigh before the Oklahoma City bombing. It is believed some of the robbery money was used to help fund the bombing, viewed as a response to the FBI attacks on Waco and Ruby Ridge. The gang was eventually arrested, and aside from two members who committed suicide by hanging, the others were sentenced to prison terms on a range of state and/or federal charges.

Top: Mugshots of members of the Aryan Republican Army, the Midwest Bank Bandits; **Top right:** Militant Sikh leader Labh Singh, who arranged the Punjab National Bank heist in Ludhiana; **Right:** The destroyed British Bank of the Middle East in Beirut.

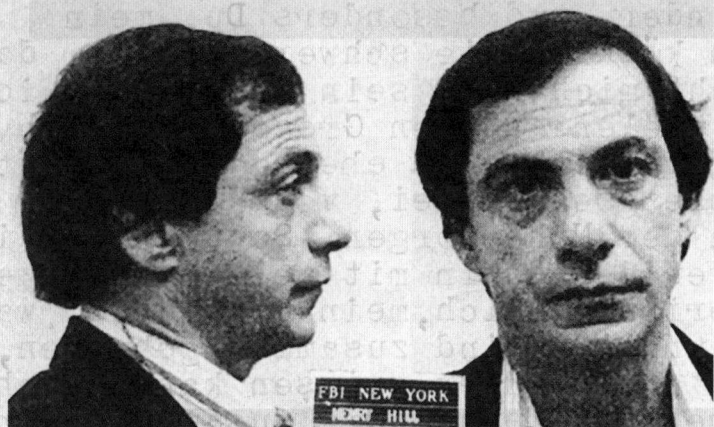

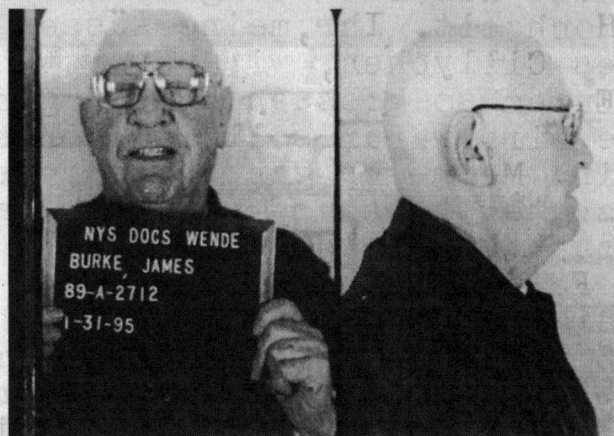

THE LUFTHANSA HEIST

Top left: Henry Hill mugshot. Hill heard about the movement of currency into the Lufthansa Cargo Terminal at Kennedy and discussed a possible heist with Jimmy "the gent" Burke **(top right); Above:** Tommy DeSimone, one of the heist gang members. The robbery was the subject of two TV films—*The 10 Million Dollar Getaway* (1991) and *The Big Heist* (2001)—and was a key plot element in Martin Scorsese's *Goodfellas* (1990). The three mobsters pictured here were portrayed in *Goodfellas* by Ray Liotta (Henry Hill), Robert De Niro (Jimmy Conway), and Joe Pesci (Tommy DeVito).

On December 11, 1978, a daring robbery took place at New York City's John F. Kennedy Airport, one that resulted in the largest cash haul up to that time in America. The theft was likely masterminded by crime boss Jimmy "the Gent" Burke, a member of the Lucchese crime family. Burke was never charged, however, possibly because he arranged the murder of people associated with the crime to prevent them from fingering him.

The theft was first conceived when Henry Hill, an associate of Burke's, heard from bookmaker Martin Krugman that the German airline Lufthansa flew currency into its cargo terminal at Kennedy Airport. Martin had learned this from airport workers Louis Werner—who owed him $20,000 in gambling debts—and Peter Gruenwald. The two had successfully stolen $22,000 in foreign currency from Lufthansa in 1976.

Burke handpicked his team of robbers—Tommy DeSimone, Angelo Sepe, Louis Cafora, Joe Manri, Paolo LiCastri, and Robert McMahon. Burke's son Frank was to drive a back-up vehicle; Parnell Edwards would dispose of the transport van later. They estimated a haul of around $2 million.

On December 11 at 3 a.m., a black Econoline van carrying the six men arrived at Lufthansa cargo building 261. A Buick sedan, the "crash car," waited in the parking lot nearby. Using bolt cutters, the team broke the padlock, entered the building and began collecting hostages—mostly workers who were on a meal break. Rudi Eirich, night shift cargo traffic manager, was forced at gunpoint to open the vault. The robbers then removed 72 15-pound cartons of untraceable money from the vault and carried them to the waiting van. Two gunmen then got into the van, while the rest piled into the Buick . . . and the two vehicles disappeared into the night. The entire theft took little more than an hour and netted the thieves a surprising $5.875 million. The hostages waited, as instructed, to sound an alarm, and so the Port Authority Police received their first call about the robbery at 4:30 a.m.

Meanwhile, the thieves drove to an auto repair shop in Canarsie, Brooklyn, where the cartons of cash were transferred to the trunks of two

other cars. The telltale van was meant to be driven by Parnell Edwards to a junkyard owned by mob capo John Gotti, where it was to be destroyed. Instead, Parnell left it parked outside his girlfriend's apartment, where the police impounded it two days later. DeSimone was ordered to kill Edwards for his lapse, which he and Sepe did, firing five bullets in his head. But the police had already lifted a number of fingerprints from the van that pointed to Burke's crew.

Alarmed by the subsequent police surveillance, Burke grew paranoid and arranged the murder of anyone who might implicate him in the crime:

- **Martin Krugman**—murdered by Burke and Sepe after nervous demands for his cut of the take made them suspect he might turn FBI informant.
- **Richard Eaton**—a con man tortured and

murdered by Burke for skimming heist money while it was being laundered. Burke was sent to prison for this murder, where he died in 1996.
- **Tony Monteleone**—club owner, associate of Easton, killed for skimming heist money.
- **Louis Cafora/Joanna Cafora**—Burke's former cellmate, a money launderer, bought his wife a gaudy pink Cadillac with heist money instead of lying low; both Caforas disappeared.
- **Joe "Buddha" Manri/Robert McMahon**—night shift supervisors for Air France, helped plan the Lufthansa heist; found dead in a car, shot execution-style.

Police surveillance yielded little in the way of real evidence, and so the only person actually convicted in relation to the robbery was airport worker Werner.

Main image: Kennedy International Airport in the 1970s, at the time of the Lufthansa Heist; **Above, from left:** Director Martin Scorsese, Joe Pesci, Ray Liotta, and Robert De Niro on the set of *Goodfellas*.

The most obvious problem with stealing famous works of art is that the thief—or the "client" they sell to—can't ever display them in public. But that hasn't stopped a number of famous paintings from being taken. Sadly, some have never been recovered and possibly now reside in private vaults where only their lawbreaking owners can gaze upon them.

STEALING MASTERPIECES

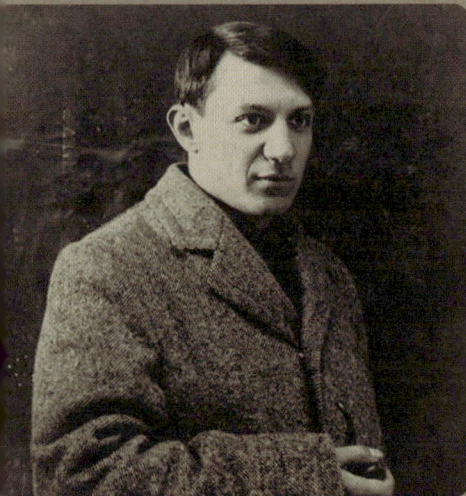

> "Remember, for practically every piece of stolen art, a murder was committed...." RONALD S. LAUDER, WORLD JEWISH CONGRESS PRESIDENT, SPEAKING ON NAZI PLUNDER

The Last Judgment Gdansk, Poland

The first documented art heist of the modern era was of a 15th-century triptych by Dutch artist Hans Memling. The work was on a ship bound for Florence, when it was stolen by Paul Beneke, a Polish privateer. The altarpiece was placed in the Basilica of the Assumption in Gdansk, Poland, and it remains there today in that city's national museum.

Mona Lisa Paris, France

Arguably the most famous painting in the world, Leonardo de Vinci's portrait of a mysterious-looking, bemused woman had a place of honor in the Louvre Museum in Paris. Then on August 21, 1911, an amateur painter busily set up his easel near the spot where the painting hung, but when he looked up, he realized *La Giaconda* was not there. Someone had stolen her. For more than two years French detectives searched for the priceless painting, even questioning poet Guillame Apollinaire and artist Pablo Picasso about the missing masterpiece. It was not until December 1913 that an Italian house painter contacted a well-known Florentine art dealer, claiming to have the portrait. After police arrested Vincenzo Peruggia, the former Louvre employee explained he had walked into the museum, removed the Mona Lisa from its frame, and hid it under his clothing before exiting. Hailed as a patriot in his native Italy for wanting to return the painting to its homeland, he served only six months for the crime.

The Scream Oslo, Norway

This expressionistic painting of a man clasping his face and crying out in anguish is another immediately recognizable work of art. Norwegian artist Edvard Munch created

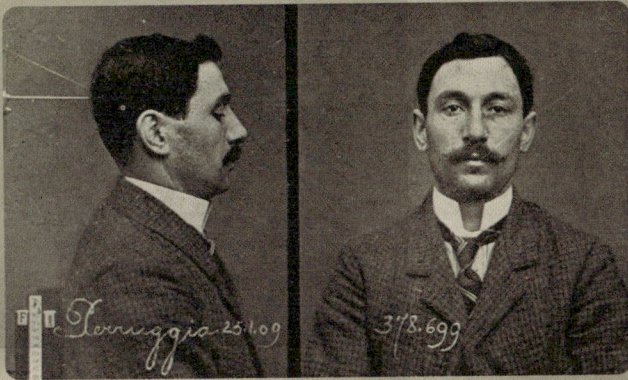

Opposite, top: *The Last Judgment* by Hans Memling; **Above:** Leonardo Da Vinci's *La Giaconda*, the *Mona Lisa*; **Opposite page center:** Pablo Picasso in the early 1900s; **Opposite page bottom:** Guillame Apollinaire (right) and his counsel, during the stolen *Mona Lisa* affair of 1911; **Left:** The Italian Vincenzo Peruggia, eventually unmasked as the man who stole the Mona Lisa; **Above right:** Peruggia returned the painting to the Uffizi Gallery in Florence.

several iterations of it, two of which have been stolen. In February 1994, four men broke into the National Art Museum in Oslo, stole their version, and left a note that said, "Thanks for the poor security." Fortunately, a sting operation three months later recovered the work. Then in August 2004, two masked robbers held tourists and staff at gunpoint in Oslo's Munch Museum, and yanked another version of *The Scream*—along with Munch's *The Madonna*—off the gallery wall. Norwegian police nabbed the thieves and recovered the paintings in 2006, but both had sustained tears and water damage.

Isabella Stewart Gardner Museum Boston, Massachusetts

On March 18, 1990, one of the biggest art thefts in history took place at the former home of a major collector. During Boston's St. Patrick's Day parade, two thieves dressed as police officers entered the Boston museum, telling guards they were looking into a disturbance. They carried off 13 paintings, including works by Rembrandt, Vermeer, and Manet. In spite of a $5 million reward and a massive FBI investigation, nothing has been recovered.

Plundering Europe's Heritage

From 1933 to 1945, both before and during World War II, the Nazis confiscated or looted an estimated 20 percent of Europe's art heritage—paintings, sculptures, jewelry, religious and decorative objects—treasures either owned by Jews or found in the museums of Nazi-occupied cities. Hitler, a failed painter, intended to amass an incomparable collection for the unrealized Führermuseum in his hometown of Linz, Austria. The Allies created the Monuments, Fine Arts, and Archives program to track down, retrieve, and safeguard much of this lost art. Some notable masterworks, such as the exquisite Amber Room stolen from Russia's Catherine Palace, were never found.

THE BRINK'S-MAT BREAK-IN
BULLION GALORE

This high-profile robbery took place on November 26, 1983, at 6:40 a.m. at the Brink's-Mat warehouse on the Heathrow International Trading Estate, close to the airport in West London. The thieves, a South London gang of six armed robbers, headed by Brian Robinson and Mickey McAvoy, gained entry from security guard Anthony Black. Inside the warehouse, they rounded up the staff, poured gasoline over them, and threatened to ignite them if they did not reveal the combination to the safe.

The gang had estimated a take of around **£3.2 million, but within the vault they** found 98,000 troy ounces of gold bullion. They ended up making off with £26 million in gold, diamonds, and cash. The bullion had been the property of Johnson Matthey Bankers Ltd, which collapsed the next year due to large loans made to fraudulent firms.

Several days later a couple in Bath noticed a white-hot crucible in a neighbor's garden hut and alerted the police. The property was just

beyond their jurisdiction ... and they never followed up on it. A year later the property was raided, and the owner, jeweler and bullion dealer Robert Palmer, said he had no idea the gold was stolen property. Robinson was fingered by his brother-in-law, Anthony Black ... whose family connection to Robinson was also soon discovered. Black confessed to giving the robbers a key and details of the security systems.

Mickey McAvoy had entrusted part of his share to associates Brian Perry and George Francis. Perry brought in gold expert Kenneth Noye to melt down the bullion and recast it in order to make it salable, mixing in copper coins to disguise its origins. But when large sums of money began moving through a Bristol bank, the Bank of England grew concerned and contacted the police. Noye was placed under surveillance, and actually killed a police officer who was in his garden ... yet was not convicted of the crime. Eventually McAvoy was captured and sentenced at the Old Bailey to 25 years; Black received six years. Noye, the gold pro, was heavily fined as a conspirator and given 14 years.

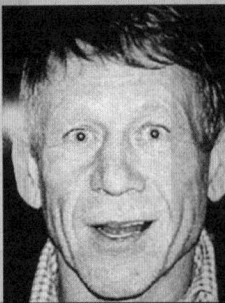

Brian Perry   George Francis   John "Goldfinger" Palmer   Charlie Wilson   Donald Urquhart   Solly Nahome

A CURSED CRIME

There is a well-founded belief that the gold cursed the robbers because so many people related to the theft met untimely ends. It's possible that the London underworld arranged these deaths to cover their involvement in laundering the gold.

▪ **In 1990,** the former treasurer of the Great Train Robbery, Charlie Wilson, was living in Marbella, Spain, and possibly engaged in drug smuggling. After agreeing to launder some of the proceeds from the Brink's-Mat robbery, he lost the investors £3 million and on April 23, 1990, was shot dead.

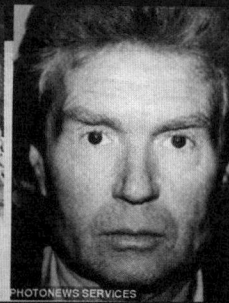

▪ **Donald Urquhart,** another one of the launderers, was shot dead in January 1993 in Central London. Informant Kenneth Regan assisted police with information about Urquhart's murder. Graeme West was subsequently jailed for the killing, as was accomplice Geoffrey Heath who planned it.

▪ **Hatton Garden** jeweler Solly Nahome was shot dead outside his home on December 5, 1998. Nahome's associate, jeweler Gilbert Wynter, had earlier disappeared on March 9. It was thought they were murdered over the disappearance of £800,000, most probably from a cannabis deal.

▪ **In mid-2001,** robber Brian Perry was shot dead.

▪ **On May 14,** 2003, robber George Francis was shot dead by John O'Flynn outside Francis's courier business in Bermondsey. Francis, a Kray associate, was probably also involved in the gold laundering.

▪ **On June 24, 2015,** John "Goldfinger" Palmer was shot dead.

Opposite page top: The Heathrow International Trading Estate, located by the airport, stores freight going to all points around the globe; **Opposite page center:** The two leaders of the gang: Brian Robinson (left), and Mickey McAvoy. **Opposite bottom and this page top:** Police seal off the Brink's-Mat warehouse after the robbery was discovered. In spite of the police nabbing the key suspects, the bulk of the stolen gold was never recovered; **Above:** A cursed crime: the six villains shot dead in the aftermath.

THE KNIGHTSBRIDGE SECURITY DEPOSIT ROBBERY

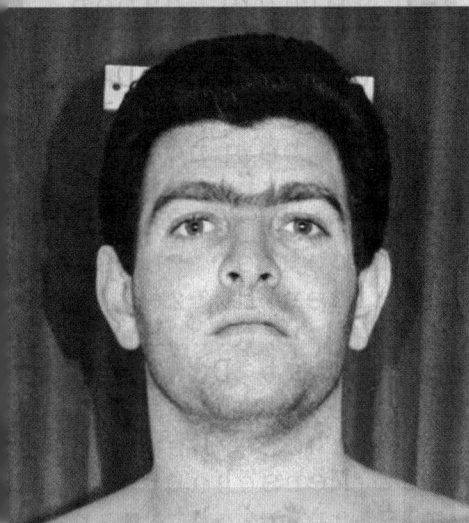

Top: Knightsbridge in the 1980s; **Above:** International playboy and career criminal, Valerio Viccei; **Opposite, main image and inset:** The robbed safe deposit center in Knightsbridge, after the robbery. Although the Knightsbridge theft netted from £40 to £60 million, only £10 million of it was ever recovered; **Opposite, far right:** Valerio Viccei wrote two autobiographies, *Too Fast to Live*, from 1992, and *Live by the Gun, Die by the Gun*, which was published posthumously in 2004.

The Knightsbridge Security Deposit theft occurred in London on July 12, 1987. The robbers were led by the colorful international playboy and career criminal, Valerio Viccei. The son of an Italian lawyer, Viccei had dabbled in Neofascism and political bombings before becoming a thief. And what a thief he was! When he traveled to London in 1986, he was being sought in Italy for 54 armed robberies.

Once in England, Viccei renewed his criminal activities, mainly to finance his glamorous lifestyle, which included driving fast cars and seducing beautiful women. He enjoyed nicknames like the Wolf and the Italian Stallion. He modeled himself on Al Pacino's role in the movie *Scarface*, with his gold machine gun keychain and his designer accessories. He was often quoted as saying, "I always wanted to reach something that was top of its field." Unfortunately, the things he reached for usually belonged to someone else.

For the Knightsbridge job, he arranged inside help from the managing director, Parvez Latif, a cocaine addict who was deeply in debt. On the day of the theft, two men simply walked into the safe deposit center and said they wanted to rent a box. They were shown to the vault, where they pulled out handguns and restrained the manager and security guards. To avoid any interruptions, they placed a "Closed" sign on the door, then let in their additional accomplices. After breaking into 114 safe deposit boxes with metal cutting equipment, they fled with money and goods worth between £40 and £60 million. The victims of the theft were members of royalty, celebrities, millionaires, and criminals. At least no shots were fired, and no one was injured.

A Bloody Fingerprint

When the shift changed an hour later, the incoming staff discovered the robbery and contacted the police. Forensics identified a bloody fingerprint that traced back to Valerio Viccei. The police set up surveillance, and the accomplices were captured during a series of raids in August. Viccei, who had fled to South America, eventually returned to England to arrange shipment of his Ferrari Testarossa to his new home. The police, who had been alerted to his presence in England, set up a roadblock and

VALERIO VICCEI
TOO FAST TO LIVE

The Life and Death of Millionaire Gunman Valerio Viccei

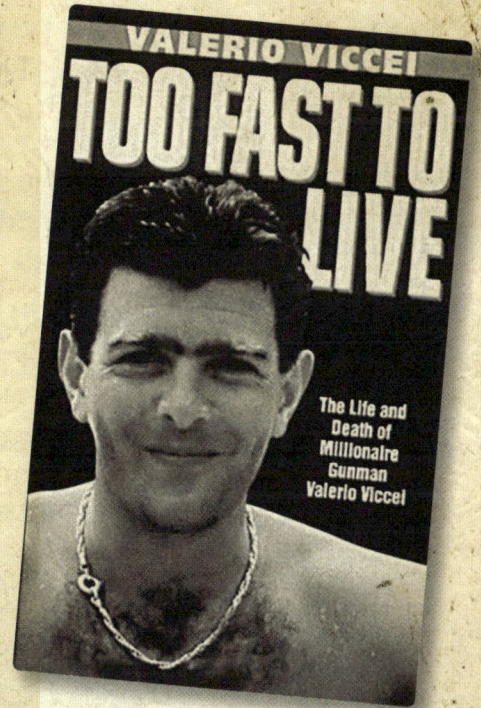

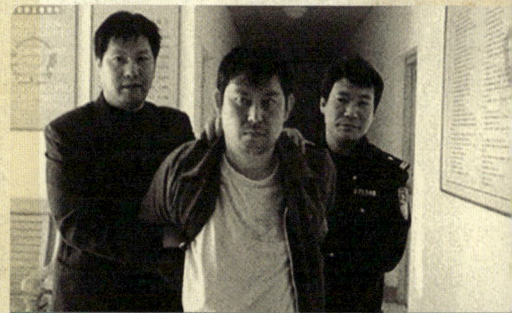

ANOTHER INSIDE JOB

In the fall of 2006, bank vault manager Ren Xiaofeng of the Agricultural Bank of China "borrowed" money to buy lottery tickets. He finally won enough to replace the money, but instead bought many more tickets, to the tune of $6.7 million, enlisting another manager, Ma Xiangjing, to help move two tons of currency. He never won enough again to replace the money and the men were eventually caught . . . and executed due to China's harsh penal code. Poor Ren had even helpfully offered security suggestions to banks, like counting the money in the vault occasionally or watching surveillance footage.

apprehended him by smashing in his windshield and dragging him from the car.

Viccei was sentenced to 22 years in Parkhurst Prison on the Isle of Wight. He eventually formed a friendship with Flying Squad member Dick Leach, who had led the arresting officers, and the two often corresponded over the years. In 1992, Viccei was deported to Italy to finish serving his sentence. Now in an "open" jail,

he could again pursue his lavish lifestyle and even run a translation company, providing he returned to prison each night. During a day release in April 2000, he and an accomplice became involved in a gun battle with two traffic cops while planning either a robbery or kidnapping, and Viccei was killed by submachine gun fire. The flamboyant thief was only 45.

During the first decade of the new millennium, the Middle Eastern country of Iraq came under attack from America and her allies. War had been declared based on reports that dictator and strongman Saddam Hussein had mobile labs where weapons of mass destruction—including nuclear, biological, and chemical weapons—were being manufactured. Furthermore, Iraq was considered a haven for terrorists, including members of al-Qaeda, the group behind the attacks of 9/11.

TARGETING IRAQ—TWICE

Two major bank heists took place during the conflict, perhaps because, as the Nazis had learned in World War II, it was much easier to steal enormous amounts of money during a time of war than during a period of peace.

Above: Qusay Hussein, Saddam's second son and the man responsible for the largest bank heist in history.

The Central Bank of Iraq

On March 20, 2003, the United States declared war on Iraq. On the morning of March 18, a day before American cruise missiles would begin battering Baghdad, three large trucks pulled up in front of the Central Bank of Iraq. An endless stream of metal boxes was carried from the bank's vaults and loaded into the trucks. But this was no break-in; these "robbers" had presented a handwritten note to the bank's governor explaining that the removal was to prevent the money from falling into enemy hands. The note was signed by Saddam Hussein himself, and it was delivered to the bank by his son (and heir), Qusay Hussein. Saddam had the larcenous notion he could loot his country's cash reserves, more than $920 million, mostly in US currency, in what became the largest bank heist in history.

During subsequent US military raids much of the money was recovered, including hundreds of aluminum boxes found in one of Saddam's palaces, each containing $4 million. The money was transferred to Kuwait where a group of American soldiers was recruited to count the cash—enormous piles of $100 and €100 bills. Some soldiers gave in to temptation and pocketed hundreds of thousands of dollars. In all, 35 service members were caught and convicted of theft.

The Dar Es Salaam Bank

Iraq was the site of yet another major heist in 2007, when $282 million was stolen from the Dar Es Salaam Bank, a private institution in Baghdad and one of the largest commercial banks in the country. It was later confirmed that the money was American dollars, though why an

A CLOSER LOOK

When US forces found $650 million dollars hidden behind a false wall in the palace of Saddam's son, Uday Hussein, they believed it was from the Central Bank robbery. But it turned out to be Uday's own "private stash." A shocking example of a dictator's embezzlement of national wealth.

Iraqi bank should be holding so much US currency was never explained. The details of the crime remained sketchy; basically two, possibly three, bank guards carried out the robbery and then used their contacts within local police force and the militia in order to pass through checkpoints across the war-torn city. At that time in Baghdad, chaos and carnage reigned supreme: eighteen residents of the city were murdered on the day of the heist. The robbers clearly took advantage of all the disruption to escape detection. When the bank staff came to work the next morning, they found the front doors unlocked, the vault open, and the guards, who normally slept at the bank, missing. The Interior Ministry and the Finance Ministry immediately set up a committee to investigate the theft. Alas, no information came forth about the robbers or the fate of the money, and the culprits were never caught.

Main image: The Central Bank of Iraq. Built in 1983, it had practically no windows. The only way in and out was through the front door; **Above:** US soldiers with the recovered stolen Iraqi treasure; **Inset:** Uday Hussein (left), Saddam's eldest son. Saddam Hussein, the absolute and despotic ruler of Iraq, (center). Qusay Hussein (right), Saddam's second son, and heir apparent.

HOSTAGE-BASED HEISTS

The perpetrators of these two headline-making bank robberies employed a very similar *modus operandi*, or MO—coerce a bank supervisor or key employee to cooperate with the robbers by threatening their family with harm. The Northern Bank theft set the record for the most money stolen in the UK ... until that amount was supplanted by the Securitas heist.

THE NORTHERN BANK ROBBERY

Above: Chris Ward, the Northern Bank employee who was kidnapped along with his supervisor, Kevin McCullen. Unless they cooperated with the robbery, both their families would have been harmed. Ward was actually tried for conspiracy but acquitted.

In 2004, the Northern Bank, now the Danske Bank, was the largest retail bank in Northern Ireland, with headquarters located in Belfast's Donegall Square West. It was one of only four banks in the UK allowed to print its own banknotes, producing notes in denominations of £5, £10, £20, £50, and £100.

On the night of December 19, two bank employees, Chris Ward and his supervisor Kevin McMullen, were kidnapped by armed men. Gunmen remained at Ward's home with his family, while McMullen's wife was taken to an undisclosed location. Both men were told to go to work the next day, as normal, and informed they would receive further instructions by cell phone. The next day McMullen was ordered to bring £1 million in a bag to a bus stop and pass it to one of the gang. That dry run went perfectly, so the robbers returned that night and forced Ward and McMullen to open the vaults ... threatening that their wives would be killed otherwise. The

gang loaded crates of bank notes onto trolleys and placed them in a white van. It took multiple trips to carry away their takings. They ended up stealing £26.5 million, much of it in uncirculated Northern Bank currency.

The police quickly assigned 50 detectives to the case. Assistant Chief Constable Sam Kincaid observed of the robbery, "This was not a lucky crime, this was a well-organized crime." Soon after the robbery, The Northern Bank announced it would replace its £10, £20, £50 and £100 notes with new versions in different colors, with new logos and altered serial numbers. This new look meant that the stolen, uncirculated banknotes would be hard to spend without sparking suspicion.

A Fruitless Investigation

The hunt for the robbers went on for weeks, and then months, without any real results. The police began to suspect the Provisional Irish Republican Army was behind the theft. On

January 5, 2007, Hugh Orde, Chief Constable of the Police Service of Northern Ireland, officially blamed them for organizing the robbery. Both the IRA and Sinn Féin, the Irish republican and democratic socialist party, denied any involvement, but many people continued to believe the IRA guilty. The controversy even imperiled the delicate multiparty peace talks that were taking place in the strife-torn country.

A number of people were arrested in connection to the theft of the money, but no one was convicted. Chris Ward, one of the bank employees who was coerced, went on trial as a possible "inside man" but was acquitted. The only person jailed over the crime was Cork resident Ted Cunningham, a financial advisor found guilty on ten counts of money laundering after the discovery of roughly £3 million in his possession that traced back to the robbery. Otherwise, the mystery of who or what was behind the theft continues to thwart investigators.

Main image: The Northern Bank in Belfast's Donegall Square West (now the Danske Bank); **Above:** Sir Hugh Orde, Chief Constable of the Police Service of Northern Ireland. He laid the blame for the robbery squarely at the feet of the Provisional IRA, though both the IRA and Sinn Féin strenuously denied their involvement.

HOSTAGE-BASED HEISTS
THE SECURITAS DEPOT ROBBERY

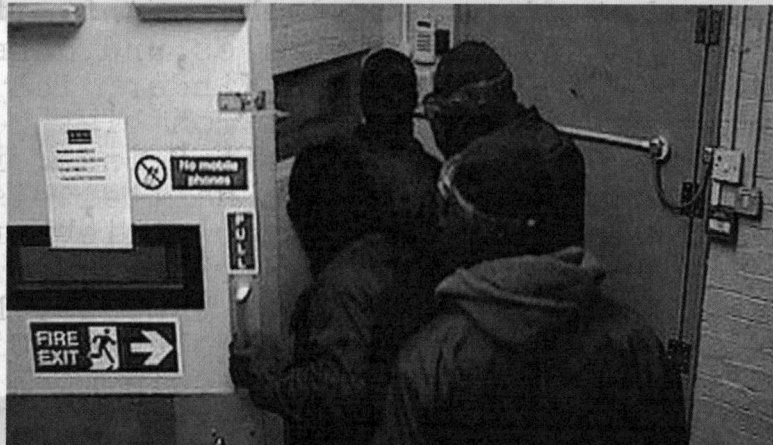

Above: The Herne Bay home, on the Kent coast, of Securitas Depot manager Colin Dixon and his family; **Center sequence, from left:** The Securitas Depot in Tonbridge, The gang enters the Depot; the CCTV cameras about to be turned off, the staff are held at gunpoint, removing the cash; **Opposite, bottom:** Six of the convicted men from top row, left: Ex-cage fighter and mastermind Lee Murray, Lea Rusha, Stuart Royle, bottom row from left, Roger Coutts, Emir Hysenaj, and Jetmir Bucpapa.

The Securitas Depot robbery, the UK's largest cash robbery up to that time, took place in Tonbridge, Kent, England, on February 22, 2006. It began with the kidnapping of the depot manager and his family on February 21. Colin Dixon was driving near Maidstone in Kent when he was pulled over by what he thought was an unmarked police car. Dixon was ordered into the other car, placed in handcuffs, and taken to a farm in Staplehurst. His wife and eight-year-old son were also abducted from their home in Herne Bay by men dressed in police uniforms and taken to the farm as well. Dixon was told that if he failed to cooperate with the gang, he and his family would be harmed.

The next day they drove Dixon and his family to the Securitas location and, under duress, he let them inside. The gang, wearing balaclavas and body armor, then entered the depot carrying assault rifles and a Skorpion submachine gun. They forced employees to open the gates, allowing entry to their Renault truck and other vehicles. After tying up the Dixon family and 14 staff members and locking them in cash cages, the gang collected more than £53 million in used and unused Bank of England sterling banknotes and placed them in the truck; they ended up leaving behind another £154 million for lack of room. The next day a reward of £2 million was broadcast for any information regarding the robbery, the largest reward ever offered in the UK.

Closing the Net

Within the next week most of the getaway vehicles were found, one still containing £1.3 million in notes and several arrests were made; by June 2006, more than 30 people had been arrested, and a police raid at a car yard in Welling yielded another £7 million in banknotes. Held in London's Old Bailey, the trial of the eight key players began on June 26, 2007. These included inside man Emir Hysenaj, an Albanian who worked at the depot. Michelle Hogg, who had made prosthetic disguises for the men, turned Queen's evidence and implicated the other conspirators in exchange for her charges being reduced. On January 28, the jury returned guilty verdicts on Stuart Royle, Jetmir Bucpapa, Roger Coutts, Lea Rusha, and Emir Hysenaj; sentences ranged from 20 years for Hysenaj and life for the others, with a minimum time served of 10 and 15 years respectively. Charges were dropped against a number of people who had only peripheral involvement in the robbery.

Lee Murray, a former cage fighter and the purported mastermind, was arrested in Morocco and eventually jailed there, receiving a sentence of ten, then 25 years. Murray had incriminated himself, leaving an accidental recording about the robbery on his cell phone, which was left behind at the site of a car crash just before the heist.

Keyinde "Kane" Patterson, likely a key player in the robbery, is thought to be residing in the West Indies, living well off the stolen money. In February 2013, Malcolm Constable, also possibly associated with the robbery, was found dead of a self-inflicted shotgun wound. As of 2016, £32 million of the Depot's money had not been recovered.

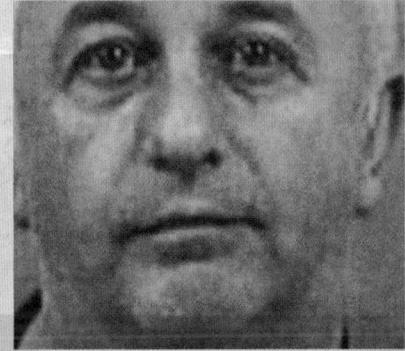

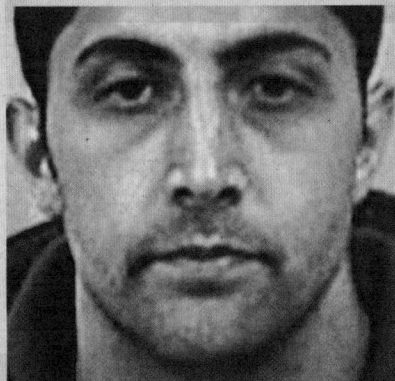

GOING UNDERGROUND
THE BANCO CENTRAL

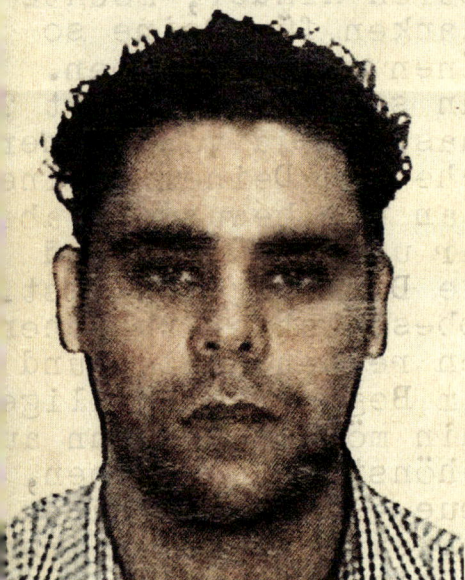

Above: Luis Fernando Ribeiro, one of the likely leaders of the gang that carried out the Banco Central heist. Ribeiro was destined not to enjoy his ill-gotten gains though. He was kidnapped, and despite his family paying the ransom, Ribeiro was shot to death. Local police were suspected of the assassination; **Opposite, main image:** The Banco Central do Brasil building in Fortaleza; **Far right, top and center:** Police discover the entrance to the tunnel which extended two city blocks and ended directly under the bank vault.

On Saturday, August 6, 2005, a determined group of burglars tunneled into the vault in of the Banco Central in Fortaleza, the state capital of Ceará in northeastern Brazil. Once inside, they stole five containers of 50-*real* notes valued at the equivalent of 71.6 million US dollars and weighing more than three tons.

The Banco Central is the bank charged with controlling the country's money supply. Because the insurance premiums would have been so high, the bank managers had chosen not to insure the money in the containers. The burglars were able to override the bank's alarms and sensors and, since no alarms were raised, the banking staff did not discover the theft until the bank opened again on Monday.

The burglars had been particularly clever, and their plan was well thought out. Three months before the robbery they rented a property in the center of the city, advertising themselves as a landscaping and gardening service. When van-loads of dirt were seen being carted from the business, their commercial neighbors thought nothing of it. Meanwhile, the group of six to 10 men was creating a tunnel 13 feet deep and 256 feet long, that extended for two city blocks and ended directly under the bank vault. The tunnel was lined with plastic and even had its own lighting and air-circulation systems. On the weekend of August 6, the gang succeeded in drilling through more than three feet of steel-reinforced concrete and entered the vault. Because the bank was closed, they had plenty of time to move all that money through the 2.5-foot-square tunnel.

Identifying the Gang

At the now-abandoned landscaping company, police located a pick-up truck marked *Grama Sintética* (Synthetic Turf) that still held many of the tools the thieves had used. Inside the rented space, the gang had used burnt lime to obscure their fingerprints. The Brazilian Federal Police also began investigating a connection between the thieves and car resellers in Fortaleza. On August 20, 2005, likely acting on a tip, they arrested two men driving a car-carrier. The three pick-up trucks being transported proved to contain more than R$2.13 million of

stolen currency. Another five men were arrested in late September with more than R$5 million of the money. They confessed that they had helped dig the tunnel. Apparently, they revealed, the gang leaders had tried to charter a plane to get their crew and the money out of the country, but were not successful.

In October 2005, one of the leaders, Luis Fernando Ribeiro, 26, was found outside Rio de Janiero handcuffed and shot to death. The police were sure the crime was a result of the robbery. His family admitted he had been kidnapped. They said they paid the R$900,000 ransom, but Ribeiro was not released. Local police were suspected of the murder, and three were arrested. At least another six robbery-related kidnappings occurred, and all ransoms were paid. Altogether, the police arrested 54 suspects, but only R$20 million of the money has been recovered.

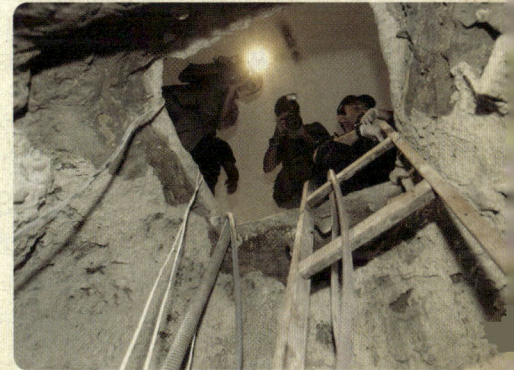

A CLOSER LOOK

In legal terminology, bank robbery is the act of entering an open bank and extracting money by force or threat of force, while burglary constitutes breaking into a closed bank. Although bank "jobs" remained common from the late 18th to the late 20th century, the evolution of modern anti-robbery technology—exploding dye packs, security cameras, and silent alarms—has made it increasingly difficult for criminals to rob a bank and get away with it.

"I was extremely greedy and lost my moral compass." ANDREW FASTOW, ENRON CFO

Con Men and White-Collar CRIMINALS

Confidence men, or con artists, prey on our natural tendency to trust others. Even savvy business professionals can get lured into confidence schemes by sharp operators. "Who would buy the Eiffel Tower or purchase bonds from a fake country?" you ask. Plenty would, it turns out. White collar thieves are a type of con man: they create a bond of faith with their customers, clients, or companies, then take them, as the saying goes, "to the cleaners."

IVAR KREUGER
THE MATCH KING

Top: Ivar Kreuger, around 1920; **Above:** Kreuger photographed on his transatlantic crossing to America in the spring of 1930.

At the peak of the "roaring twenties," a wealthy Swedish financier with ties to the match industry offered loans to countries still suffering the effects of World War I. In return he received "matchstick monopolies"—the sole right to sell or manufacture matches in those countries. He was lauded as one of the few success stories during the early years of the Great Depression.

The son of an industrialist in the match industry of Kalmar, Sweden, Ivar was a bright boy who skipped two grades and entered Stockholm's Royal Institute of Technology at 16. He graduated at 20 with combined master's degrees in civil and mechanical engineering and then spent seven years abroad working as a civil engineer and visiting different countries, including the US. In South Africa he encountered the patented Kahn System for concrete-steel constructions, a new technique not yet introduced to Sweden. Kreuger obtained the representative rights for the system for the Swedish and German markets and then formed two construction firms: Kreuger and Toll in his

homeland and Deutsche Kahneisengesellschaft in Germany. His Swedish firm eventually won several desirable contracts—the Stockholm Olympic Stadium, foundation work for the Stockholm City Hall, and the NK department store. The firm was the first in Europe to commit to finishing a building by a fixed date and was so prompt they received completion bonuses on every project.

While Kreuger took an interest in his father's match factories, his main focus was creating new companies or getting control of existing ones. By 1929 his fortune was estimated at $100 billion in modern dollars; he owned banks, mining companies, railways, timber and paper firms, and film companies. He had apartments in Stockholm, New York, Paris, and Stockholm, and a summer house on a Swedish island. He never married, but maintained an open-minded relationship with Ingeborg Hässler, a physical therapist.

In spring of 1930 he again visited the US, lecturing on world economics at the Industrial Club of Chicago and meeting with President Hoover. But by then Kreuger had

KREUGER'S FINANCIAL INNOVATIONS

Ivar created the playbook on innovative financial products meant to support businesses or retain control of them, yet many were precursors to the financial instruments currently undermining today's markets.

Dual class stock ownership: Stocks were separated into A shares, with full voting power, and B Shares, with greatly reduced voting power.

Convertible gold debentures: These securities were not secured by physical collateral or assets. They typically matured in 20 years and could be converted to shares in International Match.

American depository receipts: This combo of bond, preferred stock, and profit-sharing option allowed investors exposure to foreign companies paying dividends of 25% . . . and backed by large loans to their government.

Off balance sheet entities: Here, a parent company's financial statements do not include details of certain enterprises. Recently, this practice helped speed the demise of Enron, Bear Stearns, and Lehman Brothers.

grown reckless, speculating with the funds from the companies he controlled. He began introducing questionable practices—using shell corporations in tax havens, fudging accounting figures, even resorting to forgery. By 1931 rumors were spreading through Europe that Kreuger's empire was shaky. While in Paris preparing for a meeting in Berlin, he took his own life with a pistol. In a note to a colleague he wrote: "I have made such a mess of things . . ." His death revealed the dark, and surprisingly crooked, underside of this financial genius. After the Kreuger Crash, his empire crumbled, leaving millions bankrupt, especially in the US and Sweden.

Top and above left: The Stockholm Olympic Stadium, Sweden, built using new construction techniques by Kreuger & Toll for the 1912 Olympic Games; **Center:** Villagatan No. 13A & 13B, Kreuger's apartment in Stockholm; **Above:** Panic followed the Wall Street Crash of 1929 and Kreuger's debts were called in. By 1931 his financial Tower of Babel was on the point of collapse, and he shot himself. After his death, his empire was swiftly taken over. His family maintained that he had been killed; his brother Torsten even wrote a book on the subject. As more documents from the case have come to light, other researchers now support the claim.

"PSST, BUDDY, WANNA BUY

"There's a sucker born every minute." Those words were attributed to American showman P.T. Barnum, and he likely wasn't confining himself to the citizens of the US.

People around the world have proven surprisingly easy to hornswoggle. The mark's greed, or the yen for easy money is often at the root of a swindle, and it makes the job of real estate tricksters a lot easier.

Most swindlers operate from a similar playbook, utilizing the same human weaknesses: they exploit the need to feel part of a group, they falsely advertise exclusivity and scarcity, and they pretend to fill in knowledge gaps. Some even resort to intimidation and force.

Above: George C. Parker, "the greatest con man in American history," who was such a cultural icon that the phrase "If you believe that, I have a bridge to sell you," became the go-to expression for indicating gullibility; **Main Image:** The Brooklyn Bridge at night, with the Manhattan skyline behind.

George C. Parker New York City

George C. Parker, sometimes called the "greatest con man in American history," was a native New Yorker of Irish descent who operated at the turn of the 20th century. He was infamous for repeatedly selling New York landmarks like the Brooklyn Bridge, Madison Square Garden, Grant's Tomb, and the Statue of Liberty. He sometimes sold the bridge twice a week, and one time raked in $50,000. New "owners," typically recent immigrants, were known to set up their own toll booths in the middle of the bridge—until removed by the police. Parker was eventually caught, convicted, and sentenced to life in Sing-Sing . . . where he died in 1936. One wonders if he ever tried to "sell" the prison to any of the guards.

THE GREAT EAST RIVER SUSPENSION BRIDGE.

A BRIDGE?"

THE MYSTIQUE OF THE BRIDGE

The Brooklyn Bridge is a graceful steel-wire suspension bridge that spans the East River, connecting Manhattan to her sister borough. Engineering and construction were overseen by John Augustus Roebling; his son, Washington Augustus; and Washington's wife Emily Warren Roebling. Composed of limestone and granite, the two massive Gothic revival towers stood 278 feet tall. The steel cables that suspended the bridge, however, were supplied by a swindler—J. Lloyd Haigh—who mixed inferior wire with the higher grade. Roebling did not find out until the cables were spun, so to make them safe, he added extra wire to each cable. When the Brooklyn Bridge was completed in 1883, it was a structure of such monumental scale that it earned instant public adulation. Over the years it became a cherished part of the New York City landscape, not only for its history but for its enduring beauty.

William McCloundy Asbury Park, New Jersey

William McCloundy was an early 20th century con man. He often impersonated men of stature—the captain of an ocean liner and a prison warden. Known as I.O.U. O'Brien by the police, he served a two-and-half-year sentence at Sing Sing for convincing a tourist to buy the Brooklyn Bridge in 1901.

Victor Lustig

Victor Lustig, who operated during the 1920s, was born in Austria-Hungary (modern Czech Republic). A gifted young man, he took to gambling before he'd even turned 20. Using his skill with languages to bilk the public, his cons soon gained him money and property. He especially liked plucking wealthy pigeons during transatlantic crossings on luxury ocean liners, sometimes posing as a theatrical producer seeking backers for a non-existent Broadway musical.

In 1925, he traveled to Paris, where the famous Eiffel Tower was deteriorating badly. Some Parisians even wondered if it shouldn't be torn down. Lustig had a brainstorm—he invited a number of scrap metal dealers to a meeting and with forged documents offered the monument to the highest bidder. After André Poisson, who was eager to be noticed in Paris business circles, "bought" the tower, Lustig fled to Austria. When he tried the same scam again in Paris, the police were informed and Lustig fled to the US, where he conned people into buying a machine that "replicated" US paper money. After being arrested for counterfeiting, he was sent to Alcatraz, where he died in 1947 of pneumonia.

Right: Victor Lustig, a notorious con man in both Europe and the USA. He would set up swindles whilst traveling on luxury liners between the French sea ports and New York; **Top right, inset:** 19th-century print of the new "Great East River Suspension Bridge."

The term Ponzi scheme began making the news in 2009, after the conviction of mega-schemer Bernie Madoff for securities fraud. But what exactly is a Ponzi scheme and why is it illegal?

PONZI SCHEMERS

Above: Charles Ponzi, a major financial swindler of the early 20th century.

"The whole government is a Ponzi scheme..."
BERNARD MADOFF

The scheme starts when a financier attracts a group of investors by promoting a venture with high returns and little risk. They are then paid profits from the money that comes in from the next group of investors. The first investors, meanwhile, believe that they are earning profits from a legitimate business venture. In legal terms a Ponzi scheme scheme is a type of fraud—intentional deception to secure unlawful or unfair gain or to deprive a victim of a legal right.

Charles Ponzi Boston

Charles Ponzi, an Italian-American swindler from Boston, was doubtless influenced by an earlier scammer, William Miller, who was nicknamed "520 Percent" for the exaggerated returns he promised investors in a late-19th-century con. In the 1920s, Ponzi honed his version of this corporate con and elevated it, raking in huge sums of money. The basic premise has not changed over time: A crooked broker touts a surefire investment, guaranteeing lavish returns.

Ponzi's plan began legitimately, based on the arbitrage of international reply coupons (IRCs),

but before long he was using new investors' money to pay previous investors . . . and to pay himself. Unlike similar schemes from the 1870s and 1880s, this one got a lot of press coverage in the United States—and internationally—both while it was operating and after it collapsed. Ponzi became so notorious, his name will be forever linked with this form of financial scam.

Bernard Madoff New York City

Bernard "Bernie" Madoff was a powerful New York stockbroker and financial advisor who numbered celebrities and politicians among his clients. In 1960 he founded a penny stock brokerage (one that deals in common shares of small public companies selling for less than a dollar), which eventually grew into Bernard L. Madoff Investment Securities. He served as the company's chairman right up until his arrest on December 11, 2008. That year, the firm was the 6th largest market maker in the Standard & Poor 500 stock index.

His MO was simple: he'd deposit his clients' money into one Chase account, and if he needed funds for a client's cash out he withdrew the

sum from the same account. He invested in nothing. He primarily targeted wealthy Jewish communities and Jewish individuals and organizations including Hadassah, the Women's Zionist Organization of America, the Elie Wiesel Foundation, and Steven Spielberg's Wunderkinder Foundation. Jewish hospitals lost millions and some were forced to close.

When financial analyst Harry Markopolos began investigating Madoff in 1999, it took him one afternoon to calculate that Bernie was lying about his profits. One clue: Madoff kept reporting profits even when the S&P 500 index was falling. Markopolos filed his first Securities and Exchange Commission (SEC) complaint against the financier in 2000, but was ignored. In 2005 a sluggish SEC investigation was begun but never followed up on. Bilked investors later raged at the SEC, which could have been more rigorous early on and saved them millions.

Madoff was eventually unmasked during the financial crisis of 2008; his investors rushed to withdraw their money, and Madoff did not have enough funds in his Chase account to cover the dispersal. He told his sons Mark and Andrew, both members of the firm, about the massive scam and how it was all collapsing . . . and they reported him to the feds the next day.

On March 12, 2009, the financier pleaded guilty to 11 federal felonies, including securities fraud, wire fraud, mail fraud, money laundering, and perjury. The criminal complaint stated that for 20 years Madoff had defrauded his clients of close to $65 billion, by far the largest Ponzi scheme in history. He was sentenced to 150 years in prison and died in 2021 of natural causes. The great irony of Madoff's swindle was that he didn't need the money. By the late 1980s his firm was legitimately making $100 million a year. When interviewers asked why he did it, he said he wasn't sure. At least the IRS allowed his defrauded investors' capital losses to be treated as business losses, so that they could be claimed as tax deductions. But the public viewed the Ponzi scheme as emblematic of a greedy, manipulative Wall Street that had helped bring about the Great Recession of 2008.

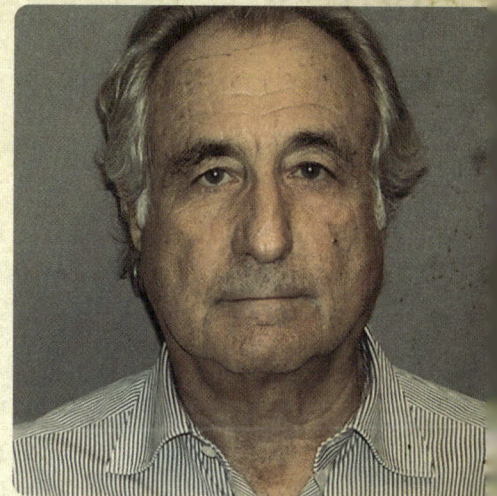

Above: Bernie Madoff, the powerful New York stockbroker and financial advisor who pleaded guilty to 11 federal felonies, including securities fraud, mail fraud, money laundering, and perjury. Over twenty years he had defrauded his clients of close to $65 billion; **Main image:** Madoff arrives at court.

209

Investors Beware!

Below are warning signs that a tempting investment opportunity could be part of a Ponzi scheme:

High investment returns with little or no risk. Every investment has a degree of risk, and investments with high yields usually carry more risk. Any "guaranteed" opportunity should be carefully investigated.

Suspiciously consistent returns: The value of investments fluctuates, especially those with high-returns. When the same payout arrives each time, regardless of market movement, something is fishy.

Unregistered investments. Schemes offer investments that are not registered with financial regulators like the SEC or FCA.

Unlicensed sellers US federal and state securities laws require the licensing or registering of investment professionals and their firms. Most Ponzi schemes involve unlicensed personnel and unregistered firms.

Secretive or complex strategies Be wary of investments that cannot be understood or on which no complete information can be obtained.

Issues with paperwork Account statement errors may indicate funds are not being invested as promised.

Difficulty receiving payments Ponzi promoters may try to prevent participants from cashing out by offering even higher returns for staying in.

TWO MORE PONZI SCHEMERS

Reed Slatkin California

Reed Slatkin, an ordained scientology minister, was a co-founder and investor of the internet provider EarthLink. He was also behind one of the United States' biggest Ponzi schemes. From 1986 to 2001 he raised $593 million from 800 investors, using the money from later investors to pay large profits to the early group. Many of those he targeted were also Scientologists, a number in the entertainment fields. In 2001 the SEC shut him down, and he faced both a civil case from the SEC and a criminal case from the U.S. Attorney. He pled guilty and was sentenced to 14 years in federal prison. He was released in 2013 and died in LA in 2015.

Sam Israel III New Orleans and New York

Sam Israel III, known as the "Bayou Guy," was a Louisiana native born into a famous trading family. Determined to make it on his own, in 1996 he founded the Bayou Hedge Fund Group, which ended up raising $450 million from its investors. But when Israel suffered losses and began misappropriating funds for personal use, he created a Ponzi scheme to cover his tracks. He even went to the extreme of starting up a dummy accounting firm that the fund "hired" to audit their accounts. This helped Bayou keep up appearances to their investors.

In 2005 Israel was indicted, and eventually declared bankruptcy. In April 2008 he was sentenced to 20 years, but failed to report to prison as ordered. His abandoned SUV

Above: Reed Slatkin, an ordained scientology minister who devised one of the United States's largest Ponzi schemes. He targeted many in his own scientology community; **Opposite and below:** Sam Israel III, the "Bayou Guy," was eventually traced and arrested after his massive financial fraud;

was found on the Bear Mountain Bridge in New York with "Suicide is painless" written in the dust on the hood. Israel had fled with the help of his girlfriend, Debra Ryan, who explained his getaway after her arrest. He was eventually traced to a campground in Granville, Massachusetts, and surrendered peacefully. Two years were added to his sentence; Ryan received three years of probation.

A CLOSER LOOK:

This type of financial scam existed well before Ponzi refined it. Charles Dickens included these schemes in two of his novels, *Martin Chuzzlewit* in 1844 and *Little Dorrit* in 1857.

Investor's To-Do List:

These basic tips will keep potential investors out of both Ponzi schemes and pyramid schemes.

Do check out the background of a broker or adviser before investing money with them. There are tools like the SEC Action Lookup and BrokerCheck, a database maintained by the Financial Regulatory Authority (FINRA) to access information on a broker's employment history, their licensing status, and complaints against them or their firm.

Do be wary of lures that are meant to get you in the door, such as offering a free meal for attending an "investment seminar."

Do resist any high-pressure sales tactics. Sketchy brokers make it sound like you are missing a once-in-a-lifetime opportunity if you don't act quickly. Take as much time as you need to decide if an investment is right for you.

Do insist anyone pushing a hot marketing or sales outfit provides you with financial statements audited by a certified public accountant (CPA) indicating that the company makes its money from selling actual products or services, not from constantly luring in new members.

The Difference Between a Ponzi Scheme and a Pyramid Scheme

Ponzi schemes involve a crooked broker luring investors to sink their money in a surefire investment. Instead of investing their money, however, the broker uses the money of new investors to pay earlier investors, while pocketing some of the money himself or herself. Eventually, this ruse becomes impossible to carry off, simply because at some point there are not enough new investors to pay the growing numbers of past investors. And so the scheme collapses.

Pyramid schemes also offer get-rich-quick opportunities, in this case via the marketing of goods and services. Those at the top of the "pyramid" build a team of entrepreneurs typically by reaching out to people on social media, offering them a chance to make money selling a "great product" if they pay an up-front fee. This second tier of people are told then can make even more money by bringing new recruits on board and earning commissions. Then the next tier gets the same spiel, "Bring in recruits, earn big bucks in commissions," and so on. Eventually a cut of all this money makes its way to those at the top of the pyramid. The reality of a pyramid scheme is that the product or service the leaders are marketing is sketchy at best, often described in vague terms. Like Ponzi schemes, when pyramids get too big, they collapse . . . and the investors are left with very little.

Embezzlers are simply thieves who steal funds from the company till. But rather than pilfering a few dollars, they aim for hundreds of thousands, even millions.

BIG-TIME EMBEZZLERS

"You don't want another Enron? Here's your law: If a company can't explain, in one sentence, what it does ... it's illegal ..."
LEWIS BLACK, COMEDIAN

Robert Vesco

Robert Vesco, called the "king of the fugitive financiers," was at one time admired as the boy wonder of international finance. After quitting school in Detroit, Michigan, he worked as an auto shop apprentice. Relocating to New York City in 1957, he was hired as an engineering assistant by a chemical company. He soon gained an interest in two small manufacturing companies in New Jersey. More acquisitions followed, then the formation of International Controls Company in the mid-1960s. In three years he increased his companies' annual sales from $1.3 million to more than $100 million. In 1971 he gained control of the Swiss-based mutual fund empire, Investors Overseas Services (IOS), which he and his associates were accused of looting to the tune of $224 million. In 1973 Vesco was indicted for secret, illegal campaign donations to Richard Nixon and in 1976, indicted for his fraudulent acts regarding the IOS. He fled the US for Central America, where he lived the high life. After moving to Cuba he was eventually jailed by Castro for financial crimes and was released in 2005. He died there in 2007.

Calisto Tanzi

Calisto Tanzi, born near Parma, Italy, dropped out of college, but in 1961 went on to found Parmalat, a dairy and food corporation—and the global leader in the production of long-life milk. In 2001, Forbes listed his net worth as more than $1.3 billion. But Parmalat collapsed in 2003, with a €14-billion hole in its accounts. In 2008, Tanzi was found to have embezzled more than 800 million euros from his firm and was sentenced to 10 years in prison for fraud. In December 2009 the authorities seized 19 works of art be longing to Tanzi, including Picassos, Monets, and van Goghs, worth more than €100 million. In 2010 he received another 18 years for fraudulent bankruptcy and nine years for bankrupting his company.

Enron

Enron became a notorious example of a corporation going from hero to zero. This massive energy, commodities, and services company rocked Wall Street—and undermined faith in the stock market—when its stocks' value shrank from $90 a share at its peak to 26 cents per share. Formed by a merger of Houston Natural

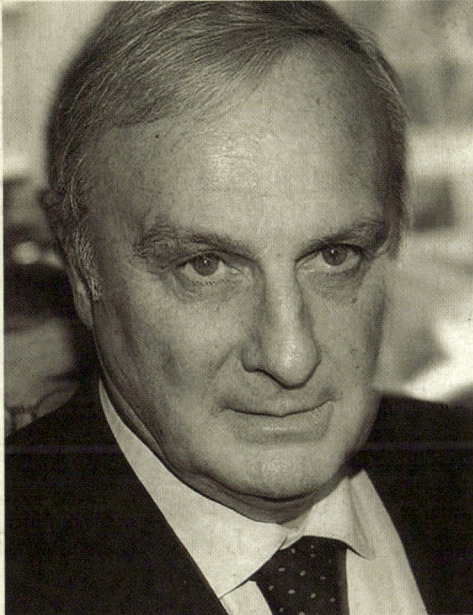

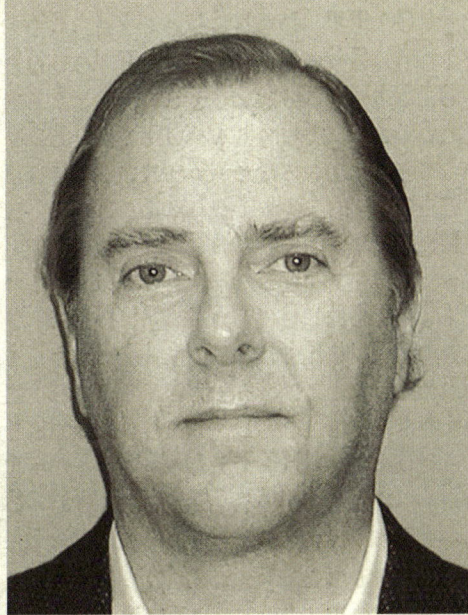

Gas with Oklahoma's InterNorth Incorporated, Enron's new head was Houston CEO Kenneth Lay. He soon created Enron Financial, with consultant Jeffrey Skilling as head. It was Skilling who changed Enron's accounting from cost accounting to market-to-market, which appraises a company's current financial situation based on "fair value," but which can be manipulated. Using this method, a new power plant enters the books already showing a profit. Enron accumulated huge debts but was able to obscure and bamboozle regulators via special purpose vehicles and entities, false holdings, and off-the-books accounting. Eventually, in 2000, Enron admitted inflating its income by $586 million. In 2001, they filed for Chapter 11 bankruptcy. After a criminal investigation, top executives received prison sentences, but Lay died of a heart attack before he was due to report.

Samsung

Samsung was another case of faith in a multinational corporation being shaken by the illegal activities of its leader. In 2017, the acting head of electronics giant Samsung, Lee Jae-yong, has was charged with bribery and embezzlement

in connection with a corruption scandal that led to the impeachment of South Korea's president. Lee had funneled $36 million to the president's confidant in order to ensure government support of a controversial merger. Lee was sentenced to five years, but only served half his term.

Opposite, center: Robert Vesco; **Opposite, bottom:** Disgraced US President Richard Nixon; **This page, left and top:** Calisto Tanzi: big-time Italian embezzler, now serving prison time; **Above:** Enron chiefs Jeffrey Skilling (left), and Kenneth Lay. Enron was named "America's Most Innovative Company" by *Fortune* for six consecutive years between 1996 and 2001; **Below:** Disgraced Samsung chief Lee Jae-yong.

Imposters are typically clever, intuitive people who have a knack for impersonating either a celebrity or a white-collar professional, or who claim a connection to a famous person.

SUCCESSFUL IMPOSTERS

"Rascality, pure rascality…"

FRED DEMARA, IMPOSTER, DESCRIBING HIS MOTIVATION

Above: Princess Caraboo's story inspired a number of books and productions, including a 1994 movie with Phoebe Cates.

Princess Caraboo England

Princess Caraboo was found wandering in Almondsbury, England, in April 1817. She claimed to be a royal from the island of Javasu in the Indian Ocean who had been captured by pirates. After a long sea journey, she had jumped overboard into the Bristol Channel and swum ashore. The local gentry feted her for 10 weeks, entertained by her primitive ways—she used a bow and arrow, fenced, and swam naked.

Furnished with exotic clothing, she posed for portraits and gained national exposure via newspaper stories. The Princess was exposed by a boarding house worker as Mary Willcocks, a cobbler's daughter from Devon. She was exiled to Philadelphia—after, purportedly, going ashore on St. Helena, where Napoleon wanted to marry her. She attempted to generate public interest in her exotic character in the US and abroad with little success. Back in England she married Richard Baker, had a daughter, and began selling leeches to hospitals. She died from a fall in 1864.

Cassie L. Chadwick Cleveland, Ohio

Cassie L. Chadwick was America's pre-eminent con woman during the country's Gilded Age. Born Elizabeth Bigley in Ontario, Canada, she passed bad checks at home and then conned people in Cleveland as a clairvoyant. After marrying a respected doctor, he threw her out when he discovered her larcenous past. She did jail time for forgery, then opened a brothel, where she met and married another wealthy doctor. She was soon living on Cleveland's "millionaire's row."

By hinting to Cleveland society that she was the illegitimate daughter of—and heir to— wealthy Scottish industrialist Andrew Carnegie, she procured bank loans worth two million dollars. She was called "the queen of Ohio," and had 30 closets full of jewels. When Andrew Carnegie denied knowing her, she was arrested. She was sentenced to 14 years, but the warden allowed her to furnish her cell lavishly due to her celebrity. She died in 1907 at age 50. Her massive

debt to the Oberlin Citizen's National Bank bankrupted it.

Ferdinand Waldo Demara
Massachusetts

Ferdinand Waldo Demara, known as "the Great Imposter," was possibly the most skilled faker in American history. He was born in 1921, the son of a prosperous movie projectionist in Lawrence, Massachusetts. Hard times during the Depression forced the family lose their home and move to a poorer neighborhood.

As a teen, young "Fred" ran away, living briefly at a Cistercian monastery before joining the army. Using a fake name he went AWOL, tried twice more to live with monks, and finally joined the navy, training as a hospital corpsman. When that did not work out, he assumed another fake name and posed as a religion-oriented psychologist and then a teacher. Captured by the FBI for desertion, he served 18 months. Afterward he studied law at Northeastern, then joined the Brothers of Christian Instruction as Brother John Payne. In 1951, he actually founded a college, LeMennais College, in Alfred, Maine, hoping to make the teaching order more prominent.

Next he embarked on his most famous exploit: masquerading as a doctor he'd once met, Joseph Cyr, he worked as a trauma surgeon aboard the *HMCS Cayuga*, a Royal Canadian Navy destroyer during the Korean conflict. Here, he was called upon to perform surgeries and dispense medications. When 16 injured Korean soldiers were brought aboard, Demara speed-read textbooks on the different procedures, including major chest surgery, and successfully treated all 16 patients.

Other professions he assumed include civil engineer, sheriff's deputy, assistant prison warden, hospital orderly, lawyer, childcare expert, editor, and cancer researcher. His success as an imposter, he said, was attributed to two things: "in any organization there is always a lot of loose, unused power lying about which can be picked up without alienating anyone," and "if you want power and want to expand, never encroach on anyone else's domain; open up new ones." Demara supposedly had a photographic memory and an incredibly high IQ, allowing him to memorize various techniques from textbooks. He lived by two personal rules: the burden of proof is on the accuser, and when in danger, attack.

After giving a *Life* interview, he was less successful at impersonations; he eventually, and legitimately, worked as a pastor in California. A good friend of Steve McQueen, he delivered the actor's last rites. Demara died in 1982 from heart failure and complications of diabetes.

Top left: Cassie Chadwick, America's pre-eminent con woman; **Top, and above:** Fred Demara, the Great Imposter, possibly the most skilled faker in American history.

"If you look at any successful professional—a salesperson, a marketer, a real estate agent, a trader— they all have the same qualities as the con man..." FRANK ABAGNALE, IMPOSTER

Frank Abagnale The Bronx, NYC

Frank Abagnale was the heir to Fred Demara, a determined and convincing imposter who inspired the movie *Catch Me If You Can.*

Abagnale, born in the Bronx in 1948, is the son of a French-Algerian mother and an Italian-American father. He began passing bad checks at the age of 15 and was sent to reform school. At 16 he enlisted in the navy, but was discharged after three months, and shortly thereafter was arrested for fraud. A year later the FBI nabbed him for stealing a Mustang from his father's neighbor in California. Not a promising start. He next decided to impersonate a pilot and went as far as renting a uniform, but was again arrested.

He served two years in Great Meadow Prison, was paroled, stole another car in Boston, and was returned for an additional year. In 1969, again impersonating an airline pilot (he was 17!) in Baton Rouge and using stolen checks, he was arrested and found guilty of theft and forgery. Sentenced to 12 years of supervised probation, he fled to Europe. After illegal shenanigans in

Sweden and France, he was deported to the US. There, in his pilot guise, he visited college campuses to recruit female flight attendants.

After cashing a personal checked doctored to look like a Pan Am paycheck, Frank was again nailed by the FBI. Released after serving two years of a 12-year sentence, he worked as a cook, grocer, and move projectionist. He then repeated the pilot role in 1974 at Texas children's camp, Camp Manison, but was arrested for stealing cameras from the staff. Still posing as a pilot, he obtained a position at a Houston area orphanage helping to locate foster homes for the children. This ruse was eventually discovered by his parole officer, who moved him into quarters above his own garage in order to keep an eye on his wayward client.

In 1975, Abagnale approached a bank with an offer to speak to the staff about various tricks that check forgers, or "paperhangers," use to defraud banks. They accepted and he began a new career as a speaker and a security consultant. Still not totally square, he falsified information on his resume indicating he had worked with Scotland Yard and the LA Police.

Top, and center: Frank Abagnale as Pan Am pilot; **Above:** Poster for the 2002 Steven Spielberg film *Catch Me If You Can*, with Leo DiCaprio and Tom Hanks; **Main image:** Frank with Leo DiCaprio at the press launch of the film.

David Hampton Manhattan, NYC

David Hampton became notorious in the 1980s for conning a group of wealthy Manhattan residents by claiming to be Sidney Poitier's son, a ruse he had used to enter Studio 54. He employed his celebrity status as "David Poitier" to gain money, meals, and even places to stay. In 1983, he was arrested and convicted of fraud. His stint as an imposter inspired John Guare's successful play and the subsequent movie *Six Degrees of Separation*.

Main image and far left: David Hampton, imposter. He frequently claimed he was Sidney Poitier's son.
Left: Actor Sidney Poitier in 1968.

A number of con men were so daring, so resourceful, so brazenly over-the-top in their efforts to bilk the public that they have become almost legendary in the annals of crime.

LEGENDARY CHARLATANS

Above: Gregor McGregor, a low-self-esteem fantasist?

Gregor McGregor: Royal Scam

Formerly a Scottish-born officer in the British Army, McGregor invented a country in Central America called "Poyais." As its appointed ruler or "Cazique" he conned hundreds of British and French businessmen to invest in this tropical paradise in the 1820s.

After serving in the Peninsular War between Britain and Napoleon's occupying French forces in Spain and Portugal, McGregor joined the republican army in the Venezuelan war for independence, where he was quickly elevated to general. After two disastrous military operations in 1819, where he abandoned the British volunteers under his command, he returned to England. There he relayed fascinating tales of how the king of the Mosquito Coast in the Gulf of Honduras had made him Cazique of Poyais, a developed colony with a community of British settlers. Hundreds of people invested in Poyais government bonds and land certificates, and around 250 Britons actually emigrated to this fictional Eden. What they found upon landing was untouched jungle with nary a settlement in sight. Fewer than 50 of the original party returned to England, the rest died or dispersed. Back home McGregor's advocates rallied to his defense, claiming the expedition leaders were at fault. Still, this failed scheme was viewed as a contributory factory to the financial "Panic of 1825."

After attempting a similar con in France, McGregor was arrested and tried. Once he was acquitted, he oversaw several lesser versions of the Poyais scam in England. In 1838 he returned to Caracas, Venezuela, where he died a hero and was buried with all military honors.

Natwarlal: India's Robin Hood

Mithilesh Kumar Srivastava, also known as Dashan Dudhat, became famous as Natwarlal, the pre-eminent con man of India. Born in 1912, in Bangra, India, he was the son of a station master. He received a bachelor of commerce degree, while a brief stint as a stockbroker gave him a working knowledge of banking. That background, combined with an uncanny ability to forge documents and signatures, became invaluable for running cons. After serving time for stealing nine tons of iron,

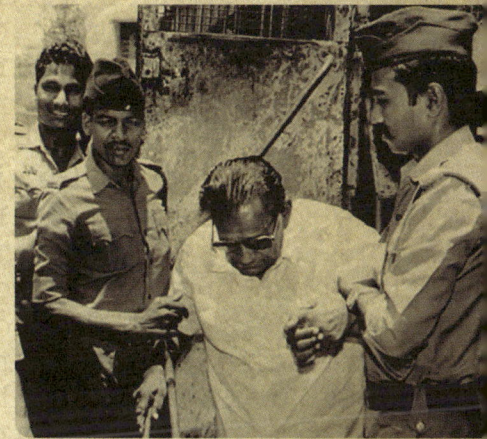

he began drugging prostitutes and stealing their cash and jewelry, then moved on to swindles. He had more than 50 disguises he adopted to bilk shop owners, jewelers, bankers, and tourists out of their money. By forging the signatures of celebrities he was able to cheat some of India's major industrialists out of large sums. He was attributed with many amazing feats of con artistry, including selling the Parliament House of India to a foreigner—including the members of Parliament themselves—and selling the famous Taj Mahal . . . three different times. In his village of Bangra, Natwarlal was considered a hero, a native son who spread around some of his ill-gotten gains. He also earned local respect for staying away from violent crimes and only targeting the rich and powerful.

Natwarlal never evaded the law for very long, however. His criminal career was punctuated by increasingly longer jail sentences. Yet he invariably escaped, once dressed as a policeman, whom the prison guards saluted. In total it is reckoned he only spent 20 years in jail. At the age of 84 he was arrested, and while being transported by train from the prison to a hospital, again managed to escape, in spite of being confined to a wheelchair! It's hard not to admire or at least be entertained by Natwarlal. His illegal shenanigans continued right up until the end of his long life.

Top left: The painted depiction of McGregor's Poyais paradise bore no resemblance to the reality of untouched, and for Europeans, dangerous jungle; **Above left:** The world-famous Taj Mahal, which Natwarlal "sold" three times; **Above right:** India's Robin Hood himself: Natwarlal.

INDEX

A

Abagnale, Frank, 216
Abberline, Frederick, 87
Abilene, 17
African Serial Killers, 134–135
Agency and the Company, 22
Agricultural Bank of China, 193
Alfred R. Rowe Jr., 62
Algarron, Jacques, 62
Allen, Arthur Leigh, 112
Allitt, Beverly, 111
The "AMBER" Alert, 174
Amber Room, 189
18th Amendment, 27
American Mafia, 34
America's Missing: Broadcast Emergency
    Response (AMBER), 174
"America's Most Innovative Company," 213
Amurao, Corazon, 138
Anastasia, Albert, 38, 39
And Children Who Kill, 64–65
"The Angarsk Maniac." See Popkov, Mikhail
Angels of Death, 110–111
Anthony, Cindy, 63
Anthony, George, 63
Antonio, Walter, 107
Antonyan, Yuri 129
Apollinaire, Guillame, 188–189
ARA. See Aryan Republican Army
Arafat, Yasser, 184
Arlington, 174
Arsenic, 51
"Arsenic. Poison for rats," 49
Aryan Republican Army (ARA), 185
Asbury Park, 207
Asian Serial Killers, 132–133
Asphyxiation, 178
Atari game, 178
Attenborough, Dicky, 90
Attenborough, Richard, 59, 145
Auburn Police, 114
Augustus, Washington, 207
Austria-Hungary, 207
"Auto bandits" (desperados), 28
Aylesbury Vale, 183
Azrac of Mazatlan, 147

B

Backus, Michael, 79
Bailey, F. Lee, 82, 92
Baker, Doyle Wayne, 78
Baksheev, Dimitri and Natalia, 159
The Banco Central (Going Underground), 200
Bank of England, 190
Barbosa, Daniel Camargo, 122
Barker, Kate "Ma," 29
Barnes, George ("Machine Gun" Kelly), 29
Barnum, P.T., 206
Barrow, Blanche, 31
Barrow, Clyde, 30–31, 145
The Barrow Gang, 30–31
Barrymore, John, 72
Bartlett, Edwin, 49
Barzee, Wanda, 177
Báthory, Elizabeth, 107
"Bathtub gin," 27
Bat Masterson, 17
7th Battalion of Combat Engineers, 147
"Bayou Guy," 210
Bayou Hedge Fund Group, 210
Bazil Thorne of Bondi, 174
Bear Stearns, 205
Beatty, Warren, 144
Beets, Betty Lou, 78
Beets, Jimmy Don, 78
Belfast's Donegal Square West, 196
Belknap, Myrta, 88
Belle Elmore. See Crippen, Dr. Hawley Harvey
Belle Starr, 16
Beneke, Paul, 188
Bennett, Keith, 127
Berkowitz, David, 98, 100–101
Bertillon, Alphonse, 57
Betty Newmar of Ohio, 79
Bexar County Hospital, 110

Bianchi, Kenneth, 114
"Big Bertha," 59
Biggs, Ronnie, 182–183
Big-Time Embezzlers, 212–213
Bill Tilghman, 17
Billy the Kid, 16-17
Bishop, William N., 19
The Black Dahlia. See Short, Elizabeth
Black Hand, mark of, 35
Black Panther member, 184
Black societies, 43
Black Widows, 78–79
Blanco, Griselda, 39
A Bloody Fingerprint, 192–193
"Bloody Nineteenth," 36
Bluebeard, 79
The Blue Dahlia, 53
Bodies in Bin Bags (Dennis Nilsen), 104–105
Bogart, Humphrey, 144
    The Petrified Forest, 144
Bogdanovich, Peter, 57
Boggs, Gerry, 79
Bolt cutters, 186
Bonaparte, Charles, 18
Bonnie and Clyde, 144–145
Born to Raise Hell (Richard Speck), 138–139
    The Borough Poisoner. See Chapman, George
Boston, 26, 39, 40, 208, 216
Boston College, 60
Boston Museum, 189
The Boston Strangler (Albert Desalvo), 92–93
Botulism toxin, 51
Boulder County, Colorado, 68-69
Bow Street Magistrate's Office, 14
Bow Street Runners, Bobbies, and Scotland
    Yard, 14–15
New Scotland Yard, 15
Sir Robert's Own, 14–15
Bradley, Stephen, 175
Brady, Ian, 126, 127
Brando, Marlon, 144–145
    The Godfather (1972), 144–145
    The Wild One, 144–145
Branson, Robert Franklin, 78
Bratva. See Russian mobs
The Brazilian Federal Police, 200
Breadwinners, 28
Bregof, Denise, 65
Bridego Bridge, 183
Bride kidnapping, 173
Bridgewater State Hospital, 93
Brighton Beach, 41
Brink's-Mat robbery, 191
Brink's-Mat warehouse, 190–191
Bristol bank, 190
British Army Officer, 182
The British Bank of the Middle East, 184
The British Rail Class, 183
British Road Transport Services, 91
British Serial Killers, 124–125
British Tanganyika Territory, 150
The Brooklyn Bridge, 206
Brooks, Stephanie, 94
Bruck, David, 62
Brutal orphanage, 162
Bryan, Peter, 159–160
Bucpapa, Jetmir, 198
"Buddha," 187
Buffalo Bill's Wild West Show, 89
Bulger, James, 64
Bulgar, Whitey, 39–40
Bullion Galore, 190–191
Bundy, Ted, 94, 98–99
Buono, Jr., Angelo, 114
Buono, Richard, 98–99
Bureau of Alcohol, Tobacco, Firearms, and
    Explosives (ATF), 13, 18–19
Burress, Troy, 107
Butch Cassidy, 16–17, 144–145
"The Butcher," 109
Butler, Tommy, 183
Butts, Lori, 65

C

Cadillac Joe, 37
Cafora, Louis, 186
Cagney, James, 144–145
    The Public Enemy and White Heat, 144–145

Calling in the feds, 18–19
Cannibalism, 165
Cannibals in Our Midst, 153
"Can't-Do-It-Christie," 90
Capital of Ceará, 200
Capone, Al, 26, 27, 36, 37, 38
Captives in the Basement, 176–177
Carlos, Juan, 123
Carnegie, Andrew, 214
    "the queen of Ohio," 214
Carroll, Lewis, 86, 87
    Alice's Adventures in Wonderland, 86
Carskaddon, Charles, 107
Carter, Jimmy, 172
Casino, 144
Catch Me If You Can, 216
Catherine Palace, 189
Catholic church, 184
"Cazique," 218
Celebrity Abductees, 172–173
Celebrity Assassin (Andrew Cunanan), 118–119
Census Bureau, 17
The Central Bank of Iraq, 194
Central Intelligence Agency (CIA), 22
Cerebral hemorrhage, 108
Chadwick, Cassie L., 214
Challenging Prohibition, 26–27
Chambers, Alison, 81
Chambers, Robert, 60
Chandler, Raymond, 75, 145
Chapman, Annie, 87
Chapman, George, 51
Chapman, Mark David, 58
Cherry, Brian, 159
Chicago, 26, 27, 29, 88
Chicago Crime Commission, 27
"Chicago Outfit," 36
Chicago's South Side, 35
Chikatilo, Andrei ("The Butcher of Rostov"),
    128-129
Childs, Chivonna, 145
Chinese immigrant communities, 42
Chisako Kakehi of Japan, 78–79
Chloroform, 51
The Chocolate Cream Killer, 50
Christie, Ethel, 90
Christie, John Reginald, 59, 90, 145
Christie: 10 Rillington Place, 91
Christmas Eve, 89, 100
Church of Scientology, 210
Cianciulli, Leonarda, 158
Cicero, Paul, 145
Cigrande, Emeline, 89
Cincinnati's Eden Park, 76
City police force (Boston), 26
Civil War, 17
The Clantons, 16
Clarke, Judy, 62
Clark, Marcia, 83
Claudia Mijangos "La hiena de Querétaro," 147
"Client," 188
Clinton, Bill, 172
Clothing stall, 159
Clottemans, Els, 77
Club of Chicago, 204
"The Cocaine Godmother." See Blanco, Griselda
Cochran, Johnnie, 82–83
"Code Adam," 178
Coit, Jill, 79
Coit, William, 79
Colombian spree killer, 146
Colosimo, Big Jim, 35
Condon, John, 170
Con Men and White-Collar Criminals, 203
Connolly, John J., 40
Controlled Substances Act, 19
Cooper, Carol Ann, 81
Coppola, Francis Ford, 35, 144
The Godfather Part II, 35, 144
Cordrey, Roger, 182–183
Costello, Frank, 38
Costello, Rena, 80
Cotton, Charles, 49
Cotton, Frederick, 49
Cotton, Mary Ann, 49
Court of Cassation, 69
Coutts, Roger, 198
The Cowboys, 16

Cowell, Eleanor, 94
Cowlings, A.C., 82
Crane, Cheryl, 57
Cranley Gardens, North London, 105
"Crash car," 186
Cream, Thomas, 50
Criminal Investigation Division (CID), 15
The Crippen Case, 74–75
Crippen, Dr. Hawley Harvey, 74
Crowe, Bernard, 142
Crown Point Prison, 29
Cult kidnapping, 173
"Cult of personality," 142
Cumpanaa, Ana, 29
Cunanan, Andrew, 118–119
A Cursed Crime, 191
Curtis, Tony, 93
The Boston Strangler, 145
Cyanide, 51
Cyprus, 184
Czolgosz, Leon, 18

D

da Conceição, Pedro Rosa, 146
D.A. Hunter, Alex, 68–69
D.A. Lacy, Mary, 68-69
Dahmer, Jeffrey, 98, 156–157
Daly, John, 182
Dangerous prisoner, 60
Danske Bank, 196–197
Dapper Don. See Gotti, John
Dardenne, Sabine, 177
The Dar Es Salaam Bank, 194
Dark forces, 43
da Rocha, Tiago, 122
DaRonch, Carol, 94
Darrow, Clarence, 169
Davy, Gloria, 139
Daybreak Boys, 34
Deadly as the Male, 107
Deadly love Triangles, 76–77
Dead Rabbits, 34
DeAngelo, Joseph James, 112, 114
Death From Above, 140–141
Death in Brentwood, 82–83
"Death to pigs," 143
Decree on Land enactment, 148–149
de França, Genildo Ferreira, 147
Delgado, Campo Elias, 146
Delmenhorst Clinic, 111
Delport, Carel Johannes, 150
Democratic socialist party, 197
De Niro, Robert, 145
The Departed (2006), 40, 144
Department of Homeland Security (DHS), 13
Department of Justice (DOJ), 13
de Rais, Gilles, 79, 87
Dershowitz, Alan, 82
DeSalvo, Albert, 92–93
DeSimone, Tommy, 186
Des Plaines River, 103
DeVito, Tommy, 145
Dewsbury Police Station, 117
Dew, Walter, 74
Dick, Evelyn, 78
    "Canadian Black Widow," 78
    "Torso Murderer," 78
Dickens, Charles, 210
    Little Dorrit, 210, 211
    Martin Chuzzlewit, 210
Diehl, John, 100
Dillinger, John, 29
Dipendra, Crown Prince, 151
Dishonorable Mentions, 162–164
Disorganized offenders, 99
Dixon, Colin, 198
DNA, 21, 52
"Doctor Death," 109
Dodge City, 17
The Doolin-Daltons, 16
Dornier, Christian, 148
Double Fantasy, 58
Double Indemnity, 144–145
Downey, Lesley Ann, 127
Drinkwater, John, 52
Drinkwater, Muriel, 52
Drug Enforcement Administration (DEA), 13,
    18, 19

Dugard, Jaycee Lee, 176
Dunaway, Faye, 145
Durham Jail, 49
"Dutch" Schultz, 26
Dutroux, Marc, 177
Dyer, Amelia (The Ogress of Reading), 124
Dzhumagaliev, Nikolai, 129, 158, 161

E
Eady, Muriel Amelia, 90
"Earthquake," 38
Eastern European mobs, 41
Eastham Prison Farm, 30
East Harlem, 36
"Eaten Loudwell's flesh," 159
Eaton, Richard, 187
Eddowes, Catherine, 86–87
Edmunds, Christina. See The Chocolate
  Cream Killer
Edwards, Buster, 182–183
Edwards, Parnell, 186–187
Eiffel Tower, 207
Eirich, Rudi, 186
Elie Wiesel Foundation, 209
Ellis, Hangman John, 75
Ellus, Jacque, 96
  The Technological Society, 96
"El Patrón." See Escobar, Pablo
English and European Cannibals, 158–159
Enron, 212
Ershov (the axe murderer), 129
Escobar, Pablo, 39
Ethylene glycol, 51
Eunick, Tiffany, 65
European Serial Killers, 128–131
European Union Agency for Law Enforcement
  Cooperation (Europol), 23
Evans, Beryl, 90–91
Evans, Eddie, 127
Evans, Timothy, 59, 90–91
Express kidnapping, 173
Express Newspapers, 179
"The Express Train," 134

F
Farris, Suzanne, 138, 139
FBI. See Federal Bureau of Investigation
F.B.I.'s Most Wanted Men, 19
Federal Bureau of Investigation (FBI), 13, 18, 22,
  96–97, 170, 189
Federal Bureau of Prisons, 13
Federal law enforcement, 18
Ferrari Testarossa, 192
Ferrin, Darlene, 112
Filho, Pedro (Killer Petey), 120
Findlay, Tom, 62
Firearms Act (1988), 149
Fire Chief Frank Worden, 155
Fish, Albert, 162
Fitzgerald, F. Scott, 76
  "The Great Gatsby," 76
Flanagan, Catherine, 78
Flanagan, Margaret, 78
Fleischer, Richard, 59
The Floradora Girl (Evelyn Nesbit), 72–73
Floral Park, 100
Florida State Prison, 106
Floyd, Charles Arthur ("Pretty Boy" Floyd), 29
Flying Squad, 183
Flynn, Billy, 76–77
Folger, Abigail, 143
Ford Deluxe Sedan (1934), 31
Forensic clues, 20
Forensic science, the advent of, 20–21
  anthropometry, 20–21
  ballistics, 20
  DNA, 21
  fingerprints, 21
  identifying Human Blood, 21
  job of, 20
  or criminalistics, 20
  toxicology, 20
Forest Hills, 100
"Foundlings," 176
Fountain Avenue, 210
Francis, George, 190–191
Franklin Dodge, 76
Franks, Bobby, 168

Freedom Club, 97
Freund, Christine, 100
Frey, Amber. See Peterson, Scott
A Fruitless Investigation, 196
Fritzl, Elisabeth, 176
Führermuseum, 189

G
Gacy, John Wayne, 102–103
A Gallery of Victorian Poisoners, 48–51
Gallichan, David, 104
Gambino, Carlo, 38–39
Gandolfini, James, 144–145
Gangs of New York, 144–145
Gang violence, 35
Garaviti, Luis (The Beast), 123
Gardner, Isabella Stewart 189
Gargullo, Merlita, 139
Garrett, Pat, 17
Garrido, Phillip, 176
Garvie, Max, 76–77
Garvie, Sheila, 76–77
Gein, Edward Theodore, 154
Genildo Ferreira de França, 147
"The Gent," 186
Géricault, Théodore, 104
  The Raft of the Medusa, 104
German-Jewish heritage, 168
Gettler, Alexander, 48
Getty, J. Paul III, 172–173
  Getty, J. Paul, 172–173
Gibson, Charles Dana, 72
Gilbert, Kristen, 110
Gillis, Lester ("Baby Face" Nelson), 29
Goddard, Henry (Scotland Yard), 20
"Godfather," 39
Godfrey, Susan, 149
The Golden State Killer, 112–115
Goldman, Ron, 82
Golovkin (the child killer), 129
Gonzalez, Maria and Delfina
  (Las Poquianchis), 123
Goodfellas, 144–145
Gooding Jr., Cuba, 145
Goody, Gordon, 182
Göring, Nazi Hermann, 51
Gotti, John, 39, 187
Gough, Lynda, 81
Grachev, Peter, 148
Grama Sintética (Synthetic Turf), 200
Grand larceny, 162
Granger, Farley, 169
Grantham and Kestevan Hospital, 111
Gravano, Salvatore, 39
Gray Man, 162
Graysmith, Robert, 112
Greasy Thumb, 37
The Great Depression, 28, 204
"Great East River Suspension Bridge," 207
Greater China, 43
Greater São Paulo, 120
"The Great Imposter," 215
Great Recession, 209
The Great Rock 'n' Roll Swindle, 183
Great Scotland Yard, 15
The Great Train Robbery, 182–183, 191
Greco, Giuseppe, 128
Greene, Danny, 40
"Green Man," 92
The Green River Killer, 115
Green River, Washington, 115
Greenwood, Graham, 117
Gregory, Ron, 117
Grim and Grisly (Fred & Rosemary West), 80–81
Gruenwald, Peter, 186
A Gruesome Discovery, 154–155
Gualtieri, Paul "Paulie Walnuts," 145
Guare, John, 217
  Six Degrees of Separation, 217
Gulf of Honduras, 218
Gulf of Thailand, 132
Gull, Sir William Withey, 86–87
Gumb, Jame, 94
Gunness, Belle, 108–109
Gunness, Peter, 108

H
Hagerman, Amber, 174

Haigh, John (The Acid Bath Murderer), 124
Hamer, Frank, 31
Hamilton, Patrick, 169
Hamilton, Red, 40
Hamilton, Polly, 29
Hampton, David, 217
Han Chinese, 43
Harrison, Carter, 89
Harris, Thomas, 144
  Hannibal, 144
  Red Dragon, 144
  The Silence of the Lambs, 144
Hauptmann, Bruno, 170–171
Hazelwood, Roy, 98
"Healter Skelter," 143
Hearst, Patty, 172
Hearst, William Randolph, 172
Heathrow International Trading Estate, 190–191
Heavy Goods Vehicle (HGV), 116
Hefner, Hugh, 57
Helm, Boone, 162
Helter Skelter, 145
Hennessy, David, 36
Henry Gurholt of Wisconsin, 105, 108
Herne Bay, 198
Heroin, Cocaine, Methamphetamine Drug
  Cartels, 44–45
Herschel, Sir William, 21
Hickey, Eric W., 107
Higgins, Mary, 78
Higgins, Thomas, 78
High Body Counts (Belle Gunness), 108–109
High-value package coach, 182
Highway Homicides (Aileen Wuornos), 106–107
Highway patrol, 12
Hill, Henry, 145
The Hillside Stranglers (Cousins Bianchi &
  Buono), 112–113
Hindley, Myra, 126, 127
Hinman, Gary, 142
Hitchcock, Alfred, 169
Hitler, Adolf, 126
  Mein Kampf, 126
HMCS Cayuga, 215
Hobson, Jim, 117
Hodel, Steve, 53
Hoffman, Anna, 162
Hogan, Mary, 154
Högel, Niels, 110–111
Holliday, Doc, 16–17
Holloway Jail, 124
Hollywood Homicides, 57
Holmes, Henry Howard, 88–89
  "Murder Castle," 88–89
Holmes, Imogene, 76
Holmes, Stephen, 104
Home Office Large Major Enquiry System
  (Holmes), 117
Homicidal Husbands, 66–67
Hong Kong triad, 43
Hoover, Herbert, 27, 204–205
Hostage-Based Heists, 196
"House of Horrors," 81
Hughes, Michael Anthony, 176
Hughes, Tony, 157
Humphreys, Charles "Dick," 107
Humpty Jacksons, 34
Hungerford massacre, 148
Hussein, Saddam, 194
Hussey, Jim, 182
Hysenaj, Emir, 198

I
Ice Pick Willie, 36–37
"Implements of Hell," 162
International Criminal Police Congress, 22
International Criminal Police Organization
  (Interpol), 22–23
International law enforcement, 22–23
  The CIA, 22
  Europol, 23
  Interpol, 22–23
  UNODC, 23
International reply coupons (IRCs), 208
Investors Overseas Services (IOS), 212
Iqbal, Javel ("Kukri"), 132
IRCs. See International reply coupons (IRCs)
The Irish and Russian mobs, 40–42

The Irishman, 144. See also Bulgar, Whitey
Irish Republican Army, 184
Isle of Wight, 193
Israel III, Sam, 210
Israel's intelligence service, 184
Italians, 34

J
Jack "Legs" Diamond, 26
Jack's Forebears, 87
Jackson, Emily, 116
Jackson, George, 184
Jack the Ripper and His Victims, 86–87
Jack the Ripper, 20, 86–87
James Bond, 15
James, Frank, 17
James, Jesse, 16, 17, 28
James, Roy, 182
Jane, Mary, 66
Jazz-fueled energy, 26
Jeffreys, Sir Alex, 21
Jennings, Margaret, 78
Jennings, Patrick, 78
Jewish Eastman Gang, 37
Jews, 34, 189
Jin Ruchao, 151
The Joe Boys, 42
John D. Long Lake, 62
Jones, Genene, 110
Jones, Harold, 52
Jones, W.D., 31
Jordan, Mary Ann, 138–139
Judy Buenoano of Florida, 79

K
Kaczynski, David, 97
Kaczynski, Theodore John, 96
  Industrial Society and Its Future, 97
Kahn System, 204
Kampala wedding massacre (1994), 150
Kampusch, Natascha, 177
Kamwenge Trading Centre, 150
Kardashian, Robert, 82
Keddon, Thomas, 162
Kelly, Mary Jane, 86
Kelly, Paul, 36–37
  Five Points Gang, 36–37
Kemmler, William, 95
Kemper, Edmund, 99
Kennedy, John F., 186
Kennedy, Ludovic, 59
Kidman, Nicole, 77
  To Die For, 77
Kidnapping consequences, 175
Kidnappings That Created Change, 174–175
Kidnappings, types of, 173
"Killer Clown" (John Wayne Gacy), 102–103
King Birenda, 151
"King of Cocaine." See Escobar, Pablo
"King of the Bootleggers." See Remus, George
"King of the Underworld," 39
Kiss of Death, 144
The Knightsbridge Security Deposit Robbery,
  192–193
Knowlton, Teresa, 132
Komakech, Richard, 150
Krasnodar, 159
Kroll, Joachim, 158–160
Krueger, Ivar, 204
Krueger's Financial Innovations, 205
Krueger & Toll, 205
Krugman, Martin, 186–187
Kunigunde Mackamotzki, 74

L
Labbé, Denise, 62
La Cosa Nostra: The Mafia in America, 36–37
Lambeth Poisoner. See Cream, Thomas
Lamphere, Ray, 105, 108
Lancaster, Burt, 144
  The Birdman of Alcatraz (1962), 145
  The Killers (1946), 144
Landru, Henri, 79
L'Angelier, Pierre Emile, 50
Land Rovers, 183
LáPree, Melinda Rose, 108
Laptew, Andy, 117
Larson, Erik, 89

The Devil in the White City, 89
Las Vegas Strip, 39
Latin American Serial Killers, 120–123
Law enforcement, branches of, 12–13
Lazarus, Joel T., 65
Leach, Dick, 193
Leach, Kimberly, 95
Leatherslade Farm, 183
Legal Attaché (LEGAT) offices, 18
Legendary Charlatans, 218–219
Leibacher, Friedrich, 149
Le Neve, Ethel, 74–75
Lennon, John, 58
Leopold Jr, Nathan, 168
Lê Thanh Van, 133
Levin, Jennifer, 60
Lewis, Damien, 184
LiCastri, Paolo, 186
The Lindbergh Abduction ("The Crime of the Century"), 170–171
Lindbergh, Charles, 170–171
Liotta, Ray, 145
"Little Italy," 36–37
"Little Red Riding Hood Murder," 52
Little, Samuel, 108–109, 115
Liverpool, 78
Locusta of Gaul, 87
Loeb, Richard, 168
Loesch, Frank J., 27
London's East End, 87
London's Metropolitan Police, 20
Longo, Christian, 66
Longo, Zachary, 66
Lopez, Pedro (Monster of the Andes), 120
Lorain, 108
"The Lord high executioner," 39
Los Angeles region, 114–115
Loudwell, Richard, 159
Louvre Museum, 188
Lucas, Frank, 39
Lucas, Henry Lee, 178
Luciano, Lucky, 36, 37, 38
Ludeña, Pedro (The Apostle of Death), 120
Ludhiana, 185
The Lufthansa Heist, 186–187
Lui Pengli, Han prince, 87
Lumumba, Patrick, 68
Lupino, Ida, 144
Lustig, Victor, 207
Lyman School for Boys, 92
Lynn, Jeffrey, 144

M
MacLennan, Hectorina, 91
MacMurray, Fred, 145
Madden, Owney, 40
"Mad Hatter," 38
Madison Square Garden, 206
Madoff, Bernard, 208
Mafia, 35–41, 44
The Mafia's origins: Italy and America, 34–35
"Mainland Chinese criminal organizations," 43
Malakhov, Vladimir, 41
Maleshoff, Ivan ("The Bluebeard of Kharkiv"), 128
Mallory, Richard, 106–107
Maloney, Kathleen, 91
Mam'zelle Champagne, 73
Mandalay Bay Hotel, 141
Manri, Joe, 186
Manson, Charles, 142, 145
Manson Murders, 142–143
Mansour, Ramadan Abdel Rahim (al-Tourbini), 134
Marconi, Guglielmo, 74
Marie, Anna, 80–81
Markopolos, Harry, 209
Marmon, Doris, 124
Martinez, Sergeant Ramiro, 140
"The Marrakesh Arch-Killer," 134
Marsh, Maud, 51
The Master of "Murder Castle", 88–89
The Match King (Ivar Krueger), 204–205
"Matchstick monopolies," 204
Matsuzawa Hospital, 164
Matusek, Pat, 139
Ma Xiangling, 193
Maybrick, Florence, 49, 86

Maybrick, James, 49, 86
Mayhem in the Midwest: Bonnie & Clyde, 30–31
Mayhem in the Midwest: Depression Desperados, 28–29
Mayhem in the Midwest: In Cold Blood, 54–55
Mayo, Virginia, 144
McAvoy, Mickey, 190
McCann, Wilma, 116
McCloundy, William, 207
McCoy, Patrolman Houston, 144
McCoy, Timothy Jack, 102
McFall, Anne, 80
McGregor, Gregor, 218
McMahon, Robert, 186–187
McMullen, Kevin, 196
McNeill, Isa, 80
"Measuring Man," 92
Medellín Cartel, 39
Media circus, 168
Media storms, 178
Melcher, Terry, 142
Melrose Avenue (Cricklewood), 104
"Mementos," 165
Memling, Hans, 189
The Last Judgment, 188–189
The Menendez Brothers, 60–61
Menendez, José, 60
Menendez, Mary "Kitty," 60
Mesfewi, Hadj Mohammed, 134
Metal Fang, 158
Methvin, Henry, 31
Metropolitan Museum of Art, 60
Metropolitan Police, 15
Metropolitan Police Force on Whitehall Place, 14–15
Metropolitan regions, 12
Met's robbery unit, 183
Mexico, 67
MI5—Counter-Intelligence Service, 15
MI6—Secret Intelligence Service, 15
Miami Beach, 119
Midway Avenue, 89
"Midwest Bank Bandits," 185
Miglin, Lee, 118
Mijangos, Claudia, 147
Milkins, Neil, 52
Miller, Bruce, 74
"Millionaire's row," 214
Mills, Jack, 183
The Milwaukee Monster (Jeffrey Dahmer), 156–157
Mitchell, Brian David, 177
Mithilesh Kumar Srivastava. See Natwarlal
Miyazaki, Tsutomu, 164
Missing Children's Assistance Act, 178
Modern policing concerns, 13
Moe, John, 105
Mogilny, Alexander, 41
Mona Lisa, 188
Monmouth, 138
Monster, 145
Moon Maniac, 162
"Moonshine," 27
The Moors Murders, 126
Morello, Giuseppe, 36
Morrow, Anne, 170
Morton, Samantha, 90
Moscowitz, Stacey, 100
Mosquito Coast, 218
Mosser, Tom, 97
Mott, Juanita, 81
Mowbray, William, 49
Mudgett, Herman Webster, 88
Mulberry Street, 36
Munch, Edvard, 188
Munchhausen Syndrome, 111
Murders, 127
Murray, Gilbert, 97
Murray, Henry, 96
Murray, Lee, 198
Mustache Petes, 36
The Mystique of The Bridge, 207

N
Naidu, Padmaja and Purushottam, 63
Nassar, George, 92
National Art Museum, 189
National Maritime Union, 138

Natwarlal, 218–219
Nayfeld, Boris, 40
Neapolitan Camorra, 36
"Neat operation," 185
Necrophilia, 123, 165
Nelson, Rita, 91
Nene Valley Railway, 183
Neo-Nazism, 185
Nesbit, Evelyn, 72
New Hampshire, 88
Newman, Paul, 144
New Orleans Times, 36
News of the World, 91
New York City, 37, 58
New York Police Force, 18
New York's Auburn Prison, 95
New York's Lower East Side, 34
Nichols, Mary Ann, 87
The Night Stalker, 114–115
Nikolayev, Vladimir, 159–160
Nilsen, Dennis, 104–105
Nilsen, Elizabeth, 104
Nixon, Richard, 212
Norris, Charles, 48
The Northern Bank Robbery, 196–197
Northern California, 42
Northern Ireland, 197
Nottingham, 109
Nykopp-Kosk, Aino, 111

O
O'Banion, Dean, 40
Odessa Mafia, 41
Office of Strategic Services (OSS), 22
O'Flynn, John, 191
Ogre, 159
Ogwang, Alfred, 150
Oklahoma, 185
Old Bailey, 198
Oldenberg Clinic, 111
Oldfield, George, 117
Ono, Yoko, 58
Onoprienko, Anatoly ("The Terminator"), 129
Opium, 51
Oregon, 162
Organized Crime, 33
Organized offenders, 99
Oslo's Munch Museum, 189
OSS. See Office of Strategic Services
"Otaku Murderer," 164–165
The "Other" Peterson Murder, 67
Outlaw, 28
Overbye, Dagmar ("The Angelmaker"), 128
Oziel, Dr. Jerome, 61

P
Paddock, Stephen, 140–141
Paget, Sir James, 49
Palace Station Hotel, 83
Palestine Liberation Organization, 184
Palmer, Dr. William, 51
"Panic of 1825," 219
Paranoid schizophrenia, 117
Parents Who Kill Their Children, 62–63
Parker, Bonnie, 30
Parker, George C., 206
Parliament House of India, 219
Pasion, Valentina, 139
Peel, Sir Robert, 14
"bobbies" ("peelers"), 15
father of modern policing, 15
Peist, Robert, 103
Pembroke, Danny, 182
Pentonville Prison, 74, 91
People Against Sex Offenders (P.A.S.O.), 174
The People's Republic of China, 133
The People v. O.J. Simpson, 145
Peoria County Court House, 139
"Perfect crime," 168
Perrault, Charles, 79
Perry, Brian, 190
Peruggia, Vincenzo, 189
Peterson, Kathleen, 67
Peterson, Laci, 67
Peterson, Michael, 67
Peterson, Scott, 66–67
Philippines, 118
Picasso, Pablo, 188–189

Pichushkin, Alexander ("The Chessboard Killer"), 129
Pickton, Robert—"The Butcher," 109
Pinkerton, Allan, 17
Pitchfork, Colin, 21
Pitezel, Benjamin, 89
The Plainfield Ghoul (Ed Gein), 154–155
Poison, 48
Poitier, Sidney, 217
Polanski, Roman, 142
Polaroid, Richard, 115
Poles, 34
Police force, goal of, 12
Police Service, 197
Ponzi, Charles, 208
Ponzi scheme, 208, 210
Ponzi Schemers, 208–211
Popkov, Mikhail ("The Werewolf"), 129
Port Authority Police, 186
"The Possessed," 62
Post-9/11 Patriot Act, 13
Postal Inspection Service, 18
Potenza, 172
"Poyais," 218
Praia da Luz, 179
Prendergast, Eugene Patrick, 89
"Preppy Murderer." See Chambers, Robert
Price, John, 163
Prince Gyanendra, 151
Princess Caraboo, 214
Princess Diana, 58
Pritchard, Dr. Edward, 51
"Private stash," 195
Privileged . . . and Deadly, 60–61
Procrustes of Greece, 87
Profiling: Portraits of Psychopaths, 98–99
Profiling: A Six-Step Process, 98–99
Apprehension, 99
Constructing a decision process model, 98
Crime assessment, 98–99
Criminal profile, 99
Input, 98
Investigation, 99
The Prospect of Prison, 29
Provisional Irish Republican Army, 196
"Psst, Buddy, Wanna Buy a Bridge?," 206–207
Psychiatric hospital, 158
Puch, Robledo (The Black Angel), 122
Puerto Rico, 168
The Punjab National Bank, 185
Purvis, Melvin, 28

Q
Queen Aishwarya, 151
Queen Anula, 87
Queen Victoria, 86
Quintanilla Jr., Abraham, 59
Quintanilla-Pérez, Selena, 59

R
Raghav, Raman, 150
Railsback, Steve, 145
Raman Raghav, 150
Ramirez, Miguel, 115
Ramirez, Richard, 99, 115
"the Night Stalker," 99, 112, 115
Original Night Stalker, 112
Rampage Killers of Africa & Asia, 150–151
Rampage Killers of Europe, 148–149
Rampage Killers of Latin America, 146–147
Rampton Secure Hospital, 159
Ramsey, JonBenét, 68–69
Ramsey, John Bennett, 68–69
Ramsey, Patsy, 68–69
Ransacker, Visalia, 112
"The Rat Man," 164–165
RCA Records, 60
Reade, Pauline, 126, 127
Redford, Robert, 144
Reese, William, 119
Regan, Kenneth, 191
Reggio Emilia province, 160
Remus, George, 76
Rena, 80
Renault truck, 198
Renczi, Vera ("The Black Widow"), 128
Ren Xiaofeng of the Agricultural Bank of China, 193

Reserve Bank of India, 185
Reynolds, Bruce, 182–183
Ridgway, Gary, 98, 115
Rillington Place, 59
10 Rillington Place, 90, 145
Rio de Janeiro, 146
Ritchie, Guy, 144
  Lock, Stock, and Two Smoking Barrels, 144
  Snatch, 144
Riverside Hostel, 159
Roach Guard, 34
The Roaring Twenties, 144
"Robbers," 194
Robin Hood, 29
Robinson, Brian, 190–191
Robinson, Edward G., 144
Robinson, Shirley, 81
Rochester, 114
The Rock (VX), 51
Roebling, Emily Warren, 207
Roebling, John Augustus, 207
Roosevelt, Theodore, 18, 22
Rossi, Michael, 103
Ross, Valentin, 20
Roth, Tim, 90
Rotten, Johnny, 183
Royal Fusiliers (West Germany), 104
Royal Institute of Technology, 204
Royal Mail, 182
Royle, Stuart, 198
Ruby Ridge, 185
Ruchao, Jin, 151
Ruhr region, 158
Rusha, Lea, 198
Ryan, Debra, 210
Ryan, Michael, 148–149

S
Sacramento region, 112
Saddleworth Moor, 126, 127
Sagawa, Issei, 164
Saldiver, Yolanda, Selena fan club, 59
Salt Lake City, Utah, 115
Sam Bass, 16
Samsung, 213
San Diego, 118
San Francisco, 42–43, 118–119
San Francisco Bay, 67
San Francisco Police Gang Task Force, 43
San Joaquin Valley, 112
San Quentin Prison, 184
"Scarface," 38, 192
Scheele, Carl Wilhelm, 20
Schizophrenia, 155
Schmale, Nina Jo, 138, 139
Scientific and surgical investigation, 20
Scorsese, Martin, 144
  Mean Streets (1973), 144
  Taxi Driver (1976), 144
  Goodfellas (1990), 144
  Casino (1995), 144
  Gangs of New York (2002), 144
  The Departed (2006), 144
  The Irishman (2019), 144
"Scotland Yard," 15
The Scream, 188
Scrutton, Hugh, 97
Sebring, Jay, 143
Second Mafia War, 128–129
Second World War. See World War II
Secret Intelligence Service, 22
Secret Service, 18
The Securitas Depot Robbery, 198–199
Securities and Exchange Commission
  (SEC), 209
Selena Y Los Dinos, 59
Sepe, Angelo, 186
Sevakis, Suzanne Marie, 176
The Sex Pistols, 183
Sexual fetishist, 162
Shapiro, Robert, 83
Shaw, Bernard, 172
Shawcross, Arthur, 99
Sheriff's department, 12
Sherlock Holmes, 15
Sheth, Nisha, 159
Shipman, Harold, 109
Shocking Deaths of Music Legends, 58–59

Short, Elizabeth, 53
Sicily, 34, 36
Sickert, Mr Walter, 86–87
Siegel, Bugsy, 39
Siems, Peter, 107
SIG Sauer pistol, 149
The Silence of the Lambs, 94, 155
Simons, Norman Afzal, 134
Simpson, Nicole Brown, 82
Simpson, O.J., 82–83
  "a trail of blood," 83
Sinclair, Stephen Neil, 105
Singh, Labh, 185
Sing Sing, 162
Sirico, Tony, 145
Sitole, Moses, 134
Skrynnik, Alexander, 159
Slatkin, Reed, 210
Smart, Elizabeth, 177
Smart, Gregg, 76
Smart, Pamela, 76–77
Smith, David, 126, 127
Smith, George (The Brides in the Bath), 124
Smith, Harry, 182
Smith, Madeline, 50
Smith, Susan, 62
Smythe, Julia, 89
Smyth, Judalon, 61
Snider, Paul, 57
"Soapmaker of Correggio," 158
Sobhraj, Charles ("The Serpent"), 132
Somers, Marcel, 77
Son of Sam (David Berkowitz), 100–101
Soprano, Tony, 145
  The Sopranos (2006), 145, 183
Sorenson, Mads, 108
Sorvino, Paul, 145
"The South African Ted Bundy," 134
South Side Gang, 35
Southwick, Alfred P., 96
"Riding the lightning," 95
South Yorkshire Police, 117
Soviet Russia, 41
Soviet Union, 40–41
Spahn Ranch, 142
Spears, David, 107
Special Air Service (SAS), 184
Special Branch, 15
Speck, Richard Benjamin, 138
Spink, Mary Isabella, 51
SS Montrose, 74–75
Stanwyck, Barbara, 144, 145
State Bureau of Investigation, 12–13
Stateville Penitentiary, 169
"The Station Strangler," 134
Statue of Liberty, 206
Stavis, Roger, 60
St. Bartholomew's Hospital, 49
Stealing Masterpieces, 188–189
Steven Hicks, 156
Steven Spielberg's Wunderkinder Foundation,
  209
Stewart, James, 169
Stockholm City Hall, 204
Stockholm Olympic Stadium, 204–205
Stockholm's Royal Institute of Technology, 204
Stockholm syndrome, 177
Stompanato, Johnny, 57
The Strand Shopping Centre, 64
Stratten, Dorothy, 57
Strauss, Richard, 119
  Capriccio, 119
Stride, Elizabeth, 87
Strychnine, 51
St. Valentine's Day Massacre, 38
Successful Imposters, 214–217
"Suicide is painless," 210
The Sundance Kid, 16, 144
Suradji, Ahmad, 133
Sutcliffe, Peter, 116
Swiss city of Zug, 149
Sydney Opera House, 174
Sydney suburb, 175

T
Taming the Wild West, 16–17
"Tania," 172
Tanzi, Calisto, 212

Tarantino, Quentin, 144
  Reservoir Dogs and *Pulp Fiction*, 144
Targeting Iraq-Twice, 194–195
Tate, Lionel, 65
Tate, Sharon, 142
Taylor, Bessie, 51
Tennis rackets, 168
Terrorist attacks of 9/11, 22
Terrorists and militants, 184–185
Tevendale, Brian, 76–77
The Texas Chainsaw Massacre, 155
Texas's Huntsville Unit, 79
Texas Ranger, 31
Thaw, Harry, 72
Thaw, Russell William, 73
Theodate, Lucy, 88
Theron, Charlize, 145
  Monster (2003), 107
They Drive By Night, 144
Thief takers, 14
Thompson, Robert, 64
Thorne, Graeme, 174
Threlkold, Ronnie, 78
Thrill Killers, 168–169
Tick-Tock, 37
Tiger kidnapping, 173
Tkach, Serhiy, 129
Tombstone, 17
Top Crime Bosses of the Past Century, 38–39
Tongs, Triads and Yakuza Asian Crime
  Syndicates, 42–43
Torrio, Johnny, 36, 38
"Total possession," 94–95
The Tragic News, 175
TREVI, 23
Triad (2014), 42
Trail, Jeffrey, 118
"Trial of the Century," 73
Tuomi, Steven, 156
Turner, Cora, 74
Turner, Lana, 57
Two More Ponzi Schemers, 210–211

U
UC Berkeley, 176
Uffizi Gallery, 189
Uhlenhuth, Paul, 21
Uhlenhuth test, 21
"The Ulsterman," 182
The Unabomber (Ted Kaczynski), 96–97
Unek, William, 150
United Nations Office on Drugs and Crime
  (UNODC), 23
United States, 35, 41–42
United States Code, 13
University and Airline Bomber (UNABOM), 96
University of Michigan, 96
University of Perugia, 68
University of Washington, 94
Unsolved Murders, 52–53
"The Untouchables," 27
Urschel, Charles F., 29
Urquhart, Donald, 191
U.S. Attorney, 210
U.S. Congress, 178
US Customs and Border Protection, 19
US Immigration and Customs Enforcement, 19
US Marshals Service, 13
U.S. Parks Police, 18
US serviceman, 146
US Stock Market, 28
U.S. Treasury, 36

V
Van Doren, Els, 77
Van Houten, Leslie, 143
Van Tassel, Edna, 89
Venables, Jon, 64
Versace, Gianni, 118–119
Vesco, Robert, 212
  "King of the fugitive financiers," 212
Veterans Affairs Medical Center, 110
Viccei, Valerio, 192
Volstead Act, 26–27, 36, 76
Voskerichian, Virginia, 100
Vowing vengeance, 148
"Vulcana" (Kate Williams), 75
VX, 51

W
Waco, 185
Waddington, Ethel, 90
Wagner, Ernst, 148
The Wah Ching, 42
Wall Street Crash, 205
Walsh, Adam, 178
Walsh, John, 178
Wanamaker's Department Store, 72
Ward, Chris, 196
Ward, George, 49
War-torn Lebanon, 184
"Weird dude," 157
Welch, Bob, 182
Werewolf of Wysteria, 162
Werner, Louis, 186
West Coast Killers, 112–115
West Coast Main Line, 182
West, Fred, 80–81, 98
West, Rosemary, 80–81, 98
West Yorkshire Police, 117
Westies, 40
Whack-Whack, 37
Whitechapel, 87
White City, 88–89
White, Jimmy, 182
Whitman, Charles, 140
Whyos, 34
Wickersham Commission (1929), 27
Widmark, Richard, 144
Wild Bill Hickok, 17
The Wild Bunch, 16–17
Wilder, Billy, 145
The Wild Rose, 72
Wild West, 17
Wilkening, Pamela, 138–139
Willcocks, Mary, 214
Williams, Kate, 75
Williams, Minnie, 89
Wilson, Charlie, 182–183, 191
Wilson, Dennis, 142
Wilson, Robert, 93
Winnacunnet High School, 76
Winnenthal, 148
Winter Hill Gang of Somerville, 39
Wisbey, Tommy, 182
Wojas, Pamela, 76
"Woke Up This Morning," 183
Wolf Lake, 168
Women's Zionist Organization of America, 209
Woo Bum-Kon, 150
Worden, Bernice, 154
World's Columbian Exposition—"The World's
  Fair," 88–89
World War I, 52, 90, 189, 204
World War II, 20, 22, 41, 90, 128
Wuornos, Aileen, 98, 106–107, 145
Wyatt Earp, 17

Y
Yale, Frankie, 36
Yang Xinhai ("Monster Killer"), 133
Yoke, Georgiana, 88
Yoo Young-chul ("Raincoat Killer"), 133
The Yorkshire Ripper, 116–117
"Young Turks," 36, 39

Z
Zhitnik, Alexei, 41
The Zodiac Killer, 112
Zug massacre 149

CREDITS

Images are for the most part in the Public Domain but in all cases are courtesy of: **Shutterstock**; **Alamy**; **Wikipedia**; **Wikimedia Commons**; Associated Press; The Paris Review; Old Police Cells Museum; UK National Archives, Kew; Wall Street Journal; Reddit; Folklife Today; FBI/Bureau Of Investigation (HarrisEwing); History Site; FBI Fingerprint Files; PNAS; Alchetron; Biography; Famous Bio; Medium; Mob Museum; Pinterest; Tumgir: Tumblr; Rare Historical Photos; New York Times; IMDb; Chloe Jafe/ Huck Mag; Ang Yi; Vintage Everyday; Adelstein; ABC News; Stratfor 2011; Wikiwand; The BBC; Wales Online; Police Bulletin; Finney County Museum; People.com; OutNow. Ch; Heather Monroe Site; The BFI; Witzel; Crime Online; ETV Bharat; Quint; International Business Times; Brian Hamill; The Telegraph; Buzzfeed News; Rich Addicks/Atlanta Journal Constitution; UPI Photos/Paul Aikens; Reuters/Rick Wilking; Globe Photos; Zuma Press, Inc.; Women's Health Mag; Bio; iNews; DailyStar.co.uk; All That's Interesting; NBC News; E!Online; Scoopnest; Independent.ie; CBS News; MirrorOnline; DailyMailOnline/AssociatedPress; The Daily Record; Skeleton Key Chronicles; Corbis; The Liverpool Echo; The Japan Times; New York Daily News; The Irish Sun; Hamilton Spectator; CNN; The Telegraph; The Sun; Reel Urban News; The Chicago Tribune; Library of Congress; Chicago Architecture Center; The Daily Express; Murder Friends; The Independent; Dick Leonhardt/Vintage Everyday; The Boston Globe; The Herald Sun; This is an Exclusive; The King's Necktie; Criminal Minds Wiki; NYPD; Getty Images; ITV Productions; News Groove; La Porte County Historical Society Museum; Texas Monthly; Liaison Agency; Crime Museum; True Crime Magazine; San Francisco Chronicle; South Yorkshire Police; Bustle; Telegraph & Argus; Leeds Live; The Guardian; Julian Blanco @ Murderpedia; History of Yesterday; Medium; Famous People; Hell Horror; Sky News; Serial Killer Database Wiki; Biograph; Dallas Sheriff's Dept.; The Schmale Family; The Whitman Family; NY Daily News/Associated Press; L'Est Republicain; Get Reading; The Hanneman Archive; Wikiwand; Vocal Media; Mirrorpix; Business Insider India; Grave Reviews; The Daily Mail; ABC; Film Daily; Scooper; ViceVideo; South China Morning Post; Chicagology; History; Metropolitan Museum of Art; Dallas Morning News; New South Wales Forensic Dept; Groovy History; The Hagerman Family; The Sydney Morning Herald; RTE; Lost Girl's Blog; Birmingham Mail (UK); Adam Film Advertising; The Miami Herald; The Walsh Family; The McCann Family; The Daily Mirror; The Oregonian; Marca; Goodfellas Film Rights; 9News.com; Musée Picasso; Photo News Services; China Daily; Kent Online; The Daily Star; Look And Learn; Johannes Scherman; Huff Post; Business Insider; Smithsonian Magazine; Idaho Statesman; The Times of India; Scoop Whoop; History Today; and Military Wiki. Contact Moseley Road Inc. for errors or omissions.